Russian Jazz

Russian Jazz

New Identity

Compiled and edited by
Leo Feigin

Quartet Books Limited
London Melbourne New York

This book is dedicated
to those people who have
influenced me and helped
me in my work:

Efim Barban
Felicity Cave
Susannah Fried
Alex Kan
Chris Gray
Kim McCroddan
Olivia Lichtenstein
The Ganelin Trio

First published by Quartet Books Limited 1985
A member of the Namara Group
27/29 Goodge Street, London W1P 1FD

British Library Cataloguing in Publication Data

Russian jazz: new identity
    1. Jazz music——Soviet Union
    I. Feigin, Leo
    785.42'0947   ML3509.S7

    ISBN 0-7043-2506-3

Typeset by MC Typeset, Chatham, Kent
Printed and bound in Great Britain
by Mackays of Chatham Ltd, Kent

Contents

Introduction
Leo Feigin

In 1983 Oxford University Press published a monumental study by
S. Frederick Starr: *Red & Hot: The Fate of Jazz in the Soviet
Union.* Meticulously researched, the book provided us with the
history of jazz in the Soviet Union till the end of the seventies. It is
a brilliant and complete sociological/historical analysis of the role
and place of jazz in a closed society.

However, the very end of the seventies and the beginning of the
eighties saw an incredible explosion of new music in the Soviet
Union, which is not reflected in Frederick Starr's book. The jazz
that Frederick Starr was writing about was, on the whole, derived
from the American music. It belonged, with very rare exceptions,
to the field of so-called 'light music' or entertainment, in spite of
the fact that it was perceived by jazz fans in the Soviet Union as
the manifestation and expression of someone else's freedom. In
strictly musical terms Soviet jazz neither had its own identity, nor
did it create anything new or exciting. Soviet musicians were aping
the Americans.

The emergence of new music changed the whole scene
immediately. The new aesthetic helped Soviet jazz to make the
crucial step from being light entertainment to becoming a serious
art form. New music helped Soviet musicians to find their identity.
They stopped aping Americans. They rediscovered the links with
the traditions of the great Russian culture, corroded by the
October Revolution in 1917.

The purpose of this book is to present the new music from the
Soviet Union. However, instead of continuing Frederick Starr's
line of research and writing the whole book on my own, I decided

1

to deal with the subject from all possible viewpoints and to include essays by many contributors. Thus, one can find articles written by authors from the USSR, Romania, East and West Germany, England and the USA; interviews with Soviet musicians and Western musicians who travelled to Russia and played with Soviet musicians; and excerpts from underground jazz publications in the USSR.

The title of the book has not been taken at random. It has been carefully chosen after many hours of discussions, doubts and deliberations. The majority of people in the West are not aware of the dichotomy in the terms 'Russian/Soviet'. They believe these two words are synonymous, as indeed Soviet official culture would have us believe. However, there is a whole world of difference between these two concepts. In 1917 the Soviet System was imposed on the Russian people. Many traditions of Russian culture were threatened and destroyed by the new revolutionary culture. The vices and evils of the new socialist society created Soviet official culture, which was based on the doctrine of socialist realism. Russian culture, based on old traditions and values, inevitably found itself in opposition to Soviet official culture. In simple terms this opposition, 'Russian/Soviet', means the following: 'Soviet' refers to the political system, official culture, etc; while 'Russian' refers to the people on whom this Soviet system was imposed – to unofficial culture.

Jazz in the Soviet Union has survived in spite of socialist realism, rather than because of it. Frederick Starr's book provides invaluable proof of this endless struggle, documenting the repressions, relaxations, crackdowns and new crackdowns. Jazz survived the most cruel spiritual oppression. The concept of jazz music, which is the most democratic music on this planet, is alien to Soviet dictatorship. And though new music emerged in the midst of Soviet official culture, its meaning and significance transcend the limitations of this culture. The newly acquired identity of new music in the Soviet Union belongs more to Russian art and world culture.

Soviet Jazz: The Third Wave

S. Frederick Starr

In 1983 Oxford University Press published Red & Hot: The Fate of Jazz in the Soviet Union *by S. Frederick Starr. The book attracted a great deal of attention for many reasons: one, it was the first book to be written on this subject in the West; two, it treated the subject not only from a musical point of view but in the context of the history of art and Soviet society in general and, as a result, paved the way for interesting discussions on the subject.*

S. Frederick Starr is a professional musician, a co-founder of the Louisiana Repertory Jazz Ensemble, and a former Secretary of the Kennan Institute for Advanced Russian Studies at the Wilson Center in Washington. In 1982 he became President of Oberlin College, Ohio, USA.

A new phase in the sixty-year history of Soviet jazz has begun. Coming on the heels of the long Soviet involvement with bop and, before that, swing, the new phase is generally summed up by the term 'free jazz'. The name is not without problems. Originating as it does with Ornette Coleman's epochal 1960 album *Free Jazz*, it implies a dependence that some claim the Soviet musicians have now shed; it understates the pronounced tendency towards structure in the new music; and it is rejected by at least some of the musicians themselves. None the less, for lack of a better term, it is convenient to call this third wave 'free jazz'.

Both within the USSR and abroad, this new current is most closely associated with the person of Vyacheslav Ganelin, the intent, puckish, and immensely gifted Russian pianist–composer from Vilnius, Lithuanian SSR. By American and West European standards, Genelin is a latecomer to the new music, his groping towards free jazz having come to fruition only in the mid-1970s. Having found his new language, however, Ganelin and his trio moved swiftly. In quick order they stunned and dazzled jazz cognoscenti in Moscow, Leningrad, and other Soviet centres, played in East and West Germany, and either inspired or spawned directly the creation of a number of further groups throughout the Soviet Union. Several recordings issued by Leo Records in England brought the group to the attention of West European and American listeners, and led to its controversial London debut in 1984. Without minimizing the number, activity, and potential significance of other Soviet exponents of free jazz, Ganelin was its acknowledged pioneer and several in his circle remain its leaders.

At the same time, the new current possesses all the marks of a movement. The number of participants and the level of their talent is great enough for them to stimulate and feed off one another. Beginning with Mr Efim Barban, late of Leningrad, a number of Soviet critics have attempted to describe and promote the new current. And a devoted if limited audience has coalesced around the artistic leaders. In all these respects, free jazz in the USSR had attained by 1980 a collective identity comparable to that of Soviet bop by 1960.

That the locus of innovation in Soviet jazz has shifted to this movement is obvious. What is less clear is how much further its exponents are capable of developing it. The answer to this question lies in the artistic gifts of the musicians themselves, but it will also depend upon the expectations and support of those circles within the Soviet intelligentsia that have shown an interest in the new music. Stated differently, the future viability of free jazz in the USSR will be significantly shaped by its broader relation to Soviet culture. If free jazz taps only those energies that have heretofore flowed into bop and related movements, it will be a passing phenomenon. If, however, it creates a new place for jazz within Soviet culture as a whole, it could achieve great and lasting significance. The purpose of this essay is to address this issue.

To do so, it is necessary to construe the new current in the context of three generations of jazz in the USSR. The first phase began in the 1920s and culminated in the successful assimilation of big-band swing music by the 1940s. Syncopated and swing music elicited the same enthusiasm in the Soviet Union as they had in Western Europe and America. Their intrinsic musical appeal was great, but their significance as the bearers of subversive ideas of sexual emancipation and individual expression was greater still. Variously tolerated and ruthlessly condemned by Communist leaders, big-band jazz was a living alternative to collectivized puritanism and organized xenophobia.

The powerful appeal of jazz provoked Soviet officials to periodic and cruel acts of suppression. Because its subversive overtones were not blatant, however, jazz could also be the object of official attempts at co-operation. Increasingly down to 1946–47 and again after 1953, great efforts were expended to cultivate a safely 'Sovietized' form of jazz music. Thanks to this effort, and also to the close association between big-band jazz and the more venturesome members of the social group pushed forward by Stalin (the *vydvizhentsy*), swing gained a narrowly generational character. Those young men and women who reached maturity in the first decade after Stalin's death in 1953 were thoroughly alienated from the older jazz. They searched passionately for cultural forms that could more adequately express their autonomy from Stalinist norms, their individualism, their cosmopolitanism, and their general rebelliousness. They found this music in bop.

During the late 1950s and 1960s most tendencies evident in American and European jazz were reflected within the USSR. The 'cool' movement achieved considerable success in the sophisticated and Europeanized world of the Baltic Republics, while regional philharmonic organizations in such diverse places as Moscow, Kaliningrad (Konigsberg) and Tula patronized up-to-date big bands that had moved beyond swing. A modest 'trad' movement even sprang up in Leningrad and Moscow. However active these currents, it was bop that dominated the scene, whether in Moscow, Baku, Leningrad or Kiev. The introverted and anti-assimilationist ideals of black American bop musicians and their allies in the 'Beat' movement provided the touchstone for a true generational revolt in the USSR. The boppers' jargon, deportment and style of dress set the tone wherever the post-Stalinist youth assembled. They defined an ethos of sullen but active disengagement that swept beyond music to permeate the urgent writings of Vasilii Aksenov and other popular authors.

This many-sided phenomenon posed a fresh problem to Soviet cultural commissars. They knew better than to resist it frontally, and therefore attempted to co-opt it. For a few years after 1961 this policy nearly succeeded. It ultimately failed, however, for it could not meet the unrealistic expectations for conformity held by unreconstructed Stalinist hard-liners. Foreign-policy considerations strengthened this hard line. First the Sino–Soviet feud in 1962–64 and then the Soviet invasion of Czechoslovakia in 1968 set firm limits upon nonconformity of all sorts.

By the early 1970s the bop movement in the USSR was in disarray. When the possibility of emigrating from the Soviet Union opened up after 1973, scores of jazzmen of the post-Stalin generation packed their bags. The departure of many of the leading talents for New York and points west heightened the difficulties for those who stayed. What cynical opponents of jazz had earlier claimed now seemed to be borne out: that jazz (specifically bop) in the USSR was the rallying point for anti-Soviet elements led by Jews and other malcontents.

Had these been the only significant developments, there would have been no soil in which free jazz could grow. In these same years, however, the astonishing rise of rock music to popularity in the USSR put jazz in an entirely different light. With the emigrés gone and the remaining leaders of the bop movement reaching serene middle age, jazz appeared decidedly as the lesser evil. In yet another of the *volte-faces* that are so common in Soviet cultural life, jazz suddenly gained a new respectability. The Communist youth organizations sponsored over six dozen regional jazz festivals, Melodiya issued various recordings, and local philharmonic societies extended their patronage to touring ensembles playing jazz–rock fusion music. The Union of Soviet Composers went so far as to reverse earlier policies and foster the teaching of jazz at forty institutes throughout the country.

This suffocating embrace, no less than the political and cultural crisis that led to the defection of so many Soviet jazz musicians, defined the milieu out of which free jazz would spring. To review, the regime laid down strict limits on political and artistic expression and showed itself ready to hound out of the country any jazz musician who violated them. Within those limits, the regime opened an umbrella of patronage which extended official support to jazz but at the price of turning it into a formalized and institutionalized ritual. All of this occurred at a moment when the bop movement in the West was passing from middle age to senility.

For Soviet musicians, the obvious path out of this impasse was to develop a new form of jazz with the following characteristics: it had to substitute individual expression for collective rebellion; it had to distance itself from rock music and at the same time exist in a state of detente with the classical Establishment; it had to protect itself from the charge of cosmopolitanism by rejecting overt references to American or West European sources; and, finally, in order to gain artistic integrity, it had to declare its independence from the ritualistic expectations of official jazz audiences and ally itself instead with truly knowledgeable and supportive devotees, however small their numbers.

There is no reason to believe that any of these objectives were consciously pursued by those who lead the establishment of the free jazz movement in the USSR. In fact, the rise of free jazz was not unlike the earlier growth of both swing and bop. American and Western recordings were carefully studied. A pleiad of new names entered the consciousness of Soviet musicians, among them Ornette Coleman, Archie Shepp, Bill Evans, McCoy Tyner, Anthony Braxton, Roswell Rudd and Henry Threadgill. Frank imitation led to mastery of the new forms, and eventually to the development of an independent musical voice. In short, the leaders of Soviet free jazz followed Stravinsky's recommendation that aspiring musicians submit themselves to an external discipline as the best means of evolving their own language of expression.

This is not the place to assess the distinctive contributions of Vladimir Chekasin, Oleg Molokoedov, Vladimir Tarasov, Gediminas Laurinyavichus and other leaders of the movement. Instead, let us take note of a number of characteristics of Soviet free jazz that define its place in Soviet life and establish its position within the global world of jazz.

First, the new jazz has, so far as its public exposure, no overt links with civic issues. It embodies no ideology of rebellion. The fierce contentiousness of Archie Shepp has no parallel among his Soviet disciples. If the Soviet avant-gardists are angry, it does not show in their music, which is shot through with irony, droll asides and outright humour.

Cosmopolitanism constituted an important theme in the early free-jazz movement in America. The conspicuous use of the Japanese koto and Indian sitar carried with it an implicit criticism of the narrowness of European culture. Free jazz in the USSR initially drew heavily on the work of the Art Ensemble of Chicago and on other American groups. It also has been enriched by direct contact with the music of central Asia and other non-Western regions. Yet both the American and non-Western elements are fully assimilated. They are neither waved as banners nor exhibited as evidence of the artists' polyglot sympathies.

A further characteristic of the free jazz movement in the USSR is its close ties with avant-garde movements in other arts. Something similar can be found in the pioneer generation of post-bop innovators in America. Ornette Coleman's spectacular rise owes much to the support of Gunther Schuller and Leonard Bernstein, both of whom heard him at the Five Spot in New York. The 1960 album *Free Jazz* featured a Jackson Pollock painting on its cover, while Anthony Braxton in the late 1970s opened up channels of contact with avant-garde musicians in Europe.

Similarly, Vyacheslav Ganelin is himself an avant-garde composer, while his drummer, Vladimir Tarasov, is a devoted student of architecture and painting. At times, Soviet free jazz approaches avant-garde theatre, complete with Dada gestures and carefully staged 'happenings'. By contrast, the mimetic repertoire of Soviet bop musicians was limited to postures of sullen introversion.

The *démarche* of Soviet free jazz towards the avant-garde arts is timely. Liberation from rules of composition, tonality, metre and style is common to the experimental fringe of many media of expression in the USSR. However, the ability of free jazz there to reach out successfully to other avant-garde artists is heightened by more conservative considerations. The Soviet Union's strongly classical tradition of pedagogy leaves its stamp on avant-gardists in virtually every field in the arts. The strong compositional element in Ganelin's music reflects this heritage and provides a bridge with other experimental arts, especially those with a strongly architectonic\ strain. Soviet avant-gardists on the whole seek to liberate themselves from conventionalized language, but not from the discipline of language as such. Their relative conservatism on this point opens different media to each other and draws jazz into a generalized avant-garde movement. For better or worse, free jazz in the USSR has positioned itself as a high art, with few links to popular and mass culture.

It is tempting to conclude that Soviet free jazz is the result of a process of subtraction. It has been stripped of nearly all political and cultural references; it has been freed from constraints of style, conventional chords, tempi, bar lines, etc. In all these respects its freedom is negative, the freedom *from* rather than the freedom *to*.

There is, however, a strongly positive dimension to the freedom of free jazz in the USSR. Compared with all earlier forms of jazz in that country, the new movement stands for a broader, more complex, and hence freer ideal of the human personality. Roswell Rudd used to extol the way in which American free jazz liberated him from the bonds of musical convention – in short, he praised the negative freedoms it made possible. By the time the new movement reached the USSR it had long since lost this rebellious edge. Its task was no longer merely to demolish old conventions but to leave the artist free to create an entirely new universe. To use a literary comparison, free jazz in America was initially akin to the *Sturm und Drang* movement in eighteenth-century Germany, a revolt of Schilleresque heroes against stagnated cultural forms and values. The present Soviet free jazz movement is more calmly Kantian in character; it begins with the assumption of absolute freedom, invites the artist to create his or her own categories and forms, and then challenges him or her to use them as a new language of expression. The emphasis is not upon rebellion, which is assumed already to have been pushed to its conclusion. Instead, Soviet avant-gardists concentrate on the playful diversity of expression to which a genuinely free personality is open. To be sure, this element is evident among the American pioneers. Among the Russians, the absolutely free play of personality is everything. To establish and then give voice to the free human personality is the very essence of the new movement in Soviet jazz, and accounts for its significance to Soviet culture as a whole.

One might charge that the new jazz musicians of the Soviet Union have 'dropped out', abandoning activism in favour of a mystical quietism. A similar charge was levelled against those

Russian writers in the early nineteenth century who abandoned
civic causes following the failure of the Decembrist Revolution of
1825 and devoted themselves instead to the maintenance of a 'pure
soul' (*Schone Seele*). One such critic was Alexander Herzen.

The charge was unjust in the nineteenth century and it would
miss the point today. It can be granted that Soviet free jazz lacks
the direct social content of bop, let alone of the popular and
subversive guitar ballads of Vladimir Vysotskii. More than any
movement before it, however, it actively cultivates a counter-
reality. It may be 'the music of an agnostic civilization', as Efim
Barban has argued. But if the new jazz is agnostic regarding
community values, it is passionately affirmative of the individual
personality as such.

Again, a historical comparison is in order. Herzen regretted the
passing of the old activism. Later, he was harshly critical of his
own cultivation of a 'pure soul' as a form of escapism. And yet he
also acknowledged that it was precisely this phase that was most
essential to his own eventual emergence as a dauntless crusader on
behalf of new cultural values. By concentrating over many years
on the freedom of personality, Herzen and his contemporaries
were later able to take the lead in promoting the Great Reforms of
the 1860s and 1870s.

It is too early to know whether the movement for free jazz in the
USSR will follow a similar course. Under any circumstances, its
musical significance should be judged by more narrowly aesthetic
standards. None the less, there are grounds for thinking that the
current movement may eventually exert a stronger influence on
the culture as a whole. Anyone who has observed the rapt,
cult-like engagement that exists between performer and audience
at a concert by the Ganelin Trio cannot doubt that the significance
of the occasion transcends music. While infinitely more limited in
scale, these performances bear closer comparison with the epochal
public readings by the poets Andrei Voznesensky and Yevgeny
Yevtushenko in the early 1960s than to any recent events in the
sphere of Soviet jazz. Indeed, it is unlikely that the newest jazz
anywhere has called forth the degree of passionate commitment
among audiences that can be seen in the Soviet Union. To the
extent that this is so, it defines the significance of the development
for the history of Soviet culture.

Soviet Jazz: New Identity
Efim Barban

Efim Barban, born in 1935, graduated from Leningrad State University. He is the author of three books on jazz: Black Music, White Freedom, Jazz Experience *and* The Soviet Jazz on Records. *His book* Black Music, White Freedom *is one of the most profound books ever written on jazz. It deals with the philosophy, aesthetics and perception of the new music. Some parts of this book have been translated into English; the whole book has not been published in the West. For many years Efim Barban was the editor and publisher of the Soviet unofficial jazz magazine* Chorus (Kvadrat). *Since 1984 he has lived in London.*

In the autumn of 1966 the Leningrad Jazz Club reopened after a seven-year interval. Soon after, a poster appeared at the entrance of the Leningrad Soviet Palace of Culture, where it held its meetings, advertising a lecture entitled: 'Jazz: Music or Religion?' The title of this lecture perfectly reflects the nature of the perception of jazz in the Soviet Union.

Jazz in that country was never merely music, or entertainment, or even serious art, as it was in the West. There were two reasons why jazz fans in Russia might suspect that their favourite music was, or might turn out to be, a religion: in the first place, jazz, throughout its history in the Soviet Union, had been the object of concentrated attention on the part of the authorities (no less than religion, or any form of ideology) and, in the second place, for its listeners it came to be an intelligible and acceptable form of spiritual resistance to surrounding reality; jazz helped them to survive in a hostile environment and to realize their spiritual and emotional aspirations. This is why jazz in Russia (particularly in the fifties and sixties) generated not only a whole system of cults and rituals but also its own slang.

Naturally, one can speculate that if jazz had not been such forbidden fruit in the Soviet Union, and if some other form of spiritual activity had existed there, no less closely linked to Western values, jazz would not have been so popular in that country. Apart from this, jazz-lovers in Russia frequently do not even suspect that, in the West too, jazz has always been a kind of musical *enfant terrible*, and that there too, jazz was not part of the cultural Establishment. But thanks to its persecution in the Soviet Union (in the last years of the Stalin era it was forbidden even to use the word 'jazz' in print), where until recently the authorities tried to convince the public that jazz was nothing more than a form of Western bourgeois propaganda – a kind of musical ideological subversion – a wide audience identified this music with the Western way of life, opposing Soviet reality and the values of official art.

It should not be forgotten, either, that there has never been a youth subculture in the Soviet Union. In popular music spontaneous behaviour on stage was forbidden for decades (all music being subject to prior censorship) and the tiniest hint of hedonism or the erotic was outlawed. Official popular music was remarkable for its gloomy 'puritanism', for its unnatural (anti-natural) sterility. Clearly, jazz with its free self-expression, swing and the Dionysian atmosphere of the contact between performer and listeners, could not fail to attract a youthful audience. When it had become part of the unofficial (alternative) culture, jazz in Russia always successfully opposed musical dogmatism and Party prescriptions. Crucially, jazz became a form of escapism, of flight from odious and depersonalized reality. In a world where natural and sincere manifestations of emotion were impossible, where everything was stifled by 'social necessity', jazz became a safety-valve, an outlet for the realization of individual life, for the manifestation of human privacy in an alienated world.

With time, as jazz began to change its aesthetic stamp, becoming an increasingly serious and elitist art (with the appearance of new jazz) rock took over the social function of jazz for the general youth audience – and here Russia was by no means exceptional. The 'ecstatic revelations' of rock proved to be more effective for sexual sublimation than the comparatively sophisticated art of jazz.

If this process of aesthetic reorientation among young people occurred in the sixties in the United States and Western Europe, in the Soviet Union it began five or six years later – the country's isolation from the process of world art made itself felt.

At the end of the seventies the 'domestication' of jazz by the State began in Russia. State concert organizations allowed several groups to appear with genuine jazz programmes and to tour the country with them. Before this only stage bands and pop groups had been taken on by the State concert organizations, the only employers for the country's musicians. In this way amateur jazz ensembles in the Soviet Union turned professional for the first time. At present there are five (!) such professional combos in the Soviet Union, and one big band. Side by side with these there are scores of ensembles and orchestras, with amateur status but made up of first-class professional musicians. To earn a living, their members are forced to work in restaurant dance bands, in studio orchestras for the radio or in pop groups, and to play jazz in their spare time. The majority of the participants in Soviet jazz festivals in Moscow, Leningrad, Riga and other towns are such musicians. Their orchestras and ensembles can be heard only at infrequent festivals.

The Soviet Union has not escaped the aesthetic division of jazz, worldwide, into 'old' and 'new'. Naturally, as has happened everywhere in the world, the more creative element among Soviet musicians has opted for free (avant-garde) jazz. The paradox of the Soviet avant-garde's social position lies in the fact that while in the West new-jazz musicians have reputations as political and artistic dissidents, in Russia the authorities regard them as propagandists of decadent bourgeois culture, fundamentally hostile to the revolutionary idea of socialist realism. This is why it is impossible for new-jazz musicians in the Soviet Union to become part of official jazz life. Essentially, musical nonconformism, in the West as in the East, has proved to be the lot of free-jazz musicians. But if in a pluralist society the worst fate of the jazz avant-garde, unpopular as it is, is simply to be left to its own devices, in Russia there is no room for anything which does not fit into the framework of officialdom (in the words of the traditional Soviet formula, 'He who is not with us is against us.') All this, however, does not mean that new-jazz musicians in Russia take no part in local jazz life; their activity simply goes on for the most part within the limits of the second (alternative) culture.

Broadly speaking, traditional jazz in the Soviet Union, in artistic terms, displays secondary characteristics, aspiring only to the greatest possible approximation to prominent American models. In Russia, and even in some national republics, there are first-class mainstream musicians, who are *technically* the equals of the best American players. But the Soviet mainstream, programmed to imitation and mimicry, has produced nothing significant *in terms of ideas*, nothing which might give its music ethnic or artistic originality. For ideas, it is completely dependent on the birthplace of jazz.

It is possible that one of the reasons why new jazz in the Soviet Union has followed a different line of development lies in the interest it evoked in the Soviet intelligentsia. (It is certainly true that new-jazz musicians, as a group, are more widely cultured than jazz traditionalists.) The intelligentsia's interest in the new music also had an element of snobbism. Among the modern Soviet intelligentsia it would scarcely be possible to awaken interest in an art which had been entirely assimilated by official culture. The non-acceptance of new jazz by the Soviet artistic Establishment is a guarantee of its success with the intelligentsia. On the other hand, old jazz is too closely linked with mass culture, with a hedonistic sense of the world, to interest a listener who is looking for an answer to the existential questions of life, who above all seeks the vindication of his sense of social alienation. The hedonism and absence of the problematical in old jazz are perceived by this kind of listener as a form of artistic conformism.

Naturally, new jazz in the Soviet Union did not emerge from a vacuum, nor was it the brainchild of Soviet musicians. The American and, subsequently, the European influence in it was always perceptible. The first new-jazz ensembles in Russia were striking in many respects. In the mid-sixties the saxophonist

Roman Kunsman (who has since emigrated to Israel) led a Leningrad quartet whose music recalled Ornette Coleman's, and the influence of John Coltrane was discernible in the sound of the Riga saxophonist Vadim Vyadro (who has emigrated to the United States). But when it had passed through the inevitable imitative incubation period, Soviet new jazz transformed itself into one of the most significant achievements of twentieth-century Soviet art. Only the lack of systematic documentation of its attainments and the fact that official music criticism has ignored it have prevented its general acceptance as such. Certainly in the last five years, since the English company, Leo Records, began systematically releasing records of the Soviet avant-garde, and the Ganelin Trio has made several concert appearances in the West, the phenomenon of Russian jazz has begun to be widely discussed in the jazz press.

A significant proportion of the new jazz music of the seventies has of course been irretrievably lost to listeners and to historians of the art – sound recordings are the only way to preserve improvisatory art. In the Soviet Union the one State recording company which exists, Melodiya, deals only with official 'social demand' work. In the last decade only four records of the Ganelin Trio have appeared in the Soviet Union (nine of their records have been released over this period in the West). Other new-jazz musicians cannot even dream of putting out a record, since officially they simply do not, and cannot, exist in the Soviet Union. When the Contemporary Music Club was set up in Leningrad in 1979, under whose auspices free-jazz concerts were held with enormous success, it was shut, after a year, as an 'ideologically harmful enterprise'.

How many people take part in the new-jazz movement in the Soviet Union? By its nature it cannot be a mass phenomenon, since the content of its music is too serious for that, and the means of expression it employs are very far from traditional. We should remember that even in the West new jazz is esoteric enough, and so, for that matter, is avant-garde art in all its aspects. In the citadel of world jazz, the United States, no more than two to three hundred musicians can be reckoned to belong to this tendency. And that is after a period of development of a quarter of a century, which has produced dozens of stars. In England, which has evolved its own original school of new jazz, there are no more than fifty serious practitioners of the art. As for the Soviet Union, by the most careful reckoning, no more than forty people there play new jazz, that is approximately ten per cent of all jazz musicians (amateur and professional) in the country. This sort of calculation is not difficult, when one knows all the jazz orchestras and ensembles currently in existence in the Soviet Union.

But in art the criterion is quality, not quantity, and the low world percentage of new-jazz adherents does not diminish their artistic weight in the general scale of world musical production. At present everything significant and original in jazz music comes out of the avant-garde. If one can speak of some sort of artistic development in the art of jazz, of its enrichment with new content and new means of expression, this is happening today only within the framework of the new-jazz aesthetic.

New-jazz musicians are almost the only authentically creative musical force in the Soviet Union, apart from half a dozen serious composers. Furthermore, one can now speak confidently of the emergence of an original school of new jazz in the Soviet Union, with its own distinctive artistic attributes, whose significance for modern jazz reaches far beyond the geographical boundaries of Russia.

What has produced such a significant artistic phenomenon in a provincial – in jazz terms – country? Where could these people have sprung from to challenge stars of the avant-garde from countries with long and fertile jazz traditions? What is the source of the Soviet new-jazz musicians' creative work? How was it possible for an improvisatory art to survive and flourish under total censorship and the state monopoly of artistic activity?

Let us transport ourselves to a small room in a private flat in Moscow in 1984. About twenty young people are sitting on the floor holding glasses of wine. Tobacco smoke hangs in the air. On the walls are abstract paintings. A long-haired saxophonist stands in the corner improvising expressive music with a jagged rhythm. A percussionist sitting nearby accompanies him on the Indian mridangam. Suddenly a barefoot woman, a violinist, enters and joins the players. The atmosphere is something between a London pub and a New York artist's loft. As for the music, it's difficult to associate it with any fixed genre. All one can say of it is that aesthetically it has no connection with the art of mass culture. It has nothing in common with rock or pop music. At times the players' improvisations recall the form of John Cage's music, or Anthony Braxton's compositions. This is a serious and technically perfect attempt at musical self-expression. At first it is not so much the music that is surprising, as the expert and authoritative instrumental technique. Here we find another distinctive feature of the new-jazz movement in the Soviet Union: as a rule the musicians taking part have had a high level of academic training, and for them problems of technique do not exist. If rock (like traditional jazz) is the province of dilettantes, new jazz in Russia is performed by professionals who have been trained in conservatoires and have experience as serious composers. Of course earlier jazz musicians did achieve perfect musical technique. No one is going to improve on Charlie Parker's saxophone playing. But traditional jazz musicians were attracted by technique for its own sake. The main criterion of musical quality in old jazz was the quality of instrumental technique. But for the musicians of the neo-avant-garde it is not technique and the possibility of self-expression in separate solo sections that is of interest, so much as the creation of an integral (non-standard) composition, i.e. what has always interested European composers. That is why the leading Soviet new-jazz musicians are above all authors of serious and sophisticated compositions, perfectly familiar with the language of modern music worldwide. One need only name Vyacheslav Ganelin, Vladimir Chekasin, Anatoly Vapirov, Vyacheslav Gayvoronsky,Vladimir Tolkachev to be assured, on the evidence of their music, that they have succeeded in attaining a superb balance between composition and improvisation in their work, and that the level of ideas in it is qualitatively equivalent to that of the work of European composers of the post-Webern era. (The degree of talent in the music is another matter.)

All this does not mean, of course, that there are no musicians in Russia using free improvisation methods exclusively (like the Company in England or the Instant Composers' Pool in Holland). The Soviet avant-garde covers a fairly wide field. The music of Sergey Letov, the Moscow saxophonist, the cellist Vladislav

Makarov from Smolensk and the Leningrad drummer Alexander Kondrashkin, who usually play as a trio, can be compared aesthetically with that of Evan Parker or Derek Bailey. One might also put the Leningrad pianist Sergey Kuryokhin into this category of musicians. But it is the Ganelin Trio, the ensembles of A. Vapirov, V. Tolkachev/Yu. Yukechev and V. Gayvoronsky/V. Volkov which set the tone in Soviet new jazz, and they use a mixed composition technique. The musicians of the 'Arkhangelsk' jazz group led by Vladimir Rezitsky, and Pyatras Vishnyauskas's ensemble from Vilnius also use this method.

When the music of the leading Soviet new-jazz ensembles is analysed, three sources of their creative work may be clearly identified: one, the Russian avant-garde aesthetic of the twenties (not necessarily the musical avant-garde); two, the folk music of the many nations that make up the Soviet Union; three, American and European free jazz, chiefly of the post-Coltrane period.

The artistic 'bond of ages' which was broken for thirty years has only gradually begun to be revived in Russia. It was only in the sixties and seventies that Russian musicians, artists and writers began to discover for themselves Russia's avant-garde culture of the first two decades of this century. The artificially interrupted natural development of Russian culture found its continuation in the unofficial (alternative) culture of the seventies and eighties. Literature has always exerted a decisive influence on public sentiment and artistic taste in Russia. Quite often the music of the best modern Soviet composers (Sophia Gubaidulina, Edison Denisov, Alfred Schnitke and others) and the music of their new-jazz colleagues displays a greater formal (structural, rhythmic) similarity to Andrey Bely's novel *Peterburg* or Russian futurist poetry or the work of the Oberiuti (the Society of Real Art), than to the music of their direct predecessors – Sergei Prokofiev or Dmitri Shostakovich. Frequently the colourist nuances of the newest Soviet music (both jazz and non-jazz) are more closely related to the painting of Vasily Kandinsky or Kasimir Malevich than to the half-forgotten music of Lurie, Roslavets, Mosolov, Golyshev and the other founders of the Russian musical avant-garde in the twenties.

Specific geographical factors have a huge influence on the musical characteristics of new Soviet jazz. Unofficial Soviet literature, painting and art criticism are concentrated in the two capitals (Moscow and Leningrad), which are the acknowledged centres of the second culture. As far as Moscow is concerned, this is not true for the new jazz: there is not one ensemble there which plays this music. The heartland of new jazz extends over the country from Arkhangelsk in the north to Alma-Ata in the south, from Vilnius in the west to Novosibirsk in the east. In this way the centres of new jazz are to be found in such culturally diverse regions as the northernmost part of Russia (the only region the Tartars failed to reach, where an authentic Old Russian folk culture has been preserved in its original form), Central Asia, Lithuania and Siberia. I have not mentioned Leningrad – the centre of the new-jazz movement in the country, and a town which always opposed the official capital in the cultural consciousness of the Russian intelligentsia; the opposition of these two imperial capitals (past and present) is seen there as the clash of two cultures.

Russian new-jazz musicians, working in an environment of heterogeneous national cultures, fuse them with the pure jazz (Afro-American) components of their music, using elements from ethnic music of the numerous peoples of the Soviet Union. Thus the trumpeter Yuri Parfenov, after he had played in Tashkent, and subsequently in Alma-Ata (Central Asia), said in one of his interviews that he was 'steeped in Eastern music'. Another new jazz musician, the Novosibirsk drummer Sergey Belichenko, stated in an interview for the unofficial jazz journal *Chorus* (Kvadrat), that the music his group plays is derived from Buryat and Touvin folk music, which is connected with that of India and Tibet. V. Rezitsky's 'Arkhangelsk' ensemble openly uses Old Russian northern folk tunes. If Russian jazz musicians use musical material from other cultures so widely, then it scarcely needs to be said that for non-Russian musicians, like, for example, Pyatras Vishnyauskas and Vitas Labutis in Lithuania, to resort to national sources is quite simply one form of struggle against cultural russification.

Soviet jazz would not be jazz if the tradition and spirit of Afro-American music were not alive within it. Despite enormous difficulties in acquiring musical information, and the isolation of Soviet jazz musicians from world jazz, they have succeeded in assimilating the achievements of Afro-American culture and in making its music an organic element of their own language. One has only to listen to Anatoly Vapirov's music, original and inventive as it is, to understand straight away that the lessons of John Coltrane, Archie Shepp and Anthony Braxton have not been in vain. The polystylistic character of Vladimir Tolkachev's music is coloured with intonations which derive from literally all jazz styles – from the music of Johnny Hodges to the sounds of Oliver Lake. The fantastic expressive quality of the music of Vladimir Chekasin – perhaps the leading saxophonist in Europe today – could not have come to maturity without a deep understanding and mastery of the blues tradition.

But Soviet new jazz is far more than the mere sum of all the aesthetic parts which go to make it up. Just as a chord is not the sum of the notes of which it consists, but an acoustic synthesis which creates a qualitatively new sound, the Soviet avant-garde has made use of the three vital sources of its creative activity to create music which is qualitatively new and bears little resemblance to its constituent elements. The musical fusion to which they have given rise is capable of breathing new life into Western jazz, whose previously headlong progress has slowed down in recent years.

A persecuted religion always engenders great spiritual exploits. An underground church demands unwavering faith and often, heroic efforts from its disciples, while in conditions of complete religious freedom faith often degenerates into empty ritual. Soviet new-jazz musicians create their art under extremely adverse social conditions, which demand not only courage, but a deep inner commitment to this kind of creative activity. The existential character of the Russian avant-garde is one of the main intrinsic elements of its philosophy and its aesthetic. It is this element which gives Soviet new jazz that stripped emotional incandescence, that inner passion, which do not arise in music which seeks merely to solve formal problems. Soviet musicians know that one must play in order to survive in their brave new world.

Another important characteristic of new Russian jazz is its grounding in cultural synthesis and the polystylistic musical character this entails. The musicians make use of contemporary intonational resources from all over Russia, of the acoustic elements – spoken, musical, extraneous – of their environment, and this makes theirs a national music. The phonic past and acoustic present in Russia are organically reworked by the musicians into jazz forms. Russia's phonic riches (more than one hundred different peoples make up the population) can be compared only with the riches of its mineral deposits. Russia's relative dissociation from a profound jazz tradition has, apparently, proved providential for new-jazz musicians, who find it easier to experiment with jazz form than their American colleagues. The inclusion in the music of heterogeneous elements, both stylistic and cultural, is a hallmark of Soviet new jazz. Structural ideas of the new Viennese school, Stravinsky's rhythmical innovations, Stockhausen's phonic 'finds' may all be found organically integrated in the music. Polystylistics is the foundation of its creative system.

The sombre ideological background to the development of Soviet jazz, the parodic gravity of the ideological ceremonies and rituals which surround the Soviet citizen (in which he or she is forced to take part), have produced a corresponding creative reaction in art. New jazz is not alone in this; practically all unofficial Soviet art is imbued with blasphemous sarcasm and black humour, countering the sacred monolithic earnestness of official ideology. The improvisatory nature of jazz enables the music to take on a carnival air, and its spirit defies deadening dogma. One need only listen to *Exercises* by Vladimir Chekasin, or *Non Troppo* by Vyacheslav Ganelin to understand how Soviet jazz conducts its own battle against general fear and paralysis in the country, how it reworks the most human of all qualities, humour, in the struggle against artistic and political (inhuman) dogma.

But the chief reason why Russia's new jazz is the foremost phenomenon of European musical culture is the high artistic quality of its output. This music is the product of highly developed professionalism and original culture. It is perhaps the most dynamic and life-enhancing artistic manifestation of the jazz process in the world today. The virtue of this music is its all-embracing humanity. Just as the classical legacy of Russian culture became an inalienable part of world culture and considerably influenced its development, so too Russian new jazz has made a serious contribution to world art in the twentieth century.

Translated from Russian by Sylvia Trott

A Week of New Jazz In Leningrad
Graham King

In spring 1982 Graham King was part of a group of English students studying in Leningrad. While he was in the USSR he was introduced to new music and witnessed the first week of new jazz ever to be held in Leningrad. Below he gives his account of this event. As this book goes to print Graham King is working as a journalist for several British newspapers.

The saxophonist's fingers shot across the keys, seemingly with complete abandon. The sound produced was not melodious. It screeched and it grumbled, always frenetic, angry and vigorous. Above the dense, shaggy beard, divided where the mouth compressed around the reed, his eyes danced with the music. They opened wide and shining, then collapsed into dim pools as the brows knitted and the forehead wrinkled.

The audience packed the hall, but moved so little they were scarcely noticeable in the half-light. Blue curtains, pulled across the windows, parted and flapped where a gap of a few inches let in gusts of the cold Leningrad afternoon air.

Vladimir Chekasin could not hear the swish of the trolley buses as they slid through Kirovsky Prospect two storeys below. He had now broken into a familiar jazz standard and, accompanied by two other saxophonists, started swaying down the aisle through the audience. Women in headscarves, wearing heavy coats with imitation fur collars, struggled to make progress along the packed pavement below. Chekasin, now halfway down the aisle, broke into 'Bye Bye Blackbird', but the other saxophones mocked his efforts. The procession broke down, they faced each other in the aisle and a musical argument broke out between the screeching and gurgling instruments. The women shuffled on, elbowing their way through the crowd towards Petrogradskaya Metro. They cursed each other with stern faces as string bags of groceries became entwined and had to be tugged free: 'Ah, to the devil with you.' Up above, through the blue flapping curtains, the argument turned to jest, each saxophonist taunting the other with his wailing sounds. The audience beamed with joy at this twist in the musical battle.

Below, although its strains penetrated the earflaps and head-scarves of the bustling crowd, another fight was going on as the 105 bus to Nevsky Prospect pulled up. It was already full as usual, with faces and noses squashed against the steamed-up windows. But the old theory applied. If you are in the middle of the crowd the efforts of those pushing from behind will somehow, miraculously, squeeze you, too, on to the bus. Only those at the back, and others who were pushed out to the side, were left on the pavement as the bus lurched slowly away. 'Ah, to the devil with you.'

Well, what did those angry shoppers, left stamping their feet on the ice and snow until the next bus came, think of the little show that was going on above their heads? It was now reaching a vigorous climax, obviously exciting the audience, as Chekasin was again hunched over the stage, his shoulders drawn together, his head tossing to and fro and his legs and torso twitching violently. Are they mad? How, in the middle of Leningrad, could anyone be allowed to make such a row? What are these discordant ravings: the outpourings of a crazed saxophonist? But, if our shopper puts down the heavy bags, leans against a post, lights a cigarette, could those sounds, just for a minute, be beautifully illogical, carry a pleasant breath of freshness, in a world otherwise dominated by responsibility, formality, Marxist logic and classical music?

New jazz was immensely popular among my friends, who introduced me to it while I was studying in Leningrad in March and April 1982. But they would certainly consider themselves intellectuals and, although they may work as boiler stokers, electricians or God knows what, they would also write reams of never-to-be published poetry and plays. Although a crowd of 500 might attend a concert, it seemed there was scarcely a face there that wasn't also a friend, unless, of course, it belonged to, well, you know who.

But that time was also the heyday of new jazz in Leningrad. The concerts I attended over three days in March 1982 were the first ever devoted exclusively to free jazz and most of the Soviet Union's most brilliant jazz musicians were in Leningrad. There was Leningrad's own Sergey Kuryokhin; Anatoly Vapirov, appearing shortly before he was imprisoned for speculating on the black market; Vladimir Chekasin from Vilnius in Lithuania; and others from Riga and Smolensk. Among the group of new-jazz followers it was an event of enormous significance. People like poet Arcady Dragomoshchenko, one of the founders of a ninety-strong semi-official writing group called Club-81, has been talking about it for weeks. The Leningrad Contemporary Music Club organizer, Alexander Kan, had diplomatically acquired the Lensoveta Cultural Hall on Kirovsky Prospect as the club's official home. In doing so he achieved the recognition that made the club and its concerts quite official, open and above board. As he explained to me: 'In this country you can't just rent a hall for a night and hold your concert. You have to be officially associated with one of the cultural halls. The director will examine the club and if it is approved, you have the right to hold events in that cultural hall. If he doesn't approve you, your club simply doesn't exist and that's it.'

Consequently, the Lensoveta Cultural Hall, a multi-purpose building of grey, prefabricated concrete, smells very officially of officialdom. Its walls are adorned by pictures of dairymaids receiving medals, miners shaking hands with suited officials, and bronzed farmworkers, with strong Soviet faces, standing beside combine harvesters in fields of swaying corn. But upstairs, in the second-floor hall where the Contemporary Music Club was holding its concerts, unofficial artists had also hung their pictures. And the audiences that came were undoubtedly bohemian, like Olga, who wore a shiny black leather cat-suit obviously obtained from abroad.

Two days of concerts passed. Some were poorly attended, while others, like Chekasin's, drew a following. The atmosphere was relaxed. People wandered around, hung about afterwards chatting, and I felt free to bring several British students along to take pictures, meet the musicians and look at this strange phenomenon.

But, on the third and final night, the atmosphere changed. Sergey Kuryokhin was to end the concert with his 'Creative Music Orchestra', which became known in the West as the 'Crazy Music Orchestra' after somebody misheard the name. Kuryokhin was something of a crazy character. At twenty-eight this handsome dark-haired man was already a legend of avant-garde jazz. He fascinated me with his energy and impatience. As I stumbled for Russian words he hummed, danced, tapped the table with his fingers and made high-pitched blipping noises – as if conducting his own private jazz concert. 'I am quite a neurotic person,' he said. That seemed clear. But he was also very talented, having studied classical piano at a conservatory. He could sit at the piano and play Rachmaninov with great feeling and then change and play almost any Beatles song you wished to name.

I asked him once if avant-garde jazz in Russia were not ten years behind Western jazz. 'This may be true,' he replied, 'because of the difficulties in communication. But there are people who, in their creative work and creative potential, have inside them everything they need to create real art. They are really in advance of all music – East and West together. People everywhere are striving for professionalism. In the West it is easier – for instance, a musician can find more published music, has more opportunity to listen to any kind of music, Tibetan, African or whatever. Here, in Russia, it is just more complicated. There are people who do everything in their power to listen to this music, they devote their whole life to it. There are people who are able to condense energy and then pour it out – the situation here produces artists of incredible power and strength.' I have heard the same said about Russian poets and novelists. My friends in Club-81 would put all their efforts into writing pages of poetry, they would discuss it, have readings through the night, live, breathe, sleep and eat poetry. And such was the solidarity that although not a word was published and not a penny earned, it simply didn't matter.

However, Kuryokhin attributed a special value to Russian culture. 'Some people see Russian culture as dependent on the West, subordinate to it. This sense of inferiority gives Russian culture its special colouring and distinctive features – and, at the same time, an element of self-confidence. Russian culture has always been great. It has developed along less rational lines than Western culture, because it is influenced by several roots – the Tartar invasion, for example. Therefore, Russian culture could be said to be looking towards the West while being influenced by the East.'

The authorities had not been sleeping during the three days of concerts at the Lensoveta Cultural Hall and, on the final night, they proved to be more awake than ever. The hall was overflowing. From the back wall to the stage people were crammed in, while the unfortunate ones were left to fill the corridor outside. Some 1,500 people were at the concert, from as far afield as Odessa on the Crimean coast. Kuryokhin was dressed in black. From the microphone at the front of the stage he announced that his Creative Music Orchestra would play a piece called 'A Gypsy–Arabic Alliance on the East–West Divan'. The vocalist was indeed a Gypsy, Valentina Ponomareva, and Kuryokhin announced he had taken a Muslim name. He was joined by Grebenshchikov, a young man who wore make-up with an arrow painted across his face. They started together, playing the pipes, but then were joined by a flute, an alto sax, two vocalists and the rest of the orchestra, coming on one by one.

The hour-long show was under way, although there were so many changes of mood, moments of such intensity, that it seemed to last a day. There was as much theatre to the performance as music. A balloon was blown up and popped, a guitar was smashed. Then Grebenshchikov scrabbled around to pick up the pieces and attempt to play the smashed guitar. Kuryokhin's charisma held everyone captive. He conducted the audience as much as the orchestra and his expressive face followed the moods of the music. The Gypsy vocalist produced disturbing piercing screams. The piano was thumped, cymbals dropped on the floor. Everything ended suddenly during a pitch of intense activity. Kuryokhin shouted '*Vsyo*' – 'That's all' and an empty stage received ten minutes of applause and screams for more.

The paintings were soon taken down and the audience left, showing no expression. I was whisked out of the building quickly – the place was full of KGB, I was told. It was two days before I saw

any of my friends again and four days before Kuryokhin emerged.
One friend said he was in a state of despair – he couldn't sleep, sit
still, think or work. He was practically in a state of shock. Why? I
asked; everything seemed fine to me. Then I realized. The largest
concert of its type, the only exclusively free-jazz concert to be held
in years, had finished. It was an enormous outlet after years of
hope, months of planning and excitement. God only knows when,
and if, there would be another. Those three days had meant so
much and ended in such a climax . . . everyone was simply
crestfallen.

It was a year before I returned to discover the consequences of the
concert. One Russian friend explained: 'The first two days were all
right. There was music, free music; the behaviour of the musicians
on stage was decent; so everything was fine. Understanding
practically nothing of the music itelf, the authorities couldn't
object to anything. But the last concert, Kuryokhin's, was
different. It was saturated with theatrical elements, the elements
of absurd theatre. And everything was tinged with a bit of irony
and sarcasm. You just couldn't help but feel it. It was bright and
very unusual and that's why it couldn't avoid arousing suspicion on
the side of the authorities. They didn't like the performance,
surely they didn't.'

Afterwards the Contemporary Music Club was told there was a
cult of violence. Why else was a guitar smashed, cymbals dropped,
a piano thumped and a balloon burst? The situation was worsened
because Kim Ismailov, chief of the Lensoveta Cultural Hall, had
fallen foul of the authorities himself and, since he had given the
permission for this concert to be held, it was a good pretext on
which to dismiss him.

My Russian friend continued: 'They tried to use this pretext to
fire Ismailov and that's why the machinery started working. To fire
him they had to prove that the event was absolutely dangerous for
the cultural upbringing of the people. They tried and they
succeeded in proving it – on paper at least. They fired him and just
closed the club. Since the club no longer has a home, it officially
doesn't exist any more.

'But,' my friend went on, 'for the future there is still some hope.

There are fraternal literary clubs like Club-81 – and they are in a much better position with the authorities. We hope to co-operate with them and to incorporate our music programmes into their newly formed theatre. We may be able to form a new centre of modern contemporary art. If it all worked out it would be unprecedented and fantastic. The painters would be included and we would have something that couldn't have been imagined five years ago. But it's hard work; every day we are meeting to discuss it and then we must talk with the authorities. We can't be sure of anything, but we still do have hope.'

Sure enough, a year later in 1984, I returned to find that the writers' club had, through skilful negotiation with the authorities, found a home for itself. There was even talk of a book of poetry from Club-81 being published. Maybe it would be only a few hundred copies that were printed and, of course, they may never reach the bookshelves, but at least it is something.

The club's new home was, ironically, not far from the Lensoveta Cultural Hall. At the top of a large ornate block, with grand wrought-iron balconies on every floor, several apartments had been made into this 'new centre of contemporary art'. It was not luxurious, in fact quite untidy and scrappy, but at least it was a home. Below, the trolley buses still swished back and forth. People pushed their way along the pavement in the bright Leningrad sun. Buses were as full as ever, with round, plump faces pushed against the mud-splattered windows. Blackened ice packed the gutters and huge lumps lay at the base of drainpipes melting in the spring sun. Everyone felt optimistic about this new, small opportunity given by the authorities. Since they could give with one hand and take with the other, perhaps it was all the better that it was small and inconspicuous.

In that new home, that Saturday afternoon in April, there would be poetry reading and music by Sergey Kuryokhin. So it seemed the circle was complete, ready, perhaps, to begin a new turn.

The Ganelin Trio: An Unguided Comet
Efim Barban

The Musicians

In improvised music, more than in any other, the personality of the performer (the creator of the music) is a natural and organic part of the musical content. In free jazz the content emerges as the emotional and spiritual experience of the listener, to whom the essence of the musician is revealed in the process of spontaneous creation of music. In the art of improvising the quality of the music is closely linked with the characteristic spiritual and intellectual features of its creators.

Many of the artistic and stylistic characteristics of the Ganelin Trio's music are closely linked with its members' characters. The musicians themselves understand that very well. 'Our pieces,' said Vyacheslav Ganelin in an interview, 'are strictly worked out compositions. But they are ours. If they are performed by other people the music will be different. In our music the individual features of each one of us are a part of the general artistic effect.'

The high quality of the trio's music and the fact that such artistically dissimilar personalities should have worked together for so long paradoxically refutes the opinion widely held by musicologists that only the improvisers' similarity of character, interests and musical outlook can guarantee prolonged artistic collaboration and the aesthetic homogeneity of the music. The very different characters, intellectual/psychological make-up and artistic interests of the musicians disprove this popular belief.

Vyacheslav Ganelin is a composer and pianist. His eyes sparkle humorously; he is always describing with enthusiasm a musical idea which has just occurred to him, gesticulating expansively; he has an irresistible sense of humour, he constantly makes fun of himself and his friends in the trio. His paradoxical artistic quest is reinforced by his extensive knowledge of music. His non-jazz composing often draws him to exotic genres and musical cultures: from ancient music to Eskimo songs. Ganelin's vivid dramatic talent, his subtle sense of style, the acute perception of a composer are clearly felt in the trio's music. He, more often than the others, plans the strategy of the composition, determining the musical roles. It is often he who is the initiator of a frank attempt to dramatize the music on stage, an attempt to turn musical improvisation into a complete visual/acoustic act, full of musical conflicts.

Vladimir Tarasov is a drummer and a recognized master of percussion. Calm and unhurried, a pipe always in his mouth, he is quietly spoken with soft, flowing gestures. While puffing at his pipe he will talk unhurriedly on any subject except music. It is hard to imagine how much explosive energy is concealed behind this calm. At home he can often be found studying paintings of old masters and contemporary sculpture, reading monographs on the plastic arts. This genuine interest in painting, sculpture and architecture is clearly reflected in his music-making, in the architectonics of the rhythmical structures of his music.

Tarasov does not only provide a very solid rhythmical basis to the improvising of his partners. He is the initiator of many architectural or ornamental details in the musical structures which are created on the stage by the musicians. The aesthetic universality of his improvisations can be explained by the range of his professional experience (in particular by his work in the Lithuanian State Symphony Orchestra) and his excellent knowlege of non-European percussion music – from Indonesian *gamelan* to African drum choirs.

Vladimir Chekasin is a saxophonist, clarinettist and composer. On the stage he is reserved, concentrated and self-absorbed. It is his presence which gives the trio's music its highly emotional quality, the acutely tense feeling which emerges during the group's best performances. His saxophone possesses the magical ability to bring to life any, even the most lifeless, music. It adds a human presence to the rich sonority and rhythmical structures of the music.

The style of Chekasin's musical experience is so wide-ranging that it includes practically all the possible shades of emotion in music: from the simplest emphatic exclamations to black humour and tragic pathos. For Chekasin there are no low or vulgar genres; he will accept all genres and styles if the music itself is performed with talent. He was once asked: 'Which music do you yourself listen to most often?' He answered: 'It all depends on my emotional state. Sometimes I want to listen to Lutoslawski or Xenakis, and sometimes Ben Webster. Each emotional state needs a different outlet.'

The desire to give each gesture, intonation, and movement an aesthetic significance reveals the real artist in him. A subtle understanding of all shades of the improviser's spontaneous music-making, the ability to control the least nuance is combined in Chekasin with fantastic instrumental technique – he is without doubt one of the greatest European saxophonists, the acknowledged leader of the Soviet saxophone school.

The creative co-operation of these musicians is based on the principle of mutual complementation. It was a happy chance which united in a single group such dissimilar artistic personalities. It is not even a question of the significance of the musicians' talent, the range of their gifts, but of the specific nature and type of their artistic thought in the special 'structural' field which they instinctively chose in the creation of their compositions.

It is these contrasting personal and psychological features, their different ways of thinking which create that organic artistic whole which is the music of the Ganelin Trio. The players are united by a clear understanding of the fact that in the improvising art of jazz artistic truth is a combination of 'live' and heterogeneous independent characters, the manifestation and fusion of deeply intimate and sincerely felt artistic experience.

Music

The musicians were once asked in an interview how their music is composed, how they work on their compositions. Vladimir Chekasin answered: 'A piece may emerge spontaneously during a rehearsal, and then we work on the details. Or a piece may emerge "mechanically": we take a structure and then we work out textural elements, colouring, characteristic features – this is traditional composing technique.'

'But what about the idea of improvisation? What percentage of the trio's music is actually improvised?' asked the interviewer.

Chekasin explained further: 'We strictly control the "aleatory". It is essentially a performance of a chamber work which has already been composed. In principle everything we perform can subsequently be written down, the whole piece is already in our heads. As a matter of fact, our spontaneity is not of the usual kind. Our improvisations are a filling-in with textural elements of the space between the main structural landmarks of a piece, which have always been thought out in advance.'

To this Vyacheslav Ganelin added: 'I think that the chief quality of our work is the absence of purely rational, "dry" elements. Our music is always organic and natural, and audiences sense the absence of any posing.'

So what we have is a conscious striving for a mixed technique – an organic unity of composition and improvisation. Much of the trio's music consists of well-planned elements of musical structure which have been composed in advance. The basic structural 'skeleton' of their pieces is always prepared beforehand. They have virtually abandoned the traditional jazz format in which the form is dictated by the inevitable sequence of theme and variation and a regular rhythmic pulse. They hardly ever improvise in the traditional way on a theme stated at the outset. But the 'open' form of their music is not explained simply by the absence of traditional jazz structure so much as by the players' striving to be guided solely by the principle of artistic expediency. This explains the wealth of different stylistic elements in their music, from folk dance and the Baroque to the aleatory and traditional jazz.

In this respect the cycle *Catalogue* (released in 1981 as *Live in East Germany*, LR 102) often performed both at home and abroad, is particularly significant. Conceived as an artistic resumé of their ten years' collaboration, it vividly reflects the whole range of the trio's aesthetic convictions, the variety of their artistic methods and the high level of their instrumental skills.

There are virtually no weak spots, no *trous* in the music of this cycle. The structure of the music is astonishingly precise and subtly planned. The seven pieces, which are played without a break, are woven seamlessly together and structured into a single subject-line, taking into account both the laws of composition and the psychology of listening. This furnishes a great variety of emotional moods and tensions as well as a perpetual contrasting of intelligible rhythmic structures and the whole spectrum of textural variations, something hitherto unknown in jazz music.

The work is as exciting as a first-class thriller; and in fact we are listening to masters in the art of musical storytelling, able to grip our attention. What takes place in the music is so unpredictable and at the same time so logically organized, that the listener is entranced both by the depth and variety of an overwhelming aesthetic experience and by the wholly convincing intrigue of the sense-structure.

The even-numbered pieces of *Catalogue* take the form of spatio-rhythmic investigations. In texture they resemble Boulez' serial pieces, but the timbre is that of jazz. The tempo is usually moderato. There are flashes of percussion and at a deeper level saxophone and guitar (bowed) flare up, as it were, with pointillistic staccatos and phrases half meditative, half speculative, fragmentary – and the very reverse of assertions – thus constituting a whole aesthetic based on the hint – the unfinished.

The odd-numbered pieces include some extremely swinging music. With the change of the saxophone improvisation to a presto we are at a high level of emotional tension which reaches an Ayler-like paroxysm (especially in the third and fifth pieces). In the fifth Chekasin has his finest solo and he contrives to touch the mystery that only a true poet can grasp. We sense a moment at which the music and the player fuse – there is no longer a Ganelin Trio, no music that is 'theirs', only the *one*. A great moment of mutual fusion. This is the climax when we are no longer aware of musicianship, of art, of deliberate artifice or 'expression', only of reality. Man becomes an illumination of his own self, and in the act of creation the players move on to the highest level, both mentally and sensually – a sudden enlightenment and non-activity at which they are no longer subject to fate. Each at last becomes himself in a spontaneous outburst; and this is particularly noticeable in the case of Chekasin, whose primitive naturalness and profound vitality merge with the universal life-force (which also fills his listeners). In his best solos he follows the only possible path – when his concentration reaches a pitch at which the improviser ceases to be aware of himself, he leaves his body and becomes pure musical insight. The trio's artistic naturalness reaches its high point when the listener has the sensation that the music is neither written, nor composed nor rehearsed and that the players are doing nothing, discovering nothing but simply revealing something which Nature has given them. And in their best compositions their intention is not to 'create' but simply not to disturb the true nature of their inner world. It is this ability of the artist to liberate his aesthetic consciousness that removes any suggestion of 'madeness', or deliberate artifice, from their music, which thus comes to resemble the free flight of a bird.

Any formal analysis of the Ganelin Trio's music must take into account the fundamental purpose of their activity as artists, their whole musical 'conduct': to combine the free formation of personality with being.

Their profound seriousness and the element of contradiction in their thinking *must* inevitably take an ironical form, since any other would inevitably lead to aesthetic exaggeration – a hunchback mounted on a camel! In Chekasin's case frivolity consists in an understanding of reality that may be called pre-ontological. And he finds a further source of energy in the discrediting of the old idolatries and demagogies of music, the defetishizing of certain ritual commonplaces which have long been obsolete but remain the foundations of philistine self-satisfaction and totemism in the jazz world.

Contradictions are never reconciled in new jazz as they are in classical music and in old jazz; they simply become more explicit and acute (*contemporary realism*). In this sense *Catalogue* is a profoundly realistic work: there is no spirit of illusory wellbeing, no false 'harmony', no happy ending. Its finest passages are profoundly tragic, telling of the suffering and death of the musical self. The sound of the siren at the end of the cycle is symbolic – is it a distress signal, an alarm or a call to action? Only the sixth piece of the set betrays this spirit of intransigence, showing in its coda a 'classical' fear in the face of unresolved conflict. One would like to think that a relative weakness in the performance of this piece is due to the pangs of aesthetic conscience.

Aesthetic

The members of the trio were asked on one occasion to classify
their music, to explain to what genre it belongs and in which jazz
style they play. This is what they answered.

CHEKASIN: If you consider our music from the point of view of
Western European jazz, then we are fairly remote from it.

GANELIN: Our music is very remote from European jazz. We do
not play free jazz as such.

CHEKASIN: We borrow some elements not only from jazz but
from chamber music, folk music and other genres. We sometimes
even make use of 'naïve', childish gimmicks which can create very
interesting combinations that are entirely new. Children are
excellent artists.

GANELIN: Children perform naturally and brilliantly. We sometimes use non-musical formal objects and find that these fit very
well into the music.

This synthesis of aesthetically heterogeneous formal genre-
elements is in fact the most noticeable characteristic of the trio's
music, which nevertheless shows marked leanings towards the jazz
idiom. This essentially includes all the jazz elements: improvisation, swing, specific sound-making, personal expressiveness
(drive) and metro-rhythmical jazz formulae combined, of course,
with irregular rhythmic figuration. Aesthetically there is every
reason to speak of the Ganelin Trio as a jazz group. On the other
hand the aesthetic range of the players is unparalleled in the
history of jazz, covering as it does a number of widely differing
musical and cultural associations and analogies – from the
Impressionist preludes in the style of Debussy and the pointillistic
music of Webern and Boulez to Oriental pentatonic pseudo-ragas,
the blues and pop music.

The Ganelin Trio has in fact created its own musical universe by
challenging the well-defined genre of traditional jazz; and in that
universe many of the stylistic limitations of traditional jazz
disappear, dividing lines between genres are blurred and what
formally hampered the flight of the musical imagination has been
removed. This kind of music-making would be fatal to less
talented players with a less developed sense of form or rhythm.
But Ganelin, Tarasov and Chekasin have never crossed the

aesthetic boundary line beyond which lie non-art and non-jazz, and artistic form and content disintegrate. It may be that the mysterious attraction of this music lies in the fact that it involves the listener in a bold and dangerous journey, full of far-out musical adventures and leading to the very limits of genre and musical form.

It is pointless to set out to prove their non-adherence to the canons of jazz, their aesthetic illegitimacy and their stylistic irregularities; for this music does not simply exist, it exerts an immense emotional and aesthetic influence on the listener. So serious a musical phenomenon, which may well anticipate the development of new jazz, is clearly not to be explained within the framework of established, firmly entrenched jazz concepts. It exists as a musical anomaly, a challenge to the idea of clearly defined genres, 'like an unguided comet in the preordained circle of the heavenly bodies' (Pushkin).

The fact that the Ganelin Trio has broken with the inertia of traditional jazz is due to two fundamental aesthetic features: a universal sense of time and an understanding of music as something composed equally of musical 'being' and musical 'thinking'.

For the mainstream musician time is anachronistic, that is to say always restrospective: in every epoch of jazz the best period has always been in the past, the present is only a shadow of 'the golden age of jazz' with its departed 'giants'. In the music of the trio time, as a metro-rhythmical phenomenon, is genuinely universal, the players being deeply aware of the relative, illusory and purely 'historical' nature of time in any and every genre. This awareness obliges them constantly to go beyond the rhythmic organization associated exclusively with jazz, and enables them to move freely over the whole musico-cultural time-field, recognizing the artificiality and conventionality of all purely genre-based limitations of time. This temporal pluralism lies at the root of the Ganelin Trio's use of widely differing styles. The dynamic equilibrium of heterogeneous temporal forms is distinctly noticeable in their music, and it explains the different systems of values in the three players' performances.

Their art is in some way akin to the original, primeval sense of music – the actual *business of 'performance'* being related to 'music' as philosophizing is related to philosophy. Episodes of 'musical life' provide the main 'plots' of their works, which are at the same time both musical 'being' and musical 'thinking'. The old, rigid conventions of (non-free) jazz made it impossible to realize this ideal which is imminent in all types of musical improvisation.

The Ganelin Trio's approach to music-making gives music the status of a non-conceptual ontological knowledge of reality, of a system that provides an irrational explanation of being, of man's existence. It is this that raises their collective musical statements from the commonplace to the poetic, because in every artistic context 'genuine speech is pre-poetry' (Heidegger).

For this reason it was natural and not difficult to understand why the Ganelin Trio were the first to cross the 'borders' of jazz in the Soviet Union, for they possess that rarest of human characteristics, real originality.

Did we ever think that the Russian jazz-chick would ever be able to teach the American mother-hen anything? That this time has in fact come is made unambiguously clear by the music of the Ganelin Trio.

Translated from Russian by Felicity Cave

Death Dance and Rebirth Steps
for Jazz in the USSR
(Meditations on Themes by the Ganelin Trio)
Norman Weinstein

*Norman Weinstein is an American poet, literary and music critic.
He has also worked as a therapist in the Jungian tradition and has
published in* Spring: An Annual of Jungian Psychology. *All of his
writing has been centrally concerned with the life of the soul and
how to keep the soul vitally alive within the context of a pre-civilized
planet. His major work of literary criticism,* Gertrude Stein and the
Literature of the Modern Consciousness, *was published in the US
by Frederick Ungar Books in 1970. His collections of poetry include*
Nigredo – Selected Poems 1970–1980 *and* Albedo. *His music
criticism has appeared internationally in* Modern Recording and
Music, East West Journal, Jazz Forum, Op Magazine, Music
Sound Output, *and other journals. At the moment he is on the
English faculty of Boise State University and 'Writer-in-Residence'
at the Boise Senior Center. He believes that the essence of life is best
revealed in the metaphors/images of alchemy and feels that poetry
and music are the supreme expressions of the soul-in-
transformation.*

Once – and not upon any particular notion of historical time – the
word 'jazz' possessed a numinosity, an erotic charge, febrile,
tactile; suggested a constellation of rhythmic possibilities linking
old world with new, African with European/American consciousness. That 'jazz' died – along with a great deal of critical

39

vocabulary once used to pigeonhole various arts – *circa* 1945.
Parker and Powell the end of a line, theirs, ours. Roar in the ears
of the survivors of Hiroshima, what could shock anyone after that
music? Or was shock any longer the point? A new musical
language to map the quick translations of matter into energetic
configuration. Braxton's impossible opaque diagrams and calcu-
lus. The Art Ensemble of Chicago's black theatrics. And back in
the USSR the Ganelin Trio following poet Ezra Pound's impera-
tive: 'Make It New' – the 'It' in this instance being Oratorio of the
Coming of Last Judgement. When even the old mystic Novalis is
recognized as prophet: entire cosmos is at last heard as symphonic
work and all suffering personal and collective a failure to hear our
place in the total composition. . .

Nationalism in music a thorny topic. Find the Finland in
'Finlandia' that is other than a sentimental postcard. To most
Western ears true Russian music either replays the Slavic
folk/dance tradition or programmatically exploits scenes from
Russian history with all of the 'realism' of cannons recoiling in the
'1812 Overture'. Soviet music is Shostakovich, socialist realism,
etc. Soviet jazz is seen as a tepid reconstruction of American when
considered at all. So the Ganelin Trio's music comes as an assault
because clearly it breathes and thrives beyond the boundaries of
traditional American definitions of what the USSR *should* sound
like. American music critics can't see in most instances beyond
their own shadowy imperatives. Slave music didn't cease with the
American civil war. There are codes which spell: liberation. You
will not hear them if you expect music to sleepily dance to. The
heart of any nation can be traced in the popular 'standards' of the
day. Collective archetypal energies shining through clichés of Top
Forty radio pap. What Vladimir Chekasin does on his album
Exercises is to lay bare the deep structure of the old-tired-horse
tunes, revitalizes them as an old alchemist does his lead bars,
doesn't 'jazz them up' but puts the old songs through the
form-transforming sax and 'the music goes a-round and a-round'
(as the old song would have it) and comes out as: rebirth of
Russian psyche.

Which is about redemption through collective suffering. Where suffering is not meaningless or absurd as the French existentialists publish. Russian suffering is not masochistic, is pointedly moral. And ikonic. There are images insisted upon, as the name of Jesus was endlessly mantrically repeated in the Greek/Russian Orthodox prayer of the middle ages. The Ganelin Trio's musical structures are large canvases, mural art for walls as ranging in length as Kremlin walls. Or the medieval priest Campanella's vision of a city with walls so graphically illustrated that children circumambulating those walls would through images learn all that they need learn. Three musicians paint with fifteen instruments a mandala thematically unified by:

'No sane person should ever live here. Yet we survive.'

'There are four qualities essential to a great jazzman. They are taste, courage, individuality and irreverence.'

Stan Getz

Dialectic music, like a dialectical society, proceeds by taking two steps forward one back. Like revolution. Like love. Nature evolves through (unexpected) leaps. Thus this new Russian music, discontinuous, asymmetrical, bold enough to declare its own melodic/rhythmic quirks as being essential to its dialectical identity. Following the lead of the greatest Soviet revolutionary bard, Mayakovsky, who insisted that art be a journey to the unknown. If Russian jazz had followed the American thrust, then the emergent Russian psyche would still not yet be born musically. At the centre of this new Russian music is an irreverent tribute to American cultural imperialism, new wine in old bottles. Sure, Soviet jazz musicians swing, but it's how they tremble on their instruments that involves.

Mood(y) musics. What psychology has thus far (1984) failed to explain in both the individual and collective (national) psyche: how moods transform themselves seamlessly into new moods and what occurs in the interstices between moods. On the Ganelin

Trio's *Ancora Da Capo* the soul at war (drummer Tarasov keeps martial art alive) moves into peaceful resolve through Chekasin's playfully Dionysian sax (saxual) release and both are honoured within the magic circle of pianist Ganelin's keyboard boundaries. A fluid metapsychology tracking the struggle of the soul to accept its body (ailing flesh or pathologically distorted Mother Land).

Ideally, the Ganelin Trio's music should be contained on one cassette tape which can be played without interruption until the end of this century, one long opus as Whitman imagined his epic American/Cosmic poem, one long erotic embrace of the ongoing human energies of an age. Including dissonance, interferences, all possible statics, repeated images and riffs moving in and out of suites, familiar musical zones segueing into unfamiliar sonic underworlds, music capable of casting the spell to bring about the Russian Revolution to end further need for revolution. The anima come alive with the waxy Lenin-doll by its side like a dummy awaiting the sound that transforms it into true flesh and blood. Chekasin finds his tenor sax a ram's horn in his hand. What does his music owe to that poor dumb sacrificed beast?

This is a music that finds endless occasions in everyday life for getting passionate. The 'cool' face of the American jazz hipster of the fifties finds no ground in Soviet new music. The musician is set up as shaman whether or not he wants the role or wears the outward trappings. To follow the daimon living within keyboards horns drums is to define a life as a quest for new and possible form. Within the context of a society where life-shapes are mass-produced the musician finds his spiritual callings in inventing that technology which permits the odd mutation, 'odd man out'. The odd-sounding music relieves the strain of being dully ordinary. Hear, in 'idiosyncratic', 'idiot' (thank you, Dostoevsky) and 'sin' or 'syn-'. The sin of acting like a fool among those for whom the heart's music is chronic palpitation.

Notes which declare where the 'Russian' psyche starts and ends
and where the 'Soviet' psyche. . .

>   somewhere in Siberia as you read this
>   the oldest priest on earth
>   & the youngest fool
>   speechlessly encounter each other on opposite
>   corners
>   of a deserted city
>
>   & across that threshold
>   each sings a note keyed
>
>   to the sound associated
>   with end of the Twentieth Century
>
>   What follows
>   is the history of the rebirth of Russian jazz.

Prophets of New Horizons
Virgil Mihaiu

Born 28 June 1951 in Cluj-Napoca, Romania, Virgil Mihaiu is a graduate of Cluj-Napoca University. Since 1968 Romanian cultural magazines have been publishing his poems, articles, essays, literary criticism, translations from German, English, Spanish, Portuguese, Swedish, French, Russian, Italian, etc.

Since 1972 Virgil Mihaiu has been a member of the editing staff of Echinox *cultural magazine. In 1977 he was awarded the Dacia publishing-house prize for a first volume of poetry. His poetry volumes are:* The Law for the Conservation of Adolescence, *1977;* Sighiscara, Sweden and Other States of Mind, *1980;* Instructions for the Breath-contained Ballerina, *1981.*

Since 1981 Virgil Mihaiu has been a member of the Writers' Union of Romania. Since 1980 he has been a producer of the radio programme 'Jazz-Essay'. In 1982 he became Romania's correspondent for Jazz Forum. *The works of Virgil Mihaiu have been translated into Armenian, English, French, German, Hungarian, Polish, Russian, Spanish and Ukrainian.*

An entire book ought to be written about the Ganelin–Tarasov–Chekasin jazz miracle. In a music whose 'historical epochs' are consumed every new decade, these three exceptional artists have succeeded in moulding a time of their own, uncompromising and true to the essence of beauty (if Keats's obsession is still relevant in our times), and yet remaining a significant mirror for modern sensibility. Such a remark might seem paradoxical as it refers to some of the most consistent promoters of the avant-garde spirit in

44

the field of jazz. Nevertheless, their work has gained an ever more profound coherence with each new performance, with each new record. Since 1971, when keyboardist/composer Vyacheslav Gane-lin and drummer Vladimir Tarasov joined forces with reedman Vladimir Chekasin, the trio has produced a major suite every year.

However, some years had yet to pass before the trio acquired its highly deserved international reputation. The first step in this direction was marked by the Ganelin–Tarasov–Chekasin presence at Poland's Jazz Jamboree in 1976. Then an important moment in the trio's career was the release of their first Soviet album, entitled *Con Anima*. Recorded in 1975 and put on sale only at the end of the next year, *Con Anima* is one of the most magnificent blendings of the past, present, and future of jazz in the concentrated space of a record. Actually it could be defined as the proper overture for the group's achievements that were to follow. Short passages of sheer warming-up, solo exercises, fading rapidly from one loudspeaker into the other, are interpolated among longer tracks already announcing the three musicians' stunning mixture of gifts: ebullient layers of swing deftly designed by Ganelin's left hand operating the basset,[1] as well as by Tarasov's myriapodic attack on the drums, above which Chekasin's continuously shifting moods and frantic histrionics combine with some sort of unromantic playing on the piano, again by Ganelin. At times the music erupts brilliantly, then goes through long burlesque, parody-like and humorous episodes, but the kaleidoscope of rhythms, colours and states of mind gradually gives way to a paroxysmal coda, where everything becomes a virtual scream of despair. The listener is carried away by the almost narrative quality of this very dramatically organized interplay of three personalities acting simultaneously on several levels of creation/communication. The various unexpected 'tricks' and turns with which the musical phrases are strewn are a subtle means of keeping the attention alive to the point of exhaustion; thus the whole work of art attains an abstract unity, due in fact to its reflection into the multiplicity of the receivers' perceptions, a tightly conducted feedback process. A prerequisite which these musicians are always very careful about is the sound, true, honest relationship between their inner worlds and the public. Ganelin–Tarasov–Chekasin's music means im-plication and abnegation, an aesthetic experience of the same intensity as that of major existential events. Listening to their records or seeing them on stage can be compared not only to witnessing a masterpiece in any field of culture, but to the breathtaking quality of beautiful erotic encounters, of being fortunate enough to discover a city like Stockholm, or a fabulous sight such as Machu Picchu,[2] or . . . anything else able to fulfil our longing for precious emotions.

The inherent power of the music is enhanced by the visual aspect of the trio's performing on a great variety of instruments: Ganelin mainly on piano and basset (positively the best player in the world on this instrument, throwing into shade similar attempts by Sun Ra or Jimmy Smith); but also half entering the body of the piano and manipulating its viscera, pinching chords, hitting an electric guitar or a toy xylophone with vibes, mallets, etc. All this happens on the left side of the stage, as seen by the spectators. The opposite third of the stage is occupied by Chekasin who always carries lots of instruments in his huge suitcases (as well as in his pockets): from his 1913-made alto saxophone to valve trombone, trumpet, bass clarinet, violin, many self-made or collected musical devices, all of them displaying his constant preoccuption with finding fresh timbres, adding astonishing colour combinations to the already vast sound spectrum of the group. In the midst – Tarasov approaching his percussion set with a grin of almost sadistic relish on his face.

There are so many interesting things to be noticed while these three extraordinary musicians develop their empathic communication inside grandiosely outlined structures that only video tapes might convey a proper documentation to future audiences. Till such video-acoustic means come to the avant-garde's aid, we ought to be thankful to Leo Records for taking the decisive initiative in bringing Ganelin–Tarasov–Chekasin into the world's record shops. As the seven discs issued up to 1985 by this invaluable British label are live recordings, the record-mirror of the trio has greatly improved. Now the music fans have at their disposal well-balanced information concerning the trio's achievements, if we also take into account some other superb studio recordings: 'Concerto Grosso', 'Poi Segue' and 'Non Troppo'. So this essay about Ganelin, Tarasov, Chekasin is based on the above-mentioned discography, combined with the live experience offered by the 1981 and 1983 performances in Sibiu, Cluj-Napoca and Satu Mare and discussions with the musicians themselves. It also analyses a part of the already rich critical debates about this 'musical/social phenomenon of our time'.

It should be pointed out that the group's total music, integrating stylistic/historical developments and an organically assimilated cultural background, grows into some kind of musical cosmogony, impressive to the most diverse categories of listeners. Thus Ganelin–Tarasov–Chekasin achieve a level of general significance where one can speak of jazz as the representative musical idiom of our century. Of course, there are definite elements or passages belonging to an established grammar – from classic counterpoint to post-free nihilism, or from romantic outbursts of passion and lyrical playing to ragtime, blues or bop references. Minimalist tensions are subtly interwoven with expressionistic crescendos and culminations. But this extraordinary versatility serves only as a basis for an original synthesis, a collective work in progress, as if James Joyce's literary legacy had been transposed to musical terms.

To keep up the comparison, these collective masterpieces, these 'jazz Finnegans', display many characteristics of Joyce's superior prose: vast architectures made up of minutely polished details, powerful leading ideas and effervescent spontaneous wit pulsating inside each cell, a mythological outlook applied to the modern world.

In fact, the impressive Ganelin–Tarasov–Chekasin suites are nothing other than chapters of an enormous, lifelong work. They have a complete autonomy of their own, but they are also profoundly interrelated through the unifying spirit of this match- less creative trinity. Consider the titles of their suites: 1971 – 'Consilium', 1973 – 'Triptikas', 1974 – 'Ad Libitum', 1975 – 'Ex Libris', 1976 – 'Con Anima', 1976 – 'Poco a Poco', 1977 – 'Concerto Grosso', 1978 – 'Catalogue', 1980 – 'Ancora da Capo', 1981 – 'Poi Segue', 1981 – 'Vide', 1982 – 'Non Troppo', 1983 – 'Semplice', etc. Vyacheslav Ganelin admitted that the titles are deliberately neutral, offering plenty of freedom to each listener and respecting the ethereal nature of music. Indeed, one has a feeling of being introduced to huge epic/poetic frescoes, but our imagination is never restricted by any superimposed pattern of thinking. On the contrary, though based on refined structures, the music always maintains its openness. The successful outcome lies in keeping a delicate balance between extreme moods – cheerful and humorous at times; grotesque, bitterly sarcastic, despondently thoughtful or melancholy and desperate at other times. Joachim-Ernst Berendt described that as 'the wildest, yet the best organized and most professional free jazz I've heard in years', a much-quoted phrase, reflecting the German expert's gift for concocting memorable formulae.[3] A nice acknowledgement, expressing the surprise caused by the trio's first appearance in the West, therefore maybe a bit too elusory.

In a discussion with Ganelin, Tarasov and Chekasin documented by Efim Barban in the Soviet jazz magazine *Chorus* in April 1979, and reprinted by Canada's *Coda*, Ganelin once again proved his rare capacity for self-judgement: 'I think that the basic quality of our music is the absence of any purely rational "dry" elements. There is always an organic, natural driving force in our music, and audiences pick up very well the lack of any affectation.' Indeed, some sort of irrational force seems to lie at the bedrock of all the Ganelin–Tarasov–Chekasin suites, like in the case of so many works by Dostoevsky, Stravinsky, Mayakovsky, Tarkovsky and other Russian geniuses. A force tempered by humanism, in a dialectical confrontation whose poles are Ganelin's sound and Chekasin's fury. The trio's members tend to underrate themselves in their declarations of principles: talking to Alexey Batashev, in *Jazz Forum* 25 in 1973, Ganelin maintained that the goal of the trio was only 'to make music which is both intellectual and emotional', and in the above-mentioned *Chorus* (Kvadrat) interview Tarasov claimed that 'our programmes are always under-prepared. We don't work them through – we never have any time.' However, the necessity for such modesty and perfectionism is invalidated by the inherent strength of the final product, be it a record or a live performance. As far as the second, more transient aspect is concerned, this hypothetical video-jazz (which I tried to outline before) is a theatrical feat in itself. Ganelin aptly proposed the term 'psychological instrumental theatre' for it. The obvious link between the two fields of art is not incidental here: Ganelin has been working as the musical director of a theatre for years, has composed rock operas, etc. Tarasov's wife is a successful ballerina, and Chekasin's wife is an actress helping her husband put into practice daring musical experiments. The entire 'show' is an extension, a logical consequence of the music itself. Chekasin's terrific contortions, jumps, bends, stamps, his by now renowned frolics (including falling asleep while too 'boring' a music is being evoked) are adjuncts of his fantastic creativity. They are inseparable from his personality. Chekasin confessed in the *Chorus* interview that while playing he could get under a table, whereas Braxton with his rational approach to the spirit of the music would never be capable of that. An excellent analysis of the Sverdlovsk-born prodigy comes from the same Efim Barban: 'The depth of Chekasin's frivolity is in a pre-ontological understanding of reality. The discrediting of musical idolatry and demagogy, the defetishizing of certain ritual "commonplaces" in music, which have long since decayed – of these foundations of philistine self-satisfaction and totemism in jazz – these are just another source from which he draws his energy.'

If Chekasin represents the mysterious extrovert in the trinity, Ganelin appears to be its affable *éminence grise*. His mind is permanently at work, while his hands are controlling the keys or other musical devices with sovereign precision. The broad lines of the musical discourse are mainly under his guardianship. And Ganelin's witty inventiveness is unlimited, constantly stimulating/provoking his partners/equals. There is also an undeniable tension between the three temperaments involved in this adventure of the intellect. Tarasov's major part is to reconcile the opposites, to pump blood into this superb but otherwise perhaps lifeless embodiment of ideas. And thus the mental picture gets moving. The accomplished percussionist is also a high-class intellectual, a well-read, well-informed person, a connoisseur of modern art, as well as a man of the world. Quite the right grounding to play the role of a perfect *raisonneur* in one of jazz history's most important trios!

It should be stressed that never before Ganelin–Tarasov–Chekasin had jazz musicians based their activity so consistently on the suite form. Thus these three prophets of the jazz to come have created a much more appropriate vehicle for the future development of this music. In a 1971 debate on free jazz (*Jazz Forum* 13–14) Andrzej Trzaskowski said that 'actually, there are three

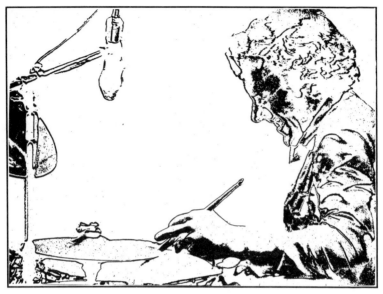

Vladimir Tarasov (Photo: A. Smirnov)

types of form in existence: theme-and-variation form, evolutionary and open. The first is probably the most traditional. Next,
evolutionary, as in Coltrane, and last, open . . . for example, a
composition that can last for two hours or two minutes, that can
start or end at any given moment.' With Ganelin–Tarasov–
Chekasin such fine differentiations lose their meaning. The suites
combine these three approaches, and obtain an ineffable new
form. Indeed, there is a suggestion of openness in everything they
play, the mind is never restricted to preconceived aims; there are
also long 'evolutionary' passages in the spirit of Coltrane's last
period of creation; but on the other hand the musicians avoid any
kind of self-indulgence. The actual form is dictated by the inherent
energies of the content, but it is also defined by critical
intelligence. The canonical theme-and-variation form, which had
provided the basis of most jazz music until the *free* rebellion in the
late fifties, is not neglected by Ganelin–Tarasov–Chekasin. This
technique is employed both in the second part of 'Ancora da Capo'
and in the second part of 'Non Troppo', which was issued by Leo
Records under the title *New Wine*. A musical motif (Argentinian

tango melody in the first case, 'Too Close for Comfort' theme by Bock, Weiss & Holofcener in the second) is hinted at, dissected, chopped up, interspersed, thickened or vaguely evoked, throughout a masterly improvisatory interplay.

Each suite offers an unexpected musical point of view, a new strategy in dealing with the profusion of spontaneous ideas. Take, for instance, 'Concerto Grosso': a refined combination of sensuality and premeditation, of emotional restraint and outbursts. Minute bits of sound are put together into a rare overdubbing experiment. In making use of the studio resources Ganelin–Tarasov–Chekasin do not overbid. Instead of moving horizontally, in vaster spaces, they prefer introspection into the realm of infinite minimalist contrivances. When they are no longer in the studio the three adventurers undertake exactly the opposite manoeuvre, namely the conquering of new horizons by instant means, which obliges the producer to print the following caveat on the jacket: 'Leo Records would like to underline that this is a live performance and no overdubs have been made.' One has to listen to the phenomenal dialogue of Chekasin on valve trombone and his two fellows on trumpets, while the 'rhythm section' contrives its own mad mad worlds, as if it were made up of other players, in order to understand this special sense of paradox and risk propelling their music towards ever new areas. A similar intensity is to be found in the middle section of 'Poi Segue', with Chekasin on trombone again, and the piano and drums in rapid fire behind, or in the thrilling splendour of the two saxophones played simultaneously and bass-clarinet episodes of 'Catalogue' (*Live in East Germany*, LR 102). What could be labelled otherwise a chain of *trouvailles* becomes a method of artistic investigation and creation in the trio's contextures.

After the Ganelin–Tarasov–Chekasin experience jazz possesses the strongest argument for fully emancipating itself from the prejudices that have always been used against it. Albert Mangelsdorff's idea that jazz means in fact any significant music of this century is magnificently supported by the Russian trio. What should be emphasized is the utmost cultural value of this phenomenon.

'The art of the Ganelin Trio is deeply provocative,' wrote Efim Barban. 'But although it stirs the consciousness it does not give the answers. It questions. It is the music of an agnostic civilization. The group's profound seriousness and antinomy of thought are bound to take an ironical form, since anything else would lead inevitably to aesthetic excess: a hunchback on a camel.' Such accurate characterizations hold true if we think of other master- pieces of contemporary art. Let's consider, for example, Andrei Voznesensky's poem entitled 'A Portrait of Maya Plisetskaya'. Mixture of biography, ballet, word, music, meditation and imprecation about the artist's condition, the text has an amplitude similar to the Mayakovskyan discharges, tempered, however, by the change in cultural background (thence implicitly including the experience of mature jazz as well). Ballet means 'vanquishing the barriers of sound', it is 'music without sound' in which 'the skin thinks and finds its words'. The synchretism of modern art is condensed in such verses: 'The empire of sound is occupied by movement. We see the sound. The sound is the line, communica- tion is the figure.' Voznesensky's capacity to maintain a con- tinuous state of excitement along kilometres of verses is the result of a vigour and freshness copiously fuelled from within. Such creative incandescence reminds us immediately of the specific mode of expression enforced by great jazzmen. The vastness of scope, the inescapable labyrinth of twentieth-century life with its terrors and hopes are given an unforgettable filmic shape by Andrey Tarkovsky (*The Mirror, Stalker*), a theatrical embodiment by Yuri Lyubimov (*The Master and Margarita*), or find their musical counterpart in the suites of Ganelin–Tarasov–Chekasin. These are works of acute cultural importance. They represent the only possible alternative as a retort to a reified, alienating pseudo-art which has become a simple merchandise to bring material profit, and/or to obliterate the general public's power of discernment in order to manipulate its taste, and subsequently its conscience.

When an unprejudiced listener first hears a work by Ganelin– Tarasov–Chekasin he or she may be struck by the novelty of the unusual sound combinations, but on the other hand cannot help noticing that an entirely novel musical universe is offered to the individual perception. Something of the raw, aggressive quality of Stravinsky's 'Sacré du Printemps' pervades the spirit of this new jazz, only the connections are certainly different nowadays. In

Bert Noglik's book *Jazzwerkstatt International* one comes across some other confessions of Ganelin, Tarasov and Chekasin.[4] They declare themselves open to ethnic music influences, not only of the peoples in the Soviet Union, but of the whole world. 'Many things that were previously developing in regional isolation have become accessible to us,' says Ganelin. And he adds: 'Our music is consciously polystylistic. We are interested in resetting different stylistic means and musical elements into a new context, defining our own way of playing.' The music thus becomes an impressive 'effigy in sound' of our troubled times, incorporating any significant impulse into a hitherto unheard *world music.*

Art's sponge-like quality of absorbing and assimilating the world's immeasurable variety (a simile belonging to Boris Pasternak, if I remember correctly) is frequently to be found in the Russian tradition. But the latter's penchant for ample expressions of a great vital force has always been alloyed with an undercurrent of human essence, an irrepressible concern for the individual. From Pushkin and Lermontov to Leo Tolstoy, in the more classical sense, but also with Dostoevsky's abyssal insights, or Gogol's and Chekhov's ironic evidence of a pre-Kafkaesque world, Russian literature was prepared to enter a radical phase after the 1905 revolution. What uncomprehending Western critics seems to ignore – at least immediately after their first confrontations with the Ganelin–Tarasov–Chekasin records produced by Leo – was an obvious fact belonging to the history of modern culture: namely that Russia gave birth to one of the strongest ever avant-garde insurrections. For about two and a half decades there was an unprecedented flourishing of what we generally define as avant-garde movements, in all fields of artistic creation, announcing, paralleling and interfering with the social transformations brought about by the creation of the Soviet Union. The innovatory spirit was present everywhere: in Diaghilev's 'Ballets Russes', as well as in Tatlin's architectural utopianism; in Malevich's black square on a white background, or in Kandinsky's and Chagall's departure from *terre-à-terre* figurative paintings; in the theatre of Meyerhold, and in the cinema of Eisenstein. Mario De Micheli pointed out in his *Artistic Avant-garde of the Twentieth Century* that 'the major centre of abstract culture, of experimenting and theoretical elaboration, besides that of abstractionism as a

movement was, initially, both pre-First World War Russia, and
the young Soviet Republic of the years immediately following the
October Revolution'.[5] In that age of proliferating '-isms' a typical
event was, for instance, the cubo-futurists' 1913 manifesto-volume
entitled 'A Slap in the Face of Public Taste' signed by such
rebellious master-spirits as David Burlyuk, Velemir Khlebnikov,
Kruchennykh and Mayakovsky. Their violent pleadings for a new
poetry would influence the development of the entire Russian
post-symbolism (including Blok, Mandelshtam, Yesenin, Pasternak, Akhmatova, etc.) It is quite significant that the same year,
1913, witnessed the founding of abstractionism by Malevich, and
the great shock caused by the first hearing of Stravinsky's 'Sacré
du Printemps' at the Champs-Elysées theatre in Paris. French
composer François Poulenc observed in an article for *Histoire de la
musique 2* that 'all arts, between 1910–13, were more or less
tributary to the Ballets Russes, but music was the one to benefit
most from Diaghilev's prophetic impulse'.[6] During that same time
Khlebnikov was concerned with finding a purely phonetical
transcription of visual image – typical of the Russian futurism
which had created the *zvukopis* concept in fine arts (meaning the
pictorial representation of sounds) – something very close to what
was later to be called 'concrete poetry'.

Naturally, a review of Soviet jazz would have to take into
consideration and reflect upon the existence of a powerful
tradition of innovation (no contradiction in terms!) in that
country. A historical development whose dimensions can only be
suggested here. The works of Ganelin–Tarasov–Chekasin can be
regarded as a continuation of the great Russian musical tradition,
following Scriabin, Tchaikovsky, Stravinsky. But they are also a
new beginning, a leading force and example within the marvellous
pleiad of today's Soviet jazz musicians. That is why another great
merit of the Leo label is to put on record other daring artists
belonging to the same area: Sergey Kuryokhin, Anatoly Vapirov,
Vladimir Tolkachev, Yuri Yukechev, Sergey Panasenko, Vladimir
Volkov, Boris Grebenshchikov, Sergey Belichenko.

In his autobiography, Ilya Ehrenburg recalls scenes from the
Poets' Cafe in Moscow, where he recited his poems during the
1917–18 winter. For instance, David Burlyuk, his face violently
powdered, a pince-nez in his hand, used to come up on stage and

recite: 'I like the pregnant man'. And Goldtsshmid, who was a sort of master of ceremonies there, dyed two curls of his hair golden-blond, declared himself *life's futurist*, and put up a monument to himself in the theatre's square – a plaster statue, not at all futuristic, but representing a nude Goldtsshmid. To those who read nowadays about Grebenshchikov picking his guitar with an electric razor, or about Chekasin conducting his free-jazz scholar/musicians from the stage while they are playing seated among the spectators, such para-artistic acts may appear as exhibitionistic as those mentioned by Ehrenburg. Yes, there is a continuity in spirit. But we cannot judge today's artistic experiments by obsolete standards. The mass media often irrationally support some sort of subculture which has lost its sense of direction. Under such circumstances the artists who still believe in progress have to be aware of their responsibilities. Simply playing the fool is no answer to the world's state of mind today, unless that modern Fronde is supported by culture and an ethical attitude in favour of humanistic deals. What I mean is that today's Soviet avant-garde is developing on more solid ground (although maybe less spectacular) than that of its predecessors. We are not so naïve as to believe that art can solve the world's problems. But nobody is entitled to deprive art of its right and obligation to propose alternatives to the dark side of reality. Even during the most obscurantist periods of dogmatism, conscientious artists continued to create valuable works, feeding hopes. The examples of Bulgakov, Ilf & Petrov or Daniil Harms immediately come to mind.[7] Thus the links between Diaghilev–Stravinsky and Ganelin–Tarasov–Chekasin may be better understood. Myriam Soumagnac wrote in *Histoire de la musique* about the extraordinary choreographer–composer couple: 'They have in common an Apollinairean taste for surprise, the surprise the genius makes to himself, and an equal respect for each work they bring to the public's knowledge.'[8] These lines apply to the new jazz trio from Vilnius perfectly.

As far as the public's reaction is concerned, there is sometimes a kind of snobbish prejudice in Eastern Europe: our artists (musicians) cannot be of world value just because they are ours. The truth is that there are far fewer means of publicity in Eastern Europe, and one is used to seeing Herbie Hancock's smile or the

Art Ensemble of Chicago's photograph on a *Jazz Forum* cover, instead of Vagif Mustafa-zade or Ganelin–Tarasov–Chekasin. On the other hand, Soviet Philharmonics have the Ganelin Trio performances programmed as the second part of ordinary classical music concerts. Jazz is regarded as a natural stage in the musical development of mankind. The emergence of so many talents on the Soviet jazz scene enabled Leo Feigin, producer of Leo Records, to express his belief that 'Russian jazz will be the jazz of the eighties and nineties'. Well, the curious thing is that large audiences enraptured by Ganelin–Tarasov–Chekasin often seem to be nearer the mark than many of those who are supposed to decide theoretically about jazz.

Some who would like to see jazz debased to nothing else but music for entertainment were outraged after watching a Ganelin–Tarasov–Chekasin performance. They accused 'Poi Segue' of being a chaotic juxtaposition of . . . non-jazz episodes!? A few jazzmen, whom I respect otherwise, even claimed that the members of the trio would never be capable of playing in any straightforward jazz form. That was a gross misinterpretation and proved a total lack of understanding for the jazz-imbued substance of this music. It was in response to such malevolent criticism that the second part of 'Non Troppo' was conceived (and later released by Leo Records under the title *New Wine*). To my surprise, Roger Cotterrell, one of Europe's leading jazz critics, did not grasp the message of this little revenge the musicians decided to have on their ignorant detractors. In his 1983 review (*Jazz Forum* 85) Roger Cotterrell is the first person in jazz criticism to complain about Ganelin–Tarasov–Chekasin confining their freedom 'within familiar forms – jazz tempi, walking bass lines, familiar harmonic structures, orthodox free improvisation – rather than bursting out of and beyond them as on some of the earlier albums'. This is as if, Sonny Rollins having decided to prove his ability to play free on a record, we obliged him to stick exclusively to the style to which we have grown accustomed. Anyway, it is not Mr Cotterrell – a fine expert in modern jazz – who would 'face the music' for the rather mistaken critical approach to the Ganelin–Tarasov–Chekasin issue, especially in the West. The sad thing is not only that some could not see beyond exterior aspects, usually connected with the 'exotic' origin of the musicians, but that there also seemed to be a difficulty in perceiving and judging each suite as a whole, as a new means of expression, with its specific laws and characteristics. This is not only a matter of quantity. It has a lot to do with cultural accumulation and the philosophical concept of the qualitative leap.

The extensive tour by the Ganelin Trio of England and Wales, organized by Britain's Arts Council in March 1984, was highly necessary. Some of the reviews published before and immediately after the first concert showed an improvement in critical perception. Graham Lock and Richard Cook in the *New Musical Express*, John Fordham in the *Sunday Times Magazine* and arts *Guardian*, Ronald Atkins in the *Financial Times*, Dave Gelly in the *Observer Review*, Charles Fox in the *New Statesman* made pertinent comments on the 'historic first ever British tour by a group of Soviet jazz musicians'. They observed that the trio's 'Russian kind of theatricality produces the right sort of balance between the tragic and the absurd', or that the group sounded at times 'like the Cecil Taylor Trio but with a more coherent internal balance', appreciating this kind of jazz 'that is vital, alive, funny, committed, virtuosic and assembled in a manner quite untypical of either European or American variants of the music'. So there are reasons to hope for more comprehensiveness on the part of the mass media, as the three musicians are becoming better known to critics everywhere. Such a development had been anticipated especially by the valuable *Jazz Forum* reviews of Norman Weinstein, Roger Cotterrell and Rolf Reichelt. And Francis Davis's acknowledgement: 'It is fair to say that the Ganelin Trio is one of the premier jazz ensembles not only in Europe, but in the entire world' (*Down Beat*, April 1984) marks a decisive *prise de conscience* in American jazz criticism as well.

When asked by *Jazz Forum* to rate the trio's music, Vyacheslav Ganelin gave the following answer: 'In my case it is perhaps connected with abstract vision. A tune is multi-dimensional, like a dream or a surrealistic painting – it incorporates unexpected happenings and a kind of weightlessness and agony – all reflected in sound' (*JF* 25, 1973). This holds true even today. And something else: like many of their forerunners (Khlebnikov in poetry, Stravinsky in music), Ganelin–Tarasov–Chekasin are universal in message, but remain deeply rooted in the Russian cultural tradition. Sergey Kuryokhin, who is not only a hope of Soviet new jazz, but also a very articulate observer of cultural phenomena, declared in an interview: 'I consider that the Ganelin Trio are developing within the framework of Russian – and I mean Russian in feeling – art. This could not have happened in the West, and I was amazed at the superficiality of Milo Fine's review of their record in *Cadence* [*Live in East Germany*, LR 102]. He didn't see anything in the record except that it was in no way inferior to the best world standards. He didn't understand the creative process. This record is so different from what is being done in the West in all ways: in structure, composition, organization of the musical material – it is a completely different principle which could never happen in the West with the pragmatic rationalism of European culture. But we are getting on to non-musical questions, questions of a nation, ethos, nature, national feeling of a kind felt by Dostoevsky, questions of social environment, climatic conditions which in many ways condition our life [laughs and looks out of the window at the mud and wet snow]. No sane person could live in this town; we are being forced to live in completely unacceptable conditions, and this forms the psyche of a person, his or her culture and so on. All the traditions of musical education, the music I heard on the radio and TV, played in school and college, in a word everything, one's whole cultural, national heritage is reflected in one's music.'

The panegyrical tone of this essay might cause certain readers to ask: is this music perfect? It would be tragic if it were, for art in general, and jazz in particular, are dynamic spiritual realities, in an unceasing process of formation, adapting themselves to, and at the same time shaping, the mentality of an age. Only those who do not toil do not err: *errare humanum est.* Humanistic art never pretends to have reached perfection. Ganelin–Tarasov–Chekasin are not always on their best form: it was amusing to notice that the recording of the second part of 'Non Troppo' (during the March 1983 Romanian tour), made for my jazz broadcast on Radio Cluj, is much richer in content than that issued on the *New Wine* record. The explanation is very simple: the latter was recorded on 26 June 1982: during the months that had elapsed between the two recordings, the general pattern was gradually filled up with even more refined individual improvisation. The fact is that musicians of such calibre cannot afford to play one and the same suite for too long. Then, if I were to make other critical remarks, I should say that the use of the electronic organ on some records is unconvincing, reminding one of Sun Ra's first awkward attempts on that instrument in the late fifties. It sounds nasty, but I am quite happy about Ganelin's lack of funds to buy himself a synthesizer.[9] This is not said out of conservatism. I simply imagine that situation to be like some encounter of the third kind between these superhuman beings and God knows what sort of mechanoid extraterrestrial. I also agree that there are a few over-extended passages in the second part of the Leon version of 'Ancora da Capo', but to a great extent they are due to the poor quality of the original tape.

At the very beginning of this modest examination I used the term 'jazz miracle' to define Ganelin–Tarasov–Chekasin. To conclude, I hope to have succeeded in making clear the following idea: these musicians are a miracle in themselves, as an entity – in their own achievements and their strength to abide by this unique formula for such a long time. And they are *not* a miracle just because they come from a space yet to be discovered by a great many, critics and audiences alike. On the contrary, that space was an essential reason for their formation. It is high time to understand, if we pretend to contribute to the enlightening of our age, that it would be ridiculous to persist in the erroneous opinion that major cultural events can be confined to certain privileged centres or areas. Vladimir Chekasin once expressed his feeling that 'obviously at the moment jazz is going through the period of waiting for the Messiah'. What if people who still believe in a better world through art were to take a closer look at Ganelin–Tarasov–Chekasin? This trinity's messianic music can offer a key to the future of jazz.

Notes

1. A small keyboard instrument which reproduces the sound of a bass
2. Best preserved of Inca cities, rediscovered in 1912 by Hiram Bingham
3. *Down Beat*, February 1981, 48 No.2
4. Noglik, Bert, *Jazzwerkstatt International*, Verlag Neue Musik, Berlin, 1981

60   *Virgil Mihaiu*

5. De Micheli, Mario, *Artistic Avant-garde of the Twentieth Century*, Giangiaco-
mo Feltrinelli Editore Milano, 1966
  6. *Histoire de la musique 2*, Encyclopédie de la Pleiade, Gallimard, 1963
  7. Prominent literary figures of the Stalinist era
  8. *Histoire de la musique*, op cit
  9. Ganelin did in fact later obtain a synthesizer

The Ganelin Trio in London
John Fordham

John Fordham was born in 1947 in London. He began writing jazz reviews as a direct result of reading Whitney Balliett's Sound of Surprise, *having been a jazz enthusiast from his teens. His first writings appeared in* Time Out *in 1970, and later in* Sounds, Melody Maker *and occasionally the* Sunday Times. *He has been principal jazz correspondent of the* Guardian *since 1978, and is currently the co-editor of* City Limits.

In May 1981 a jazz review appeared in the *Guardian* that carried an unlikely footnote. In among a collection of ruminations on a pre-comeback Miles Davis compilation album and releases by Billy Bang and Amina Claudine Myers, was a passing reference to an album called *Live in East Germany* released over here by Leo Records. The subject was a Russian contemporary jazz group called the Ganelin Trio, I was the writer and the upshot of the commentary was that the record represented 'a startling insight into a culture that many assume possesses no adventurous jazz at all. The trio puts together music of a typhoon-like energy.'

Richard Williams in the *Times* had found the Ganelin Trio the stuff that pricks the ears up as well. Instantly remarkable was the immense confidence, assertiveness and instinct for variety that the band displayed, qualities that seemed to emerge from a combination of their grasp of general jazz developments of recent times, from the length of time they had played together, and in part from their enthusiasm for composition. As a result, the music was a particularly successful combination of free-playing performance styles founded on a premeditated system.

Not that enthusiasm for the group didn't invite a certain amount of restraint and self-questioning considering the nature of their origins – something that anticipated a good deal of what was subsequently argued over as Britain and the Ganelin Trio moved slowly into earshot of each other. Was it really interesting, or was the novelty value of a thoroughly contemporary musical idiom emanating from a nation that the West presumed to be almost jazzless the overriding factor? Wasn't it simply surprising that they didn't sound like a reprise of a Glenn Miller band, or a bad fusion outfit such as the Russian one that Joachim Berendt had wearily observed at the 1980 Berlin Jazz Days performance – the same show that led him to describe the Ganelin's music as 'the best organized and most professional free jazz I have heard in years'? *Le Monde* declared 'jazz is alive and well in the land of Lenin'.

Doubts or anticipations, it could have been the beginning and the end right there: one unusual record, floating among all the rickety craft of surprising but utterly uncommercial records that get independent distribution each year. This time, things moved further. There was more to it in the case of the Ganelin Trio, and it was soon clear that not all of the incentive for further development was strictly musical.

The Arts Council of Great Britain has a £200,000-a-year touring scheme called the Contemporary Music Network. It puts out, annually, some ten or a dozen groups on national tours, dedicated to the dissemination of new, or newish, music by a mixture of straight and jazz musicians and composers. A mixture of practitioners, Arts Council officers and reasonably informed observers of the scene comprise a selection committee that chooses the touring artists each year. In 1982, a year in which I was on the panel, the subject under discussion was the programme for 1983/4. Somehow, the subject of the Russian performers came up. I was still buzzing from the *East Germany* record, and had discussed the band privately with Richard Williams and music writer Hannah Charlton, later to join the *Sunday Times*. The economic climate through which British arts funding was passing did not augur well for contemporary music, and the Network itself always feared the pressure to economize. What it needed was a big media event, to put it at its crudest, a phenomenon that was of sufficient interest outside of the rarefied world of specialist enthusiasts to put the touring scheme back on the map. Aside of that, the Ganelin Trio was clearly in ample possession of the performing excellence that the selection committee required, and represented an unusual series of departures from Afro-American jazz that could only stimulate interest in adventurous music generally. 'Apart from anything else,' I remember saying as we pondered the issue 'the press will be fascinated by a group of Establishment Russian musicians who play avant-garde jazz on their nights off and irritate the authorities. It will be the Solzhenitsyn story with music.'

There was little doubt that this would occur. Even before the earliest approach had been made it was obvious that the media – all the media, not just those which covered jazz as a matter of course – would lap up the Ganelin Trio because of what it represented in the international scene of the 1980s. Such music out in the steppes represented protest and dissent. Over here, because of the way it represents just the same thing, such music in the hands of local performers is feared and often profoundly disliked. It was much the same irony as that found in the British media's wholehearted embracing of Solidarity and wholehearted loathing of home-grown trade unionism. Still, if the opportunity was going to be there, circumstances for the publicizing of jazz were not so luxurious that such a gift horse could be looked disdainfully in the mouth.

The Arts Council's Annette Morreau, whose brainchild the Contemporary Music Network is, set out to explore the ground, and that was the last of it for a while. The group had been in the West before, on the Berlin trip that figured in Berendt's review, but negotiations were clearly going to be slow. The fact that the initiative was coming from the highest British cultural agency in the land was likely to be a help. Gradually, encouraging signs began to emerge. By the autumn of 1983 it was clearly more on than off: the band would embark on a nationwide tour that would take in eight gigs. As the event drew nearer, more records of the band were released here by Leo Records, some representing the trio in more reflective and occasionally desultory moods than the furiously energetic East Berlin gig had done. Interviews with the musicians were circulated, revealing them to be articulate, thoughtful and impressively informed about Western jazz developments. It was immediately striking that their analysis of the development of music obliged to coexist with the commercial music industry in Europe and America was more acute than that displayed by most Western performers, regardless of their musical radicalism. They also had a sharp understanding of where their own work was coming from – Western jazz, Russian folk music, classical influences, Ganelin's experience as a film composer, Chekasin's irrepressible anarchism – and where it fitted into the global scheme of things. The Ganelin Trio increasingly seemed like a very unusual phenomenon indeed.

As the likelihood of their arrival increased, so did the speculation about what would actually happen. Oxford University Press, by accident or design, published *Red & Hot* by S. Frederick Starr, which told Westerners how Russian jazz had painfully developed from the days when Prince Yusupov – Rasputin's Nemesis – recalled 'Yankee Doodle Dandy' on the gramophone in the mad monk's last moments.

In the first week after the group's arrival in the UK, it was swamped with press attention. It was interviewed for the BBC 2 'Newsnight' programme, being invited to relate some of Starr's anecdotes about how the Russian authorities over the years had got themselves into a twist about whether or not the music was actually morally and politically debilitating, and had therefore oscillated between banning it and celebrating it for decades. In Starr's book there was a tale of Ortonesque absurdity about the attempted banning of the saxophone in the years immediately after the Second World War. Moscow horn players had been gathered together to deliver up their instruments and have their identity cards altered to 'oboist' and 'bassoon player'.

The first show of the tour, at the Bloomsbury Theatre on 7 March 1984 was a sell-out. Those present were a distinctly mixed bunch. Arts Council top brass like Luke Rittner and Marghanita Laski were there, almost unheard of on the Contemporary Music Network. Russians were there in abundance: emigrés, students, officials. Musicians were there, too. British players were naturally curious because the band was from a culture such a galaxy away from them, and because there had been so much pre-match build-up. Perhaps they sensed that the Ganelin's determination to keep playing its music in the face of bureaucratic indifference, and its aptitude for vaulting over the usual channels and reaching out direct to an enthusiastic young public were not so far from the conditions experienced by unorthodox players everywhere.

The band played a mixed bag. At the time, I wrote in the *Guardian*: 'As highly organized "free" music, it will have its detractors among improvising purists, and it uses so many conventional devices as to be in danger of subjection to them. But it is a kind of jazz that is vital, alive, funny, committed, virtuosic and assembled in a manner quite untypical of either European or American variants of the music.'

The Ganelin Trio played two of its staple compositions: 'Non Troppo' and 'New Wine', both of which had been heard here on disc.

'Non Troppo' was the first – a serious, complex and tightly packed composition that opens with delicate, tinkling keyboard effects and ends by evoking a chilly winter landscape through the echoing, whistly desolation of the sound of a wooden flute. It was a more tense occasion than even the piece itself would normally suggest, since the band later revealed that it felt out of contact with such a formal audience, and Vladimir Chekasin – a slight, enigmatic figure whose expression is ambiguously mournful and mischievous at once – took matters into his own hands by a series of outrageous saxophone interventions. Throughout the piece, which was gripping, if tentative, it was apparent that the Russians had evolved an idiom for their particular combination of indigenous values and imported jazz practices that made a well-worn vocabulary like bebop, for instance, sound quite different. Generally bop is played these days to sound as *smooth* as possible – an oddity considering its prickly origins, but a method that has evolved to make the music sound sensual, relaxed, melodically rich and the proper territory of players of high techniques and effortless command of the style. The Ganelin Trio makes it sound awkward, brittle, anxious and perverse – partly a function of Tarasov's oddly static drumming. Such is the coherence of the band, however, that the effect is often of a new language being forced into life, rather than an old one inadequately absorbed.

Ganelin himself was highly impressive throughout the performance. He is a pianist with an immensely resourceful melodic imagination which he can transfer without hesitancy to the keys.

He is also capable of playing naturally in almost any idiom, can swing, and has a preoccupation with portentous, orchestral chord effects that sometimes create the dislocating sensation that George Shearing is trying to burst through the outer skin of a Cecil Taylor.

The band allowed its raucous, theatrical side to emerge in the second half of the Bloomsbury performance, in its rendition of 'New Wine', which starts with a long, eccentric drum solo from Tarasov, who sounds as if he is constantly trying to subdue his ebullience, like a speaker constantly passing a hand in front of his mouth. Chekasin then took over the event, flailing wildly Rahsaan-like on two saxophones at once, stamping frantically like a flamenco dancer, edging towards the microphone as if he suspected it of having malevolent properties, filling the hall with fierce, Brötzmann-like howls. Formal audience or no, the response was distinctly warm.

There was a reception afterwards for the musicians. Everyone was very excited about it all, and Rittner and Laski were so enthusiastic that it seemed as if the Contemporary Music Network, quite apart from Soviet–British cultural relations, had been put firmly back on a map from which some felt it had been in serious danger of slipping. The musicians themselves, though, were ambivalent.

It had been unquestionably a showcase and a propaganda exercise for many things other than a musical performance. It was an opportunity for the Arts Council to get more publicity for a single event of experimental art than it had received in a considerable time, and one that for once was not subject to the gleeful dismissals that had accompanied such sitting ducks as the Tate bricks or the South Bank tyres. It was an opportunity for arts administrators to demonstrate that the most dangerous cultural divide in the world could be bridged by creative artists and that people could be brought together under the roof of one performance space. It was also an opportunity for musicians from artistically similar territory to ponder on whether or not it was unfair that such an avalanche of publicity should have fallen on this particular tour when West European and British avantists would generally be lucky to get a footnote in the press for work not so strikingly different.

This became the torch that burned long after the Ganelin Trio had gone home, and the sense in which the musicians had become symbols for something not of their making caused a stir in the deprived and marginalized tributaries of exploratory music in Britain. While some prominent British improvisers turned up their noses at the Ganelin's carefully structured performances, or at Vladimir Chekasin's undeniably curious blend of tempestuous mid-sixties New York tenor playing, Dutch-school clowning and bullish, stamping, *uncool* bebop, was it the band that had distressed them or the accidents of circumstance that induced a kind of bitter cynicism? That they got attention because they were Russians and therefore a godsend to anybody in search of a story in the era of the reactivated Cold War was undeniable. That it should have so obscured the life-enhancing idiosyncrasy of their particular contribution to world music was unfortunate. The Ganelin Trio came to Britain to present a side of Russian life that is perceived here only in a series of caricatures of hopelessly dated bohemians taking time off from State-cultural stipends to engage in hit-and-run guerrilla wars with the KGB. They exhibited an art that unquestionably emerges from unorthodoxy and resistance, but in its widest possible senses – in subversion of routine and routine allegiances, in resistance to consensus, to moral majorities, to political shibboleths, to 'balance', to 'entertainment', to (as Efim Barban has pointed out elsewhere) 'happy endings'. As such, they were truly exponents of a world music of the 1980s. The realization of this was the happiest ending of all.

My Trips to Russia
Hans Kumpf

Hans Kumpf (born 1951) is one of those people without whom the jazz scene would not have been the same. A graduate in music, German and sociology, he works as a teacher. He is also active as a musician, playing with many European jazzmen. In 1979 he was voted No. 5 in the clarinet category of the 'Top People Poll' run by Jazz Forum.

Hans Kumpf lectures on music theory, broadcasts, contributes to Jazz Podium, Jazz Forum *and many German newspapers. He is also well known as a photographer, and has had several photo exhibitions in Ludwigsburg and Nürnberg.*

Since the beginning of the seventies Hans Kumpf has been a producer for his own record label, AKM Records, with releases featuring John Fischer, Perry Robinson, Theo Joergensmann, as well as many Soviet musicians: A. Vapirov, S. Kuryokhin, L. Chizhik, V. Ganelin, V. Tarasov, L. Saarsalu, and many others.

Preface

In the middle of 1980 the teachers of a nearby technical school had planned a study trip to the Soviet Union. Winfried Koch, my clarinet-partner in AK-Musick, a German jazz group, worked as a teacher in the school. I heard about the project and decided to go along. Of course, I was curious about the jazz scene in the USSR, because as many as fourteen years earlier, at the age of fifteen, I had read an article, 'Jazz in the USSR' by Alexey Batashev in a magazine called *Soviet Union Today.*

68

During my visits to Moscow I always got in touch with Alexey Batashev, but my other meetings with VIPs of the Soviet jazz scene happened more or less accidentally. Such was my discovery of the Contemporary Music Club in Leningrad. The friendly and cordial reception at this club made me come back to Leningrad and play with the local musicians. This was extremely gratifying because I happened to be the first free-jazz musician from the West to perform in the USSR in jam sessions with local avant-gardists. I wrote about my impressions in various newspapers and magazines, trying to throw some light on the jazz scene in the Soviet Union. Of course, I travelled as a tourist with my clarinet and I financed these trips out of my own pocket. I managed to document some performances and later on I released them on records: *Jam Session Leningrad* (featuring saxophonist Anatoly Vapirov, pianist Sergey Kuryokhin and bassoonist Alexander Alexandrov); and *Jam Session Moscow* (featuring pianist Leonid Chizhik and saxophonist Alexey Zubov). Jam sessions in Tallinn, featuring saxophonist Lembit Saarsalu, pianist Vyacheslav Ganelin, drummer Vladimir Tarasov and a pianist, Rein Rannap, were released by Leo Records as *Hans Kumpf – on a Baltic Trip*.

Leningrad (May/June 1980)

Even travelling in the Soviet Union with a regular group of tourists (which is, naturally, accompanied by the Intourist representatives) it is possible to move freely within the towns, on one's own, to get acquainted with the local jazz life. On the very first day of my stay in the USSR I heard about a big jazz concert which was to take place in the Leningrad Palace of Culture, named after Kirov (Sergey Kirov was a fellow-revolutionary of Lenin assassinated by one of Stalin's aides in 1934). It seemed a good idea for me to explore this monumental building. There were dancing halls, theatres, lecture rooms, ballet studios and many more cultural facilities. I had a chance to watch, for about half a hour, a dance in this 'Palace of Culture'. The Soviet 'Friday-night Fever' (entrance costs one rouble) took place in a quiet, subdued atmosphere and finished at eleven o'clock. There were about 150 couples dancing on the floor, most of them middle-aged. My attention was attracted by a girl wearing a T-shirt with 'Wrangler' written on it. Such clothes are considered to be a status symbol. The music was 'live' and conventional, played by the Veplinsky Big Band in a music-hall manner. A slow tune, 'Girl Talk', did not sound half as sophisticated as when it was played by Count Basie. Then the neon was turned back on, mercilessly, and the orchestra presented jazz pieces influenced by oriental folk music with Russian singing and traces of disco rhythms. In front of a greenish-red curtain embellished with folklore pictures the musicians were playing joylessly. The music lacked precision and improvisation.

After an evening of ballet with works by Stravinsky and Khachaturian followed by *pas-de-deux* to the sounds of Pink Floyd I managed to find an open restaurant on Nevsky Prospect, one of the central streets in Leningrad. A quartet with guitar, piano, electric bass and drums, joined later by a female singer, was playing numbers by the Rolling Stones and Boney M without any inspiration. They also performed jazz standards, and the guitar player happened to be an admirer and imitator of George Benson and Wes Montgomery. Three times a week these musicians played background music and each of them got five roubles an evening. However, there were problems: the manager of the restaurant found their music too jazzy and not popular enough. In the Soviet Union too musicians are frustrated by commercial considerations. When we started a conversation these young musicians wanted to know, among other things, which harmonic extensions of the blues were practised in capitalist countries abroad. The drummer had a problem. He showed me a booklet with notations of a Yusef Lateef blues, which started with a C major 7 chord. It was all new to him, but subsequently we put together the chord as C–E–G–B. We went to the piano and I had to turn my theoretical explanations into sounds. My new friends asked me about Albert Mangelsdorff and they were surprised to hear that I knew him personally. And then there came a question which was to be repeatedly directed at me in the Soviet Union: the question about the financial possibilities of Western jazz musicians. Not everyone in the East understands that what appears to glitter in the West is not always gold.

In another room of the restaurant a show called 'Disko' was on

TV. Several young people, having danced in the TV studio to a hot and jazzy version of 'Summertime' by James Last, got the chance to talk to David Goloshchekin, one of the most popular Leningrad musicians, about the blues. Their discussion was accompanied by the sounds of 'St Louis Blues' and 'Rhapsody in Blue'. At the end of that TV programme Goloshchekin himself played a modern blues on his horn assisted by his rhythm section. Then the show continued, but with less spirit and more disco hammering away.

Then, the next day, the Goloshchekin Ensemble was the main attraction of 'Bolshoi Conzert Dzhaza' (Big Jazz Concert) in the theatre hall of the Kirov Palace of Culture. The leader was blowing his horn, and by international standards he was rather mediocre. The sound of his violin was inspired by Stephane Grappelli, but he was more creative when he played it like a guitar, pizzicato. Finally, on an Erroll Garner tune he managed to create intense and emotional music.

The other pieces interpreted by the David Goloshchekin Ensemble were written by Freddie Hubbard and Cannonball Adderley. The hit, however, was the title 'Sunny', which was announced as the song made popular by Boney M at the end of 1978, when this pop group did a couple of concerts in Moscow. During the jazz concert in the Palace of Culture there were five different groups. The most interesting contribution was made by a saxophonist, Anatoly Vapirov, and a pianist, Sergey Kuryokhin. While broken Debussy chords were played on the piano, Vapirov played softly on his soprano saxophone. On the tenor sax he demonstrated the kind of fragmentary flourishes that occur in fairly modern twentieth-century classical music, and on the alto sax his reverence for free jazz. At the end of his last number things were quieter and we heard some jolly ragtime. Even in the free passages there were no wild emotional outbursts; and this seems to me a special characteristic of Soviet jazz, especially in Leningrad. Even in relaxed moods order and discipline predominate, and there is no musical exhibitionism. Vapirov, who studied the classical clarinet and now teaches the saxophone at the Leningrad Musical Academy, is regarded as the leading avant-garde saxophonist in this city of four million inhabitants, while his partner Kuryokhin, who also uses 'prepared' pianos, like John Cage, is the chief avant-garde pianist.

Dixieland is the speciality of Leningrad and Leningradski Dixieland, a group which was formed over twenty years ago, set the tone. Personally, I was disappointed by them. Dressed up as 'entertainers', what they offered were dolled-up imitations of dixieland standards. There did not seem to be any outstanding soloists and the combo had nothing like the power and vitality of the Polish old-time bands, for example.

The jazz concert was put on by the jazz club Chorus (Kvadrat), which gives a big jazz concert every month and also arranges lectures and gramophone evenings. It was explained at this, the last concert of the season, that there were temporary difficulties over publicity, and that in future there would be a concert on every second Sunday in the month, with a programme announced in advance. Anyone interested could leave an address and he or she would be contacted. Hitherto they had simply used the usual Soviet method of publicizing cultural events; a hand-written poster – and, of course, the bush telegraph.

The Contemporary Music Club is an offshoot of the Chorus and meets every Monday in the Lensoveta Cultural Hall. I was going to Moscow by the Red Arrow on Monday night, and Anatoly Vapirov therefore promised to organize a session for me that evening, offering to lend me his own clarinet. My watch let me down and I failed to be at my hotel when my jazz friends called for me. By taking a taxi I got to the concert ninety minutes late and found that some of the players – including Vapirov – had already gone, as well as a good many of the original audience. Since I had no instrument, we improvised an exchange of information about the latest developments in jazz and new music in West Germany. I was amazed to discover how well-informed these fifteen-odd intellectuals were about details of names and tendencies in modern music in the West. ECM and Mood Records discs were well-known and critically rated, and I found myself being asked such questions as: 'What are Karlheinz Stockhausen's latest works?' 'How is avant-garde jazz developing in West Germany?' 'Who is the up-and-coming personality in German jazz and new music generally?' My answers to all these questions were not very enthusiastic, as there were, in fact, no really *new* tendencies to report.

In the course of many conversations I discovered how hard it is for Soviet jazz fans to find out what is happening to jazz in their own country. Books and periodicals can be published only with government approval (and on government-allotted paper) and there is therefore inevitably a kind of 'underground press' for jazz. Even *Jazz Forum*, published in Warsaw, is rare. The chief source of information is therefore Willis Conover of the Voice of America, but he is not thought very highly of by 'progressive' jazz-lovers in the USSR on account of his conservative views. Even leading Soviet jazz players regarded an appearance at the Warsaw Jazz Jamboree as the height of their ambition.

The jazz scene in Leningrad made a rather frosty impression on me, but there was plenty of warmth in the reception that I was given. The position in Moscow is quite different, both musically and personally.

Moscow (June 1980)

In Stalin's times there used to be propaganda placards showing a young rowdy with the legend: 'It's only a step from the saxophone to the knife'; or: 'Today he plays jazz and tomorrow he'll betray his country'. Anti-jazz propaganda of this kind in the Soviet Union is a thing of the past and those in the know are aware that President Kosygin, until his death in 1980, was a great jazz-lover and collector of records. I was told by a well-informed friend that Kosygin wanted to attend the jazz festival in Tallinn in 1967 and was prevented only by the death of his wife.

The present coolness in East–West relations is not without its effect on jazz musicians in the Soviet Union. President Carter's boycott of the Olympic Games (in retaliation for the invasion of Afghanistan) was absolutely unintelligible to the average Soviet citizen. It was 'thanks to' that boycott that sax player Alexey Kozlov was giving a performance with his formation 'Arsenal', considered to be the chief jazz-rock band in the USSR. I heard Kozlov during my first day in Moscow. I had already written in advance to Alexey Batashev – author of *Soviet Jazz* and lecturer in jazz history at a music school with 600 students – and I rang him up that afternoon. It was arranged that I should telephone again that evening. He told me to go at once to the Theatre of Entertainment opposite the Kremlin, by the river, where he would give me a ticket for a Kozlov concert. We were to recognize each other by the *Jazz Forum* which we were supposed to carry.

I was hunting in vain for a taxi in front of my hotel when I was hailed by a driver of a black limousine – in fact, an official State car – which at first struck me as rather fishy. We agreed on the price for a twenty-minute ride (five roubles) and I very soon realized the advantage of such a State car, which pays little attention to speed regulations or, for that matter, to red traffic lights. Any foot passenger who gets in the way is mercilessly honked at and neither time nor sympathy is wasted on any accident that may occur.

Thanks to my express taxi I reached the theatre – which is regularly associated with jazz concerts – in good time (and even in one piece). I met Batashev and Kozlov himself, whom I agreed to meet again in the interval. He told me that he had played with the West German guitarist Toto Blanke at the Jazz Jamboree in Warsaw, his most Western appearance until then. He also asked a lot about both the financial position of jazz players in West Germany and the latest developments in the United Jazz and Rock Ensemble. He told me with great pride that Yevgeny Yevtushenko, then considered the greatest Soviet poet of the day, had been at his concert and would be writing a report of it for the German illustrated paper *Stern*. He also informed me that his trombonist, Vadim Akhmetgarev, was an admirer of Albert Mangelsdorff – a fact which was plain to any listener. The chords which Akhmetgarev produced by additional singing are even more precise than Mangelsdorff's. He uses this effect in a piece borrowed from Korean music. Otherwise there were Spanish and Indian folklore pieces and homage was paid to Prokofiev's *Peter and the Wolf* and – probably unconsciously – to the film composer Ennio Morricone. He also had some ragtime and free jazz, hard bop and cool jazz and even Jimi Hendrix cropped up. Judging from the programme, these dozen rock players model themselves on the United Jazz and Rock Ensemble. As far as instrumental technique goes, these Soviet jazz players have nothing to fear from comparison with their Western counterparts – neither the lively pianist Vyacheslav Gorsky at the synthesizer and the organ, nor Valery Kaznelson – the raw-toned tenor saxophone player, nor the percussionist Stanislav Korostelev, with his brilliant melodies, tone colours and rhythms. Individual titles were very carefully alternated with the light show put on by the normal lighting department of the theatre, emphasizing in excellent detail the various musical forms and structures. The transmission system was very metropolitan compared with that of Leningrad, and was in fact the Western Dynacord system. Performers also have stage monitors, which is not the usual Soviet practice.

In a final conversation after the concert Alexey Kozlov told me about a jam session that was to take place the next day and gave me a ticket for the performance, which was already sold out. This session was a kind of supplement to the recently ended Moscow Jazz Festival which included twenty-six bands playing everything from dixieland to rock and free jazz. That year each group had to play one 'classical' jazz piece apart from works by Soviet composers and pieces connected with folklore. Concerts were given in the concert hall of the Composers' Union, which holds 500 people. Great Soviet composers look down from the walls, from Shostakovich onwards. In the cafeteria, posters with snapshots of the artists taking part hung from the ceiling, and propaganda titles, such as 'Soldiers of the great Red Army at a concert' or 'Meritorious workers in conversation with composers', abounded. The audience for jazz concerts is in marked contrast to this official image. Part of the audience is particularly smartly dressed in Western style. The majority belong to the middle generation, the young having not yet got around to jazz, though there are quite a number of young musical intellectuals. The hall, which was at first full, steadily emptied during the first item – three-quarters of an hour of a singer called Galina Filatova, who recalled the Swingle Singers, and an Ukrainian bass player Anatoly Baby with a production rather like something of Eberhard Weber's. Musically the whole thing was too monotonous, a real non-session – there were even prepared tapes of singing and bass music thrown in. In fact with the Spanish pieces 'Concierto de Aranjuez' and 'La Fiesta', there was more than a hint of kitsch. All too short, on the other hand, was the number contributed by the ensemble of Alexander Bukharov, who deliberately (I was told) combines pre-Christian Russian texts and music with today's rock. In my view Soviet jazz displays real originality and worth when players are conscious of their own cultural history and identity and do not simply copy American models. The death, at the age of thirty-nine, of the Azerbaidjani pianist, composer and bandleader Vagif Mustafa-zade was a great blow to the Soviet jazz world, as he showed real genius in bringing new life to oriental folk music and jazz.

The real jam session began after the interval. Seven horns and a rhythm section improvised on a thirty-two-bar ballad in the modern style. The temperamental tenor saxophone player from Arsenal, Valery Kaznelson, was one of the players and everything revolved round Nikolay Levinovsky (trumpet), who is also the keyboard player and leader of the Allegro group, 'one of the best', according to Alexey Batashev. Next came a dixieland interlude, and it occurred to me that old-time jazz is played more enthusiastically and (technically speaking) better, in Moscow than in Leningrad. Meanwhile there was a queue of sixteen players waiting patiently for their solos – queueing being not exactly unknown in the USSR. . . The evening ended with 'C Jam Blues' and the modal modernists. Discipline and order rather than high spirits or *joie de vivre* were the keynotes of the evening, even here. And when it all ended at 11 p.m. there was none of the drinking that usually follows a concert in the West. I have noticed the same after other jazz concerts, both in Leningrad and in Moscow. Going back in the underground I had another glimpse of Nikolay Levinovsky. I could not help feeling that it was high time for Soviet jazz to emerge from the *social* underground.

Leningrad (December 1980/January 1981)

During my first visit to the Soviet Union I had a warm invitation from my Leningrad friends in the Contemporary Music Club to pay them another visit in the near future. What I actually wanted to do was to take my own group, AK-Musick, which was founded in 1971 and improvises free music. The group appeared at the German Jazz Festival in Frankfurt-am-Main in 1972 and five years later at the Ludwigsburg Jazz Festival, featuring the pianist John Fischer. In the end, however, I was the only one to keep my promise and go to Russia, at the end of 1980 and the beginning of 1981.

Good-quality tapes are in short supply in the Soviet Union and I therefore arrived well provided. My Leningrad friends were able to organize a 'private' recording. The players were Anatoly Vapirov, Sergey Kuryokhin and Alexander Alexandrov. The music clicked in spite of the language difficulties (the Russian jazz musicians could barely speak English) because of the common code of music. In the performance of the pieces nothing definite was prearranged except for the instrumentation and a vague outline of what was to be played.

On that occasion everything was very intellectually orientated, but next day's concert in the Lensoveta Hall was marked by more emotional moments and 'happenings'. Only the inner circle of avant-garde jazz enthusiasts had been invited and there was a certain air of secrecy about the whole thing. Once again there were no difficulties over musical understanding. Of the Russian players I was most impressed by the bass player Vladimir Volkov, with whom I played a delightful and subtle duet. I was also fascinated by the attentiveness and warmth of the audience.

Leningrad/Moscow (June 1981)

On my third visit in June 1981 I went both to Leningrad and Moscow. On this occasion John Fischer – an American born in Belgium and a well-known representative of the New-York 'loft scene' – was also there. He was invited to Leningrad quite independently of me, and he too paid all his own expenses.

In accordance with tradition the concert was again given in the Lensoveta Hall. On this occasion the Contemporary Music Club was less afraid of unpleasantness with the authorities over the presence of foreign guests, and the concert had been more advertised so that the hall was packed with an audience of about 200 people. Variety was provided by including improvisations with many different instrumental combinations. There was perhaps too much emphasis on effect and 'show' in many of the pieces, and I often missed the atmosphere of overall relaxation and interior repose. Our Soviet partners were of course Vapirov, Kuryokhin, Alexandrov, Volkov and Vyacheslav Gayvoronsky (flugelhorn), Alexander Kondrashkin (drums) and Vladislav Makarov (cello), who came especially from Smolensk.

Our next encounter took place in the more restricted space of the bar of the Palace of Culture. Here there were more opportunities for communication. John Fischer was of course asked many questions about the American scene.

At first it seemed doubtful whether we should be able to have a concert in Moscow as well, but Alexey Batashev managed to pull the necessary strings, and on the afternoon of 12 June 1981 an audience of jazz fans – summoned by telephone at the last moment – gathered in the hall of the Gnessin Musical Pedagogical College. Batashev opened the proceedings with a long talk on new jazz, and John Fischer and I then played a number of solo and duet pieces. The real 'Moscow Jam Session', though, started only after the interval, when we were joined by two players who have already made jazz history in the Soviet Union: Leonid Chizhik (piano) and Alexey Zubov (saxophone). They are, however, not really representatives of free jazz and we were therefore quite happy to make a number of musical compromises and keep comparatively traditional in style. There were a lot of swinging, tonal moments in the music which made it, to my mind, worth recording. Of course, both Chizhik, who is one of the most popular and versatile jazz pianists in the USSR, and Zubov, who works as a film composer and spends a lot of time in Los Angeles with his American wife, are experienced professionals.

Leningrad (August 1983)

Two limp and lanky figures, one of them neatly dressed in a three-piece-suit, drag in a wooden table. They are carrying it upside down, with amplifiers, speakers, etc. on top of it. A session is about to begin in the LTO–81 Club, the temporary home of the unorthodox Leningrad literati. In the fuggy room without wallpaper Timur Novikov and Ivan Sotnikov put the table back on its feet and prepare it for the session. Old irons are hung from it with chords, metal bars are fixed to it, a knife is stuck into its edge. Connection with the amplifier is provided by a pick-up microphone. Dull, shrieking and rattling patterns of sound are echoing out of the speakers while the various metal parts are set vibrating.

The two 'zero musicians', as they are called by their colleagues, practise a denial of all melodic and rhythmic conventions. But despite their rebellion they prove to have a sense of musical communication and sensitive interaction. After the concert, the two musicians go back home – no one knows where they live and when they will show up again. And they, themselves, certainly don't know that in the West, too, there are people experimenting with metal objects, only with better electronic equipment.

In one corner Alexander Kondrashkin has set up his percussion instruments. Necessity, meaning the lack of money to buy good instruments on the black market, is the mother of invention in this case. Some tin cans will do the trick. During an improvised concert, Kondrashkin proves a keen partner. He has jammed with various local free-jazz musicians but, normally, he is a member of a rock septet called Strannye Igry, which, translated, means 'Strange Games'. The fans are familiar with the group only through concerts (one even in Moscow) and cassette copies: new wave with machine-like drive and repetitive stacati. Such live music sounds too anarchistic to the ears of the culture bureaucrats. During the rehearsals, however, the ensemble develops beautiful melodies in leisurely tempo.

Eleven musicians participate in the jam session organized for me in Leningrad. Two sax players have come from Moscow just for this occasion: Igor Butman and Sergey Lyetov. After the first part of the concert, consisting of collective improvisations, we decide to play duos and trios. Boris Grebenshchikov is the first one asking me to join him. He is considered the most colourful figure among the progressive Leningrad rock musicians. Equipped with an axe, he demolishes a chair, destroys a bench and smashes bottles: a happening of a destructive kind. Before that, Grebenshchikov had produced sounds from a tea-pot, wind instruments and – with a bow – from an acoustic guitar, proving that this smart-looking guy is not at a loss for ideas for provocative experiments. His group is called Aquarium, and singer and guitarist Boris Grebenshchikov sees himself as the representative of the new Soviet wave. Many of his semi-official concerts have ended in a row. He is in trouble with the official artistic committee, where harmless texts are presented for approval, concealing the fact that during the performances more robust sounds will be heard. The pressure of their fans, he

Boris Grebenshchikov

says, is becoming so strong that the monopolistic record company
Melodiya sooner or later will be compelled to produce a record.
The thirty-year-old student of mathematics gives examples:
Mashina Vremeni ('Time Machine'), today's most popular Russian rock band, had been active in the underground for years
before receiving a contract for a record. For the time being,
however, Aquarium has to record, quite unofficially, in the studio
of some theatre. The group's latest production bears the title
'Radio Africa'. The music is rather soft and entertaining. The
concept of the ensemble – eight musicians altogether – is based on
parody of all musical genres. I ask Boris Grebenshchikov to write
down the text of one song which is important to him. In

'Rock'n'roll Dead' he goes: 'What nervous faces! It's a drag! I remember, there was a sky, I don't remember where. We meet again, we say hello. But something's wrong. Rock'n'roll is dead, and I am not.'

Such frustrated and resigned sounds have nothing in common with the officially dictated, exultant patriotism. 'It is my intention to create an alternative reality, another dimension,' Boris Grebenshchikov explains to me. The consequence: 'I can't work as a professional musician because the system in our country rejects someone like me.' Thus, he is forced to make money by working as a nightwatchman, and it is little enough.

Sergey Kuryokhin, the keyboardist of Aquarium, makes his living by playing the piano during gymnastic lessons. He also plays saxophone and has been thrown out of various conservatories on account of his nonconformist musical behaviour. He found worldwide recognition with a solo record which was released in England, but because he is not an officially recognized musician, the free jazzer can't play outside of the Soviet Union, not even in neighbouring East European countries. Restrictions, however, can't throw them off their track, these disturbing Leningrad punk rockers and jazz musicians. Boris Grebenshchikov, who calls Brian Eno his idol, says: 'I always want to continue creating different things!' But there are considerable obstacles to his ideas: although he owns an electric guitar of inferior quality, 'made in the Soviet Union', he has to find an amplifier and speakers before every concert – somehow, somewhere. . .

Moscow, the Baltic States and Leningrad (*April 1984*)

Immediately after arriving in Moscow I go to a Palace of Culture where a concert with the groups around Sergey Kuryokhin is in full swing. First, I am invited to participate, and then they don't want me to join in, arguing that difficulties might arise if a Westerner performs in public without official permission. Finally, I sneak without an announcement into a group of twenty musicians, the Crazy Music Orchestra which is reacting to the hand-signs of its bandleader.

In the crowded theatre, Kuryokhin, until recently celebrated as an imaginative avant-garde newcomer, is reaping enthusiastic applause for attempting a 'Robot Dance'. Eleven days later I am to play with Kuryokhin again. This time we create a Russian tango, together with Boris Grebenshchikov as singer and cellist. But this time the environment is entirely different, a dirty attic without furniture except for the grand piano which is out of tune: the 'new' clubroom of the unorthodox Leningrad literati.

Between Moscow and Leningrad less mysterious performances in the Baltic Republics take place. The three new republics in the west of the Soviet Union have a reputation for being rebellious, due to the fact that the omnipotent party couldn't make it up to the usual 99.9% in the last election, but only 99.7%. Moscow is far off, people think, and cultivate their national languages and keep their distance from everything that is Russian. An avant-gardistic, even seemingly destructive art is allowed to develop on the Baltic Coast which at the Moskva or Neva would be banished into subculture.

After Leningrad, Vilnius is the second Soviet centre for free jazz, thanks to the Ganelin Trio, which, according to general opinion, is the leading jazz ensemble of this huge country and which, by its concert tours, secures greatly needed currency from capitalist countries abroad. The drummer Vladimir Tarasov made a point of returning earlier from Odessa and organized a session for me. Even posters were painted and invitations printed (with the index number of censorship 6127). Solemn was the place where we improvised: the Red Room in the LTSR Meno Darbuotoju Rumai is the historical house of arts in which the chess championship had recently taken place. Vyacheslav Ganelin was playing his Japanese Roland synthesizer for the first time and dense music developed, ranging from sound arrangements to Gospel elements.

The audience, consisting mainly of artists and jazz experts, apparently enjoyed the performance in the crowded room and we, the musicians, also considered the concert a success.

In 1975 a jazz club had been founded in Riga, the Riga Dzeza Klubs, now housed in the Cafe Allegro. Of course, everything has to have permission from higher up; one is dependent on the one and only youth organization, the Komsomolzes. Occasionally, the Great Comrade Secretary-General is quoted in the club bulletin.

The club, however, is not doing too well, I'm told. The people of Riga are quite indifferent and arrogant, and progressive jazz tendencies are not promoted by the culture bureaucrats.

A session is planned for the late afternoon, in which the tenor sax player Rajmond Raubishko and bassist Ivars Galenieks are my notable partners. They belong to the most qualified musicians playing these instruments in the Soviet Union. The musical result of the meeting is comparatively traditional, concentrating on riffs, central tones and scales. And because waitresses are noisily clattering dishes, silent concentration is made impossible.

Outside of town, a further performance with my participation is to take place immediately after this one. On the wall of the entrance hall, Komsomol members are honoured by numerous awards; inside the assembly room the walls are decorated with slogans and pictures of active workers. Now, my fellow-musicians are mainly younger amateurs, inspired by rock music.

Tallinn had gone down for ever into Soviet jazz history when the American sax player Charles Lloyd had a sensational success during a festival there. But obviously, this was too much freedom for the authorities in Moscow. On a smaller scale, the conservatory is now allowed to organize festivities for students' jazz.

The finale of Tudengi Jazz '84 is a 'Jatsu Jammi' in the huge cafeteria of the university. Mainstream is in demand from the Soviet youth. The fifteen-year-old Armenian Vagan Karapetian proves to be a remarkably vital talent on piano, congas and a hot scat vocalist. I myself join in on 'Summertime' and 'Satin Doll' and create a duo of Spanish flavour with the sax player Lembit Saarsalu. The following meetings of saxophone and clarinet take place without an audience. Saarsalu, having produced two records of his own on the national Melodiya label, works as a musician in a vaudeville theatre, also for television, and has his connections in Tallinn. Thus, we get the chance to play in Niguliste Kirik, a church with an echo of ten seconds (an unforgettable experience) and in the medieval Old City Hall, which just recently has been renovated. The guide's comment: 'Today, a solemn reception will take place in the Old City Hall. War veterans and meritorious workers will be honoured, well-known orchestras and soloists will perform.' The architectural atmosphere influences our mainly modal music. The pianist Rein Rannap who, the evening before, had his own TV show on themes of Bach and Gershwin, also takes part in this festivity. As a rule he plays as a soloist, but he can also improvise in a group.

Before leaving the town there is a session with Tonu Naissoo, quite in a rush. We are making a recording in the house of the Composers' Union, during which the son of the famous composer Uno Naissoo is using a prepared piano and manipulating the strings in the interior of the grand piano. Usually, he plays in a rather conventional manner, and he writes music for advertisements on TV. Back in 'real' Russia, in Leningrad, the joviality and tranquillity of the Baltic is over. Jam sessions, either in a church or with Komsomol members, or in a house of arts with a clarinetist who had come from the West as a tourist – here, this would be an impossible thing. *Nyet!*

Translated from German by Christa Kuch and by Martin Cooper

Arkhangelsk, Arkhangelsk

Bert Noglik

Bert Noglik, born in 1948 in Leipzig, gained his PhD in 1974, having studied aesthetics at Leipzig University. He is the author of two books on new jazz and improvised music in Europe. His book Jazz im Gespraech *(Jazz in Speech), which ran to two editions in East Germany, surveys the contemporary jazz scene there. His second book,* Jazzwerkstatt International *(International Jazz Workshop), was published in 1981 in East Germany and in 1983 as a pocket book in West Germany. It uses interviews and profiles to present twenty-six leading European representatives of new jazz and improvised music. He also writes regularly for* Jazz Forum, Jazz *(Basel) and* Jazz Podium *(Stuttgart). For many years he has been broadcasting on jazz for East German radio.*

No, I didn't dream it. I have seen the northern Dvina flow into the White Sea at Arkhangelsk. Even musical curiosity, then, can be a motive for travel. In retrospect the Dvina appears to me like the sea, which is not surprising when you consider that it expands into the sea. The memory dredges up images. It calls forth sounds and noises: white sounds and snatches of song. To write of Arkhangelsk is to write of my experiences and meetings with jazz and jazz musicians from the Soviet Union. It was in the mid-sixties that I heard my first Soviet jazz group: the Igor Brill Trio. It was straight hard bop – energetic, exciting and intense. In later years the occasional Soviet group and soloist that I heard at international festivals left no enduring impression, and even my re-encounter with an expanded Brill group at the Leipzig Festival in the early eighties was colourless.

The great exception to this was the Vyacheslav Ganelin Trio from Vilnius, which soon progressed to become the hallmark of 'independent' jazz 'made in the Soviet Union'. I was fortunate enough to experience the first and truly triumphal appearance of this trio outside the Soviet Union at the Warsaw Jazz Jamboree in 1976 and later got to listen and speak to the musicians in East Germany. I wrote about the Ganelin Trio and wondered more and more — especially after the group gained international fame, released more and more records and the names of the three musicians became almost synonymous with new Soviet jazz — I wondered, then, if there were not similar (or different) original trends in Soviet jazz and improvised music.

The country is so vast, and what you learn is often by chance. So, what does one do? Initial, albeit scant information which had to be fleshed out with recordings, was offered by the reports of Soviet correspondents, particularly Alexey Batashev and Alex Kan, available in the Warsaw *Jazz Forum*. Gradually I got hold of a few of the rare Soviet recordings of local musicians, and finally there were the products of Leo Records, London, which are making Soviet new jazz internationally known. I wrote letters to the Soviet Union and got to know the names of musicians from Central Asia, from Siberia and from Vladivostok. . . Apart from Moscow, where mainstream jazz (to simplify the situation) predominates and Leningrad (which is indubitably a centre of new improvised music (suffice it to mention the pianist Sergey Kuryokhin, the alto saxophonist Anatoly Vapirov, the horn player Vyacheslav Gayvoronsky and bass player Vladimir Volkov), there are a number of jazz centres far from the above-named metropolises. For example, the Creative Jazz Unity in Novosibirsk, the Bumerang Group in Alma-Ata, the Arkhangelsk Group in Arkhangelsk. . .

Correspondence with Alex Kan, jazz expert and president of the Contemporary Music Club in Leningrad, gave me a broader insight into the Soviet jazz scene. Kan wrote his subjective impressions, mentioned a few musicians but also reported on what was just average and disappointing. All this helped me.

Since there was scarcely any prospect of being able to hear outside the Soviet Union a Soviet new jazz group which was still unknown abroad (yet how else could they become known?), I gradually resolved to go there myself. Another motive reinforced my intention: I am convinced that an understanding of music is helped greatly by hearing and experiencing the musicians in the setting from which they have sprung. I had experienced all the Western musicians only as guests, only *on the road.* To visit Soviet musicians seemed a slight chance, but a chance all the same. But which musicians, and how?. . .

As so often in life, chance came to my aid. In 1981 at the open-air festival in Peitz and shortly afterwards at the Leipzig Jazz Rally I got to know a Soviet musician who was on a private visit to East Germany. Rolf Reichelt, jazz producer and promoter, had met him a year before at the Leningrad Autumn Rhythms Festival and subsequently invited him to visit. Vladimir (I got only his first name then) was a quiet and modest guest who absorbed every impression. With his reddish beard and concentrated, at times almost penetrating gaze he stuck in my memory as a striking, but slightly introverted personality. This might have had a lot to do with his experiences – including musical ones – which he was having a bit of trouble assimilating, but it also stemmed from a communications gap. His English was confined to a couple of words and my Russian was very rusty getting started again. But still – in the bustle of the festival *small talk* was uppermost.

Brief episodes emerged. For instance, I was told how Vladimir practised his saxophone in the hotel room, using the radio as a sort of noise barrier. Vladimir spurned alcohol. Only once, I was told had he taken a stiff snort before he unpacked his instrument for a night session, way after midnight, with the stage densely populated (Perry Robinson was there too), a real power group with the clinking of glasses in the background. I'd just caught the last tram there; without that there would have been no impression of individual performances. One picture sticks in my mind: Vladimir gives Brötzmann a small present (a token, perhaps, of his reverence) – a cloth badge with the name and coat of arms of his native city. It was the first time I read Cyrillic in connection with jazz: 'Arkhangelsk'.

A year later I was reading reports on the Vasaras Ritmi Summer Festival in Riga. Sergey Khrenov wrote in *Cadence*: 'Best was the Arkhangelsk Ensemble of the city of the same name. . . The musical approach of the ensemble called to mind both the British

Company and Sun Ra's Arkestra. Vladimir Rezitsky, who is the guru rather than leader of the band, conducted the spontaneous improvisations of the musicians and controlled the mood and intensity of the music delicately. . .' Alexander Kan even wrote in *Jazz Forum*: 'It is possible to speak of Arkhangelsk as a competitor to end the decade-long dominance of the Vyacheslav Ganelin Trio in Soviet new-jazz circles.' There was no longer any question: it had to be Arkhangelsk. That's where I was going.

Letters shuttled back and forth until at last there came an officially confirmed invitation in an envelope with an embossed wax seal redolent of authority. Then, finally, a visa and a flight ticket: Berlin/GDR–Leningrad–Arkhangelsk–Moscow–Berlin/GDR.

When I arrived in Leningrad, I thought that things would continue as smoothly as the flight and arrival. They didn't. To describe all the technical travel hitches which then arose would be a long story, and that's not what I'm writing about. After long, vain efforts to confirm my flight to Arkhangelsk at Leningrad Airport I met Alexander Kan that evening, as arranged. Chernyshevskaya Metro Station; it's dark and drizzling. If I hadn't met Alexander Kan, I would never have got further than Leningrad and would probably have even had great difficulty getting home again. The very next morning we visit the Aeroflot office on Nevsky Prospect. Every day, I had been assured in Berlin, there was a flight to Arkhangelsk. Well, there was; but as a foreigner I would not be able to fly there until next week. In a week's time I had to be back in Berlin, and anyway I had no permit to stay on in Leningrad. Still, I did stay for a day and a half. There was no choice: for it was only then that I could continue my journey, by train.

The evening before my departure I paid another visit to Efim Barban, a great connoisseur of jazz and new music and a man with an enormous philosophical range. Serious conversation with reflective pauses. A little later Alex Kan delivers me to the unplanned adventure of a train journey. It's 1,134 kilometres by rail across the broad expanses of Russia towards the Arctic Circle; a night and a day, then another, short night. Between black darkness and the grey of morning I glimpse, left and right, water and a huge bridge. There is a sense of arrival and of uncertainty as to whether the telegram got there and who and what was awaiting me. We enter Arkhangelsk.

Arkhangelsk, the reference book tells you, lies where the Dvina enters the White Sea. The city arose in 1584. Until the founding of Petersburg (1703) it played an important role as the only Russian seaport. In Tsarist Russia it was also a place of exile. Arkhangelsk is a station on the north-east sea crossing that follows the northern coasts of Europe and Asia, between the Atlantic and the Pacific.

Today Arkhangelsk is a centre of the timber industry, fishing and fish processing. It has a pulp and paper combine, sail and net factories and shipyards, scientific institutes and research establishment. But above all Arkhangelsk is still an important river- and seaport on the northern sea route, free of ice from May to October.

It was mid-October when I arrived. The weather was mild although, as I later learnt, they had already had some snow. Not until November does the temperature start to drop, but when it does, it plummets.

Vladimir Rezitsky is waiting for me at the station together with Sveta, secretary of the local jazz club, who works as a children's doctor and speaks good German. Why didn't I arrive the day before, as announced? They had fixed up a concert specially for me. Well, we get over that; in the next few days there would be quite enough to hear and see. And then we are off to breakfast – and what a breakfast! Such hospitality, the outward sign of heartfelt concern, accompanies me through the next few days. Admittedly, my visit turns out much shorter than planned. Once again it's Aeroflot that sets the schedule. This flight is off, and that one too. A flight via Syktyvkar, a detour down toward the Urals, would be possible but I've no police permit for Syktyvkar. The last way out, apparently, if there is nothing else, would be back by train to Moscow. But that's out too. In the end there is one last return-possibility other than that booked – to fly back via Leningrad. That unfortunately shortens my stay in Arkhangelsk to two and a half days. A mini-stay, but then I'm glad I could do it at all. And if I got scarcely any sleep during the visit, it was because Vladimir Rezitsky and his friends arranged an almost non-stop programme for my short stay.

Willy-nilly I begin by sweating in the sauna. Apart from Sundays and Mondays, I learn over the smoked fish that follows, the Arkhangelsk group plays in a large room, the restaurant of the Yubileynaya Hotel. Since I got there on a Monday, they had put on at short notice a small concert of avant-garde music for that evening. This is no place to reflect on the problems, the end or even the peculiarity of what is called avant-garde. Avant-garde jazz or avant-garde music is what the Arkhangelsk musicians call what they play or – to be more precise – *one* field of their activity. On Tuesday, Wednesday and Thursday, also from 6 to 7 p.m., they play in the same restaurant a concert of avant-garde jazz; on Fridays they play traditional jazz. After a lengthy interval, on each of these evenings they play another three hours or so of dance music until at 11 p.m. the room lights signal the end of the entertainment.

There is still some time until our extraordinary concert. I get to know the town and the harbour. We take a trip on a little boat. It's misty. Not far from here the Dvina, a mile wide at times, flows into the White Sea. A distant and strange feeling of expansiveness. Talking to Vladimir Rezitsky and Vladimir Turov, pianist of the Arkhangelsk group, I learn a bit about the conditions in which they work. The Arkhangelsk ensemble is not, like other Soviet jazz groups, subordinate to a branch of the State agency, but comes under the hotel management. This has advantages and disadvantages: on the one hand, a certain sovereignty and an almost privileged economic status; on the other hand, few chances of securing a foreign booking. The connection with a gastronomic establishment means that popularity is of paramount importance at least in the dance music.

Since there are hardly any full-time professional jazz musicians in the Soviet Union, there are really only two possibilities: either take up jazz to some extent as an amateur and otherwise pursue a non-musical profession, or else embark in other musical fields – be it orchestral or theatre musician, composer, music teacher or the broader field of dance and light-entertainment music. Which version is best, which one the least tedious cannot be decided on theoretical grounds. Individual preference and the particular conditions and opportunities must play a role. What remains are the questions, whether one is aware of the contradictions and how you come to terms with the particular compromise.

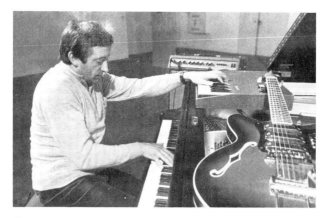

■ Vyacheslav Ganelin *(HANS KUMPF)*

■ Ganelin's first performance on synthesizer — April 1984
(HANS KUMPF)

■ Ganelin with Hans Kumpf — April 1984 *(BIRGIT HAHN)*

■ Vladimir Chekasin conducting

■ Chekasin in full flight *(A. ZABRIN)*

■ Vladimir Tarasov *(A. ZABRIN)*

■ Tarasov with a portrait of himself meeting Duke Ellington
(HANS KUMPF)

■ Tarasov, Ganelin and Chekasin (left to right) — Florence,
26 July 1981 *(FRANCESCO MAINO)*

■ The trio with (left to right) Mustafa, Anthony Smith and Don
Ayler — Florence, 26 July 1981 *(FRANCESCO MAINO)*

■ Anatoly Vapirov (left) with Vladimir Chekasin

■ Chekasin's group playing for dancing *(A. ZABRIN)*

■ The Vladimir Chekasin Quintet at Lensoveta Hall

■ Sergey Kuryokhin

■ Kuryokhin directing his Crazy Music Orchestra in Moscow
(left to right) Valentina Ponomareva, Sergey Lyetov, Igor
Butman and Alexander Alexandrov *(HANS KUMPF)*

■ Kuryokhin on saxophone

■ Sergey Kuryokhin's Crazy Music Orchestra (left to right)
Alexey Rakhov, Grigory Sologub, Kuryokhin, Alexander
Aksenov, Vladimir Bolushchevsky – October 1983 *(V. PESHKOV)*

■ Kuryokhin with Boris Grebenshchikov in the final part of a
performance of 'One Summer Evening in the Life of a
Sexually Obsessed Dinosaur' *(HANS KUMPF)*

■ Kuryokhin and Grebenshchikov *(HANS KUMPF)*

■ Boris Grebenshchikov with his group Aquarium under a slogan saying: 'The decisions of the Twenty-sixth Party Congress to be put into practice'

■ Valentina Ponomareva *(HANS KUMPF)*

■ Ponomareva with Ivars Galenieks

Before the concert starts I meet the musicians in the rehearsal room behind the stage. But rehearsal is just part of the process; it is a place to discuss music and, above all, to listen to music: records, tapes, cassettes of various origin with various types of music. Jazz, improvised music, new composed music, a lot of folk from various parts of the world. I can also listen to a selection from the previous day's concert that the local jazz club had arranged and which drew over 100 people – attentive listeners, Rezitsky assured me. In the restaurant, on the other hand, many of the guests will be just waiting for the dance music. They more or less have to put up with the concert bit. I'd soon see. It was coming up for six o'clock and the room was filling; people dressed up, among the numerous guests there were evidently quite a few travelling on expense accounts – big orders, bottles of champagne and wine on several tables.

The music starts. Vladimir Rezitsky plays alto saxophone as well as flute and keyboards; Vladimir Turov plays keyboards; Fyodor Bagretsov plays guitar; Nikolay Klishin – bass ; Oleg Yudanov – drums; Nikolay Yudanov – percussion. What emerges vaguely resembles English improvised music, although I realize there is no such thing as *the* English improvised music, just as there is no such thing as *the* Soviet jazz. They play without a continually fixed rhythm; the sound sequence is disparate and splintered, there is a large clamorous element. But a comparison with, say, recordings by Company just does not stand up. What I hear in the large hall of the Yubileynaya Hotel strikes me rather as a curious sound. But that may be due to the ambience. Most of the people are busy eating and seem barely to listen. On the cassette I recorded there is as much sound from the knives and forks as there is from the instruments. Here and there are snatches of melody, synthesizer sounds (which may explain the Sun Ra asssociation), vocal interjections by Rezitsky and Turov and enrichment of the tonality by numerous 'little instruments'. After a long set performed without a pause two young lads come on to the stage and ask what all that was supposed to be. I wonder whether the group, because I was there, played *especially* avant-garde music and how they could stand performing an hour every evening to such an audience. I also wondered whether their intention was to confront the visitors with the unusual and thus build up a following, although I doubt that:

it's easier done through a jazz club. But I never get to put these questions, for the taxis are waiting outside to take us to the studio of the painter Boris Kopylov.

Kopylov, who spends the summer in his country dacha and the winter in a studio flat in the middle of the newly built city centre, is a silent man who lets his pictures speak for him. Canvas after canvas, among them many large paintings, are placed before us: numerous landscapes, subjects from the Russian north from which all here stems and to which the people feel bound. The guests are friends of the painter and his wife and members of the jazz club. The jazz club, I was told, was founded in 1981 and arranges monthly concerts and club evenings in a house of culture and occasionally in other locations. They average 150 visitors – up to 500 for special concerts. Fifteen members are actively involved in its administration. They attract people from a wide range of professions, quite a few from the intelligentsia: doctors, teachers as well as painters and graphic artists are there. 'What we want to do,' says Sveta, the children's doctor, 'is to develop culture too here, in an economic centre.' That means get-togethers, discussions, social activities and the development of an artistic sense (the Arkhangelsk group also gives school concerts). But multifarious as the interests of Kopylov's guests may be, one senses an unspoken common denominator, the cohesion of a community which has nothing of the sectarian or the missionary about it but which simply wishes to operate in the setting in which it is placed. What comes over is a self-awareness, but no self-satisfaction; rather the desire to enrich everyday life through cultural activities. The musicians know a great deal about their colleagues in other lands. Oleg Yudanov, for example, asks me about Baby Sommer and Han Bennink. The painter, silently, props up a few more paintings, abstract landscapes in a simple and yet expressive range of shapes and colours. Kopylov paints what he sees and senses, not what you can read in them. I tell him this and after a moment's consideration he nods.

For midnight we are due at another hotel for an after-hours session. The group there is that of the pianist, composer and arranger Valentin Zelenov – a septet with trumpet, tenor saxophone, keyboards, guitar, bass guitar and drums. Zelenov's band starts to play: it is that type of swinging mainstream jazz now played almost everywhere in the world. They didn't need me to come here for that, and yet suddenly I felt good about this music; it gave me unexpected pleasure to listen to it *here*. The restaurant has long been closed, the musicians and their friends are chatting together, and one senses their pleasure in playing and listening. Tea is dispensed from huge samovars. Everything is much more relaxed than at the avant-garde concert earlier that evening.

Where and how jazz or improvised music develops does, after all, have some connection with the stylistic trends and methods of playing that this music has already adopted and which are present in musical life. What is actually or assumed to be new can only be extracted from what is already there, regardless of whether it negates or continues this. From this point of view the starting conditions for improvised musicians in different countries are not really comparable. Even the appropriation, or at best individual rendition of existing ways of playing belongs to the development of a musical scene. All this comes to mind as I listen to Zelenov playing what is certainly not avant-garde, but still music performed with dash and enthusiasm.

At last the Arkhangelsk group unpacks its instruments again. In the more relaxed atmosphere it manages considerably more compact music. Thoroughly improvised sections resound now and again in rehearsed parts. Unwittingly one is reminded of the Ganelin Trio's dramaturgically conceived suites, but the way the Arkhangelsk group handles the most varied musical material sounds, at the same time, less ordered, less respectful and bolder. At times that can run the risk of becoming a disconnected sequence of sounds, but it also offers the chance of a radical breakthrough in patterns of playing and hearing. The proportion between composition and improvisation, Rezitsky explains, varies considerably from appearance to appearance. Sometimes they agree roughly on the sequence at the start; for some time, however, the group has also occasionally played fully 'free', that is – without any prearrangement.

The total sum of impressions – live performances, tape and cassette excerpts and, finally, a jazz-rock-orientated piece very typical of the group and contained on a sampler of Soviet groups – creates no cohesive picture. Lyrical moods and sounds alternate with rhapsodic intensity (and Rezitsky's alto saxophone sometimes has a slight cool jazz touch to it); Latin rhythms contrast with sounds which call up associations with church bells and the folk music of the Arkhangelsk region. Amid this, thickly laid synthesizer sounds (the attraction of a new instrument may play a part here) punctuate pulsating free-jazz passages. Here and there there are even traces of rock and funk. There again one discerns meditative tonalities, dissolved into shrill collages which integrate even swing titles from the thirties, a sort of Gregorian chant and echoes of the chatter from children's dities. The concept – in so far as one can even talk of a concept in this context – offers further similarities with the music of the Ganelin Trio. Ganelin described his trio's music as 'deliberately polystylistic'. In the stylistic sense the Arkhangelsk group also takes a multi-track approach but makes its selection from a still greater range of musical material. Moreover, it is not just a question of subjective assessment or a decision to call this or that polystylistic or eclectic. The group's musical practice swings between musical integration and blunt contrast of the various elements.

Even its tendency towards multi-instrumentalism or (to be more precise) the enrichment of its sound with so-called 'little instruments', its interest in incorporating electronic tonality in an otherwise acoustically instrumental context, its occasional affinity to tonal improvisations such as those which developed in the circle of the Chicago's AACM, as well as its concern with European folk music (Rezitsky and Turov not long ago made a tour of provincial areas to study northern Russian folklore), but also its interest in non-European, for example African ethnic music – all this leads to a comparison with the Ganelin Trio. However, whereas the Ganelin Trio, despite its polystylistic orientation, at least in the course of a longish set, does carry the imprint of an identifiable group sound, the Arkhangelsk ensemble seems to be constantly seeking and testing new constellations and methods of playing. It has not tried to perfect a unique signature but rather dares, regardless of its many years of joint experience, to continue to experiment. Where that may lead is uncertain. Anyone taking this approach must risk making those musical skids and slips, which are never entirely avoidable, more strongly evident than in groups which essentially work on their repertoire. On the other hand, this approach can produce quite unheard of effects, in other words –

truly 'new' music. The snapshot becomes instead a picture puzzle, more exciting than many a sharply delineated view which leaves no room for the imagination.

Again the night is a short one. Next morning the group plays football. Musicians versus Teachers. I am left with no excuse to wriggle out: sports gear has been organized for me. For the Arkhangelsk group this is a regular balance to their evening work; football and sauna, also the *banya* – the Russian steam bath – followed in winter by a romp in the snow. No trace of bohemianism: they live a healthy life. I saw none of the musicians smoke or drink alcohol. Only so, I was told, can one get through in the entertainment business – and that, after all, is where they earn their living.

Somewhere I had heard that the Arkhangelsk musicians lived as a commune. That's not true. What is true is that they hold together; they meet not just on the stage but in their free time too, engage regularly in sport and discuss at length music and many other topics. This collectivity is also imparted in their music, or rather through it. Vladimir Rezitsky seems to be the one who brings in the most ideas and drives the group forward; as an instrumentalist, too, he is the most impressive. Though not, perhaps, a guru, he is the one whose playing and opinion the others attentively follow.

Between football and museum visits (the icon collection is impressive) there is still time to talk to Vladimir about his musical development. As early as 1967/68 he was playing in a cafe in his native city with the drummer Vladimir Tarasov, who also comes from Arkhangelsk but then went to Vilnius to work with Vyacheslav Ganelin and later also with Vladimir Chekasin. Rezitsky shows me a photo from his early years with Tarasov. Both have very short haircuts, apparently in their circle a sign then of radical modernity. Asked his early influences, Rezitsky names among others Monk, Brubeck, Ornette Coleman. 'What Tarasov and I played then,' Rezitsky says, 'was modern jazz without any concession to the public's taste.' When Tarasov went to Vilnius, he urged Rezitsky to follow him. For half a year Rezitsky did try to settle in Vilnius but then the two musicians parted ways. Rezitsky returned to Arkhangelsk, turned more traditional and played predominantly pop music. In 1972 he founded a trio together with

Turov, who was then mainly a singer and only specialized as a
pianist in collaboration with Rezitsky. In the space of a year this
trio grew into a sextet. In addition to dance music they played
modern jazz and gradually what Rezitsky and his friends called
avant-garde music. In 1975 the group adopted the name of their
home town, Arkhangelsk.

Since the early eighties their participation in jazz festivals in
various Soviet cities has made them thoroughly familiar to jazz
fans. But even as far as dance music is concerned, Arkhangelsk is
popular far beyond the bounds of its own region as one of the
favourite groups with an audience which is certainly not identical
to the jazz public. This popularity is also a form of regional power.

The dance I attend begins at 8 p.m. sharp so that, following
regulations, it can end on the dot at 11 p.m. A crowd is pushing to
get in; in the hall itself it is both casual and formal. The group
offers a varied menu of dance music – hits, rock titles, topical disco
hits and a good dose of stage show. Rezitsky plays alto saxophone,
keyboards and sings; from time to time a male and female singer
beef up the ensemble. Hardly any of the chairs stay occupied,
since almost everybody – young and not so young – is up dancing.
Between the numbers there is hearty applause. The musicians
seem to enjoy it all; they seem so at home that I wonder a bit. But
then how else, in the long run, could they endure such a 'double
life'.

I ponder to myself whether 'improvised (avant-garde)' music is,
for these musicians, something which they adopt, much as the way
they come to terms with new trends in pop music. . . But an
argument against this is their stylistic stubbornness and their
commitment to the push into new musical territory. I wonder, too,
whether their joint experience in the field of entertainment music
under Soviet conditions (and that means picking up new trends at
a go and quickly adapting them, usually only by ear) also makes
possible a certain flexibility which favours experiment and at the
same time prevents them from becoming fixated on any finally
determined direction. Hard to say.

As far as one can judge from a distance, the Arkhangelsk group
is one of the most interesting and certainly the most daring and
also contradictory improvising groups in the Soviet Union. Not to
cover up the contradictions seems to me one of the conditions for a

serious *rapprochement* to jazz and improvised music in the Soviet Union. Only in this way can both idealizing legends and disparaging blanket judgements be avoided. Consideration of the circumstances under which the musicians live and work is conducive to an appreciation of their music but should not, on the other hand, lead one to assess their music purely by local or regional standards. The 'Oh yes, I know all about it' attitude is uncalled for, just as is the visitor's explanation of what he or she assumes to be local exotica. What is called for is mutual familiarization.

Soviet jazz is certainly more than a foreign-currency-earning export commodity (this, anyway, applies to only a small number of groups and soloists). To build up a fuller picture of the living musical changes which are taking place an expanded cultural exchange is desirable. If it were possible to integrate into regular musical life foreign tours as well as visits by foreign musical groups and international workshops, this would do away with sheer speculation and false judgements. Nothing would be sillier (and nothing would burden the development of music more) than to see in it what one assumes to be the bearers of ideas which have nothing to do with the field of music and its public. It is not a question of doubting the social meaning of music; it is rather that we should define more precisely its relation to its setting. What I tried to do was to record and depict one moment – it could not be more – in the Arkhangelsk group's setting.

On the last day of my visit Vladimir and I sit in the packed waiting-room of Arkhangelsk Airport. Vladimir is listening to music on his Walkman. Over-tired, we feel no need for conversation. I think that's a good sign of understanding.

After a lengthy wait the Leningrad flight is called. Walking the broad stretch of tarmac, I wave to him with a large carved bird, a present to bring me luck.

Translated from German by Barry Elliot

The Ways of Freedom
(Sergey Kuryokhin's Interview)

Sergey Kuryokhin, who was born in 1954, is a representative of the new generation of Soviet jazz musicians. His brilliant piano technique and dynamic, expressive way of playing began to attract attention in 1977 when he appeared in the Anatoly Vapirov Ensemble. At the beginning of the eighties he had been performing solo, in a duo with saxophonist Vladimir Chekasin of the Ganelin Trio, in the Anatoly Vapirov Quintet, in rock group Aquarium, which he co-led with guitarist Boris Grebenshchikov, and as a leader of his own groups, including a ten-piece band, the Crazy Music Orchestra. These programmes had not only showcased his talents as a pianist but also his possibilities as a composer and a conductor of his own grotesque, eccentric shows.

*In 1981 Sergey Kuryokhin's first record was released in the West (*The Ways of Freedom, *solo piano, Leo Records, LR 107) and he was immediately hailed as a 'new Russian wizard'. John Pareles of the* New York Times *called him 'a true discovery'.*

Sergey Kuryokhin is undoubtedly one of the heroes of the new-music scene in the Soviet Union, a charismatic personality for jazz fans and a pest for the Soviet authorities. He belongs to the breed of thinking musicians. Since he has a clear way of expressing himself it is best to present his views and ideas in the form of an interview, which covers a wide variety of topics: his personal preferences and tastes; the place of improvised and avant-garde music in modern society, especially in Soviet society; the identity of Russian jazz, and so on. (Some parts of the following interview were originally published in Cadence © *1983, jazz and blues magazine, Cadence Building, Redwood, NY 13679, USA; and* Jazz

Forum, *the magazine of the International Jazz Federation,* JF *82 3/1983.)*

QUESTION: When did you begin to play the piano?

ANSWER: I started playing when I was four. At that time I liked operetta and tried to pick out my favourite tunes on the piano. Then I went to a special music school. I was born in Murmansk, but lived in Moscow and other towns. In 1971 my family moved to Leningrad. At that time young people were into rock music – I had started playing rock music while I was still in the fourth class at school. And I still like some rock-music groups and musicians: King Crimson; Emerson, Lake and Palmer; Brian Eno; Henry Cow. . . I love traditional rock and roll! I think today many young people come to avant-garde jazz through rock. You can't avoid it.

Later I went straight into the third year of the conducting and choral departments of the Music School attached to the Leningrad Conservatory, but I was kicked out after six months as I did not attend the classes. Then I tried to carry on studying but I was kicked out several more times. In the Institute of Culture, I was studying in three departments at once – piano, flute and conducting. But I was kicked out of there as well. I am totally incapable of attending classes regularly; the atmosphere there is completely uncreative, the boredom is deadly.

QUESTION: When did you really start playing, and what?

ANSWER: My development has been fairly typical of my generation: we were all playing rock at that time. I played rock in groups at school. At the same time I started listening to jazz. I didn't really like it at first, I listened to it out of curiosity. The 'Voice of America' programmes of the time were scheduled so that the jazz programme came first, before the rock programme. Gradually I got used to it. The only thing that caught my attention at the time was John Coltrane and his quartet, or rather not so much Coltrane himself as McCoy Tyner. I didn't like Coltrane much then, but I was absolutely stunned by Tyner. I never thought the piano could be played like that. Rock pianists at that time played with really only two fingers and Tyner's effect was entirely due to his mastery of the keyboard, which seemed to be unattainable – so I began to be interested in jazz. I began to play consciously some time after I left school, at about seventeen or eighteen.

QUESTION: So Coltrane was a decisive influence for you?

ANSWER: I support the theory that an interest starts with surprise. For example, Sun Ra and Mingus never surprised me – and I never liked them. I listened to Mingus only because Eric Dolphy played with him. But I can give you the names of several people who have stunned me at one time or another, although this did not necessarily mean that they influenced me. They simply broadened my interests and enthusiasm: Coltrane, Keith Emerson, Anthony Braxton, John McLaughlin, Mauricio Kagel. Recently I have become very fond of Monk.

QUESTION: Who are your other favourite pianists?

ANSWER: I have always admired Cecil Taylor. I like Muhal Richard Abrams and Alexander von Schlippenbach, but on the whole pianists have never really much impressed me, and for that reason it sometimes seemed to me that I didn't like the piano. But I really liked the saxophone and deep down I always wanted to be a saxophonist. This is probably why I often want to play with saxophonists – with Vapirov and Chekasin, whom I admire without reserve. I try not to limit myself to the piano, but to expand my means of expression.

Anatoly Vapirov is an outstanding musician. His technique is probably unequalled in the USSR, even better than Chekasin's. Vapirov is a brilliant player. But for him the music is not the end in itself. He lacks the inner world, a sense of suffering, of the tragedy of creation. In this respect Vladimir Chekasin is the complete antithesis of Vapirov. They cannot be compared.

QUESTION: You have become recognized as a pianist, but recently you have been playing the piano less and less in your programmes. Why is this? Have you had enough of it, or have you simply started thinking more orchestrally, as it were?

ANSWER: I have several answers to that question. In the first place I am not tired of the piano. It's a marvellous instrument, although I do think it's a dying one. I think it's dying out. I can't say more than that yet. So I have not found anything new for myself in 'piano thought' in the last few years. I don't think this is snobbishness – I hope I shall be understood correctly, but over the last few years I haven't heard a pianist whose playing I have liked, or even been impressed by. The only piano playing that creates any impression is in the context of a play, if it is an integral part of the play's structure. I want to give variety to my programmes; each programme should be different from the one before. Today, for example, I may be organizing a big band to play spontaneous improvisations, next time a big band with semi-traditional arrangements, then I play solo, then a duo with a saxophonist, a bassoonist, or a singer. I can make music which will not be jazz either in sound or phrasing. I want to exploit the whole arsenal of musical means available to me. And now I feel more like composing. I feel much more attracted to composing than to performing. And then . . . very recently I suddenly realized that all my life I have longed to play the saxophone. Sixty per cent of the music I listen to at home is from the saxophone. Whenever I write music, or just compose in my head, I always give the leading part to the saxophones. This is also why I work only with saxophonists – Anatoly Vapirov, Vladimir Chekasin, and with two others, younger, but marvellous musicians, who have appeared relatively recently: Igor Butman and Pyatras Vishnyauskas. I base everything on the saxophone as the main instrument – I mean I think in a linear way, not harmonically but melodically. Even when I am playing the piano now I play as though I am singing a song. I can play complex chords, complex harmonic structures, but I think in one voice.

I play less piano and more other instruments from brass to drums and accordion, and I feel this is aesthetically justified. It has to be said that non-pianists have an enormous influence on modern piano playing. Anthony Braxton, for example, and the guitarist Derek Bailey. One can also give other examples. But the piano is really dying. In my work I am striving to bring together various means of expression. Why can't I behave in a paradoxical, lunatic way on the stage? More lunacy, absurdity and shocks – this is what's needed to stir things up, not dinner jackets, black ties and dixieland. My present-day compositions can be called social art. It is a good idea to shock the public – after all their expectations are simply preconceived perceptions, standards and labels.

As I said, the piano does not interest me at all. It is an anachronism. I am totally uninterested in piano technique. At one time in Russia there was a tendency towards virtuosity and brilliance in piano technique. I would even call this the Russian piano disease. Rachmaninov is a typical example of this kind of outdated attitude in piano playing. For me his name is associated with a supreme lack of taste, and banality. Oscar Peterson is the jazz version of Rachmaninov. And yet I value inconsistency and nonconformism more than anything else in an artist. And therefore I openly admit that I love playing the piano – solo or with other musicians.

QUESTION: Theatre is becoming more apparent all the time in your programmes and Chekasin's during the last two years. The grotesque visual elements of the theatre, happenings and clowning are becoming more important. Is this a desire to give society's taste a slap in the face, or – second possibility – to avoid the deadening academic effect of 'serious art', which has crept even into avant-garde, or – third possibility – does it all have some deeper, more substantive meaning for you?

ANSWER: The first possibility can be discounted immediately. There is no slap in the face, no protest at all. The eccentricity of our behaviour on the stage is very easy to explain. Chekasin and I often discuss this question and always come to the same conclusion – that for us the behaviour is always a continuation of a musical idea, including everything: jumping about, hitting plates and stamping our feet. For me a word can grow into a musical phrase, and a musical phrase into a gesture, although some of it has, of course, been thought through in advance. I feel like – I don't know whether this is right or not, some people may like it, others may not – I feel like having fun.

And I want the audience to have fun as well – if they want to. Most people, for some reason or other, don't, they take everything absolutely straight. Anatoly Vapirov, for example, simply does not accept eccentricity on the stage – he regards his music as serious, academic – that's probably how it should be – he has his own opinions on the matter – I should like to put on a funny nose during one of his serious compositions, and all the seriousness would be dispersed. Why shouldn't one play with a funny nose on? The whole audience would react in a different way, normally. Contact would be established instantaneously. I love the theatre, I have worked a lot in it – I was the musical director of the University Theatre and wrote the music for many of the shows – I have always loved the theatre. I want my performances to be worth looking at. Our musical reality is so cut off from contemporary avant-garde jazz in the West that we only half know, from records and reviews, what goes on at Carla Bley's concerts or the Globe Unity Orchestra – they are doing just the same, after all. I have heard the recording of the Globe Unity Orchestra at the local fair. It gave me great pleasure: a brass band, a band of accordionists and the whole Globe Unity Orchestra – it was really great.

Ordinary human music, with the noises of the fair – the soloists reacted in a very lively way to every sound and played up to them.

QUESTION: Your performances at some jazz festivals – for example Riga 1981 – and the compositions of your ensemble were more like the Theatre of the Absurd than the usual free-jazz concerts. They were organized theatrical productions and not purely musical improvisation. Does this not have a bad effect on the music?

ANSWER: At the moment I am trying to go a bit further by recognizing that not only all sorts of compositions, but all areas of art are equal. But musical improvisation has to play the main part. To be more precise, I am trying to create a paradoxical 'happening' where the actions are secondary to the development of the music. Contemporary free music is connected in the most amazing way with the aesthetics of Zen, based on spontaneity and paradox, although we do not always recognize this connection. Zen (and Chinese Chang) is very close to my spiritual world, as much as this is possible for a European. Europe is only just beginning to understand this soft, mysterious language, but it is a language, a way of thinking and not a prescribed philosophy or religious system, as is often thought.

QUESTION: To what extent is your stage behaviour spontaneous? Is it pure improvisation or do you prepare something in advance?

ANSWER: It is difficult to say. Of course, something is prepared in advance, during the rehearsal, where it is spontaneous. A certain structure develops. This in its turn is filled in and comes into being only once on the stage through improvisation. In my solo performances I control about twenty per cent of the music; the rest happens spontaneously. One should not think that improvisation precludes other forms of composition technique:

aleatorics, stochastics, pointillism, serialism, new or traditional ways of notation, computerized or classical methods. One can play what one wants, how one wants, but the basis should always be the freedom of improvisation. Why should one consciously impoverish the language?

QUESTION: You said that you have recently been drawn to composing. How do you set about this? Do you write it down in traditional notation or in some other way?

ANSWER: If it has to be written down in notation, then why not? If in the music that I am writing a moment of traditionally notated music arises among the spontaneous improvisation then I naturally write it down. If I am writing a spontaneous composition which will turn into some kind of dance at the end, then I write down the tune of the dance and all the musicians simply learn it from the sheets. I use both contemporary and traditional notation systems, depending what sort of music I am writing.

QUESTION: So for you there is no dogma: playing only spontaneous music or notated music.

ANSWER: No, no, although I am a great devotee of spontaneous improvisation, which is for me the dominant form. My works have a very formal structure, then I invite those musicians whose work I know, like Derek Bailey does, but he has no structure, his is all spontaneous improvisation, whereas I construct a very exact composition with individual musicians in mind, and in my mind I fill out the skeleton, the construction, with improvisations which are characteristic of those musicians. And they improvise within the bones of this skeleton. In this way while I am constructing the composition I can already, as it were, hear it being played by the musicians I have in mind.

QUESTION: This kind of approach makes it difficult to imagine that you could work for an extended period of time with a permanent group.

ANSWER: Oh no! This is the main thing for me at the moment. I think about it a great deal. A permanent, active group is absolutely essential and the establishment of this kind of group – which must be at least a trio – is my most pressing problem at the moment. There are, of course, many, many problems, but nevertheless I hope that I shall have a permanent group to work with. Of course I shall still be working for other musicians and shall carry on doing what I am doing now. The musicians working in our group will also be connected with other groups, but we shall have our own music, we shall have what I call a real ensemble, something which takes years to build and demands a great deal of mutual understanding. I think it'll probably happen with Anatoly Vapirov. You could not really call what we have an ensemble at the moment, it's almost a duo – the musicians who do play with us are changing all the time. If we just had another two permanent people then we'd have the kind of ensemble we are looking for.

QUESTION: Imagine that you have unlimited financial and organizational resources. What kind of project would you try and tackle?

ANSWER: Oh, I love huge projects. I would take, say, five or six symphony orchestras, set them out on a stage of five square kilometres, give it amplification, add a lot of electronics, invite something like thirty or forty soloists – musicians that I like or respect – Braxton, Parker or Bennink. Chekasin would conduct a professional choir, for which I would write music. I want action on a totally global scale, what Scriabin called 'action in a total harmony', I want the metaphysics of total unity, I want to come close to mystery, I love mystery, I love the very spirit of this ancient ritual. This is, of course, totally unrealistic, although if the Guggenheim Fund would give me a grant I would be prepared to go to Paris to work with some orchestra, choirs and soloists.

QUESTION: Have you got any definite plans?

ANSWER: I have a lot of plans, but I lack the facilities. I need a choir, I need a symphony orchestra, I need a circus with all its characters, a zoo and a gypsy camp. I love gypsy songs. I need a lot of synthesizers and a lot of other things which I'll never have. But speaking seriously, I try to introduce elements of opera into my performances, elements of operetta and other genres taken to the limits of absurdity. At the moment I am seriously taken up by collage and I am trying to do it without any prerecorded tapes. I use these tapes because I am poor. In our Contemporary Music Club we tried to include Leningrad poets in our improvised performances, but unfortunately these attempts were unsuccessful as the poets did not understand what to do, how one can improvise in front of an audience. So the results were pathetic. I am working on a production of the opera *The Cherry Orchard.*

QUESTION: Can one call your music jazz?

ANSWER: I think not. I consider jazz aesthetically dead. That's why the most radical black musicians (and jazz is above all black music) like David Murray, the Art Ensemble of Chicago, Chico Freeman, Sun Ra, Pharoah Sanders and many others have gone backwards. More and more, they play music which is closer to bebop than to avant-garde. One can't say that of white jazzmen. I think that contemporary white improvised music is more up to date, spiritual and significant. Examples: Evan Parker, Derek Bailey, the Globe Unity Orchestra, ROVA, Gunter Hampel, Han Bennink and many others. Roughly speaking, I am a supporter of the most radical experimentation, the most extreme avant-garde, the boldest eccentricity, which has not become automatic, and total nonconformism, but only, of course, when it is done by people who understand what they are doing and see the meaning of it.

QUESTION: If you don't want to call the new music jazz, if this is out of date, then you obviously can't deny that there is a connection between improvised music of today and the so-called 'serious' avant-garde.

ANSWER: I have no intention of denying the merits of jazz. It is because of jazz that this freedom of improvisation was reborn in musical culture. And 'serious' avant-garde is an essential part of contemporary European culture, noticeably influencing almost exclusively white free jazz and white improvised music. Black musicians, with rare exceptions (Leo Smith and Anthony Braxton), do not turn to 'serious' avant-garde. I am not personally interested in all 'serious' avant-garde musicians, but I love Stockhausen, Xenakis and Luc Ferrari.

QUESTION: What place does the sort of music you play occupy in world culture?

ANSWER: This is a very complicated question. I could answer it properly only if I had a full and objective picture of world cultures, but this is almost impossible for one person, especially if we take into consideration the isolation we are in. It is very difficult to understand what is going on in the world of contemporary music when one is taking part in it. John Fischer was telling us that in America practically any kind of creative experimental music is played – any. Everything is played together, all the traditions are merged, all concepts. Rock musicians play classical music, classical musicians play jazz and jazz musicians try to experiment with folk music. An experiment is being carried out in all fields of art, everything is fused. It is not possible to separate anything out. Complete confusion – in a positive sense.

QUESTION: Do you agree with Leo Smith who maintains that the whole world is moving towards 'world music', as he calls it?

ANSWER: Yes, I think that there is this tendency. But I don't know whether it is good or bad. Leo Smith is sure that the prospects are very bright, that it will lead to the unity of all nations. I don't know how interesting, or how long-lived this would be. For me the questions of folklore and epic are very important. I somehow feel that this 'universalization' is a negative process which destroys the distinctive features of personality, and this will lead to the degeneration of culture. Perhaps I am wrong, I don't know, I don't want to insist on my point of view. If we were talking about the philosophical basis of the problem, then we could talk for hours. We could talk about Russian spiritual traditions. I am a nationalist-chauvinist, you know.

QUESTION: Is jazz a fairly alien phenomenon in Russian culture?

ANSWER: Yes, it is. Especially if we consider the concept of jazz. The fact is that I share the opinion of Panassie, who is criticized by everyone: that bebop is already not jazz. Someone has said that Parker's music is Parker's, Ellington's music is Ellington's. Ellington never called his music jazz – he carefully avoided this word, although he is considered one of the giants of jazz. That is why jazz in its original meaning, as it developed in the beginning, is certainly alien to our Russian understanding of art.

QUESTION: In that case how do you see your own original, independent creative work and the work of the other best Soviet jazz musicians – the Ganelin Trio, for example – within the framework of the traditions of Russian culture? Can one talk of this?

ANSWER: Of course one can. It is not only possible, but essential. I consider that the Ganelin Trio are developing within the framework of Russian – and I mean Russian in feeling – art. This could not have happened in the West, and I was amazed at the superficiality of Milo Fine's review of their record in *Cadence* [*Live in East Germany*, Leo Records, LR 102]. He didn't see anything in the record except that it was in no way inferior to the best world standards. He didn't understand the creative process. This record is so different from what is being done in the West in all ways: in structure, composition, organization of the musical material – it is a completely different principle which could never have happened in the West with the pragmatic rationalism of European culture. But we are getting on to non-musical questions, questions of nation, ethos, nature, natural feeling of a kind felt by Dostoevsky, questions of social environment, climatic conditions which in many ways condition our life [laughs and looks out of the window at the mud and wet snow of late November]. No sane person could live in this town; we are being forced to live in completely unacceptable conditions, and this forms the psyche of a person, his or her culture and so on. All the traditions of musical education, the music I heard on the radio and TV, played in school and college, in a word everything, one's whole cultural, national heritage is reflected in one's music.

QUESTION: How would you define the place of the jazz musician in present-day Soviet reality?

ANSWER: That is a very complex question. Every musician who has anything to do with jazz tries to find his or her own way. It's all very difficult. . . A great many musicians work in restaurants, some tour with all sorts of variety groups, others teach, but as a rule all jazz musicians, with very few exceptions, are not doing what they would like to be doing. If their own kind of music were well paid they would never work, of their own volition, in touring groups. They would not accompany singers or work in restaurants or variety and so on. We're not talking about huge sums of money – only enough to live on.

QUESTION: You play new jazz, avant-garde. Jazz pianists always maintained that in order to play avant-garde, the higher mathematics of jazz, one had to have worked through the arithmetics of traditional jazz. What do you think about that?

ANSWER: In the first place I don't agree with the statement itself. I don't regard avant-garde as 'higher mathematics', or the earlier stages of jazz arithmetics. The mathematical approach to art seems to me to be incorrect, even ridiculous. Music of any kind takes many forms. In the case of jazz there is bop, dixieland, jazz-rock, avant-garde, etc. When it reaches a certain level, say genius level, then these forms merge. In every kind of music it is possible to achieve the highest level of spirituality which transcends the framework of this level. Every music has its peaks and heights and I don't understand why one should play only rock, avant-garde, or whatever.

QUESTION: So you would say that there are no aesthetic gradations of style?

ANSWER: Yes, I think I should. But again only at a certain level, when dealing with genius. It's much more interesting to listen to good bop, say Max Roach or George Adams, than uninteresting avant-garde.

QUESTION: So we are really talking about musicianship?

ANSWER: No, not at all. It is not musicianship. There has to be a sense of spirituality. Without it the musicianship has no meaning at all, it's quite naked. And there is another thing. . . I regard it as . . . degradation. There is an enormous number of record labels documenting practically every performance by well-known musicians. Any musician, who plays constantly, gives ordinary, even downright unsuccessful concerts, as well as outstanding ones. But when Braxton or Taylor comes to Europe every concert is recorded, all the records are released and you have five records which are rubbish, while every sixth is brilliant. One has to extract some kind of music from this flood of information. At the moment everyone is pushing the same thing – avant-garde and more avant-garde, which can only be bad. Take someone who has never heard avant-garde – he or she listens to one of these records and, naturally, does not like it, it is repellant. So avant-garde music, like any other, has its few masterpieces which are heights, and the rest is mediocre. Real music, real creativity starts only above this level, and then the styles merge.

QUESTION: Don't you think that the boundaries between various kinds of music are becoming vaguer than ever before?

ANSWER: In my opinion it is quite pointless to try to divide music up into trends and styles or anything of this kind. Each kind of music has its peaks, its geniuses, and when one is dealing with genius the boundaries are eliminated. This is self-evident, no doubt, but I do not see any dividing line between time, style and space in music. One can play anything and call it whatever one likes, but what is important is a creative attitude towards tradition.

I mean that music should be improvised. This is one of my principles.

QUESTION: You support the most radical experimental ideas in art. But what do you feel about tradition?

ANSWER: I think that the Ganelin Trio is involved in experiments which are no less interesting than mine. But for me the Ganelin Trio is above all Chekasin. Perhaps I am biased because of my affection for Chekasin. But I can answer your question with a fairly obvious truism: a musician exists because of tradition. Tradition nourishes him or her. The mechanism of the influence of tradition is hidden somewhere in the subconscious. Even if we don't use tradition directly, at a subconscious level it still forms our language. But only on the basis of a negative attitude to tradition, and not ignorance of it, can one build a positive programme, or anything new. Otherwise, communication won't happen, and music as a language loses all meaning. But to find the meaning of music is our basic task. When the creative spirit can be felt in music and the musician sees the meaning, his or her musical language becomes clear, simple and complete.

QUESTION: In the summer of 1981 John Fischer and Hans Kumpf took part in concerts with Leningrad musicians. You also took part. What were your impressions?

ANSWER: These unofficial concerts were staged by the Contemporary Music Club of Leningrad. Unfortunately, there are very few concerts like this. I am glad of any contact, and was therefore delighted to play with Fischer and Kumpf. Hans Kumpf is a very pleasant person, and in his presence one feels an abundance of warmth. Fischer's playing really thrilled me. Many expected something supernatural from him. But I was impressed with his awareness of what he was doing. In my perception there are two sorts of music: just music, and music about music. Fischer plays the second. When we listen to such music we don't hear the music but what the performer thinks about what he or she is playing. This seems to me to be the most profound meaning of creative music. This is why ordinary music feels dead to me, impersonal, devoid of spirit. The contemporary listener is critical of any pathos in music, questioning both the heroic and the tragic. And only the sincerity of the comical is not doubted. And the search for freedom.

QUESTION: You once said in an interview that the meaning of art is to be found outside art. . .

ANSWER: For me there is a definite contradiction between art and creative work. Creativity is a spirit, a liberation from the burden of matter, and when the spirit leaves, what is left is a dead work of art, a museum exhibit, an object of worship. That's why I think that the real essence of art is to be found outside art, but is contained in the creative process. A real artist is always a nonconformist.

Siberian Jazz

Siberia is a vast territory covering one tenth of our globe. The climate is ferocious. Its cultural capital, Novosibirsk, is thousands of miles away from the cultural centres of the USSR, Moscow and Leningrad. The Urals, which separate Europe from Asia, seem to be too high for even a tiny stream of information to get over them. And yet, despite the lack of jazz records, books, magazines and recording facilities, jazz managed to establish itself in Siberia. Jazz enthusiasts put on two all-Union festivals in 1976 and 1977, and the Symposium of Contemporary Music in 1978, which was unparalleled in Soviet jazz history. It featured not only jazzmen but also many avant-garde 'classical' musicians. During the afternoon sessions the participants of the Symposium gave nineteen talks and reports, covering the widest possible range of problems related to new music.

Foreign jazz visitors are very rare indeed. In 1978 jazz fans in Novosibirsk had a special treat. They were visited by the New England Conservatory Ragtime Ensemble led by Gunther Schuller. After the concert there was a jam session, and later on Gunther Schuller shared his impressions in an interview with Chorus *magazine. This is what he had to say: 'Everything that happened in Novosibirsk really gladdened us. The character of the jam session, musicians, listeners – everything was friendly and on an equal footing. I liked very much the local pianist Igor Dmitriev – a very emotional, very sincere musician, a real jazzman. I'm in raptures over his playing. Trombonist Victor Budarin left a great impression, he is a first-rate musician. I also remember the altoist Tolkachev who used modern ideas for creating the rather traditional sound of Coleman Hawkins's style. What they do in Novosibirsk in the field of jazz is just fantastic. My Novosibirsk encounters are unforgettable.'*

In 1983 the first recording of Siberian musicians was released in the West (*Homo Liber,* Siberian 4, *LR 114). How was it perceived by the Western jazz critics? Here are some examples: 'This free jazz from the cold reaches of the Soviet Union has a peculiar flavour – a cross of Asian folk musics and "great black music", beginning with Coltrane. This music has such spiritual intensity, such drive, such impact. . . Ironically, the music breathes of freedom and boundlessness more than most American and European free jazz' (Michael Fitzgibbon, OP magazine); 'The influence of Keith Jarrett and Sun Ra are often apparent, but the overall effect is one of daring originality. The quality of improvisation heard from Homo Liber is, in fact, the kind one would expect to hear in a quality Soho loft or in Paris. All in all, it's one of the most passionately executed recordings of experimental jazz in some time'* (Norman Weinstein, Music Sound Output*); 'Their cool, spacious jazz (lots of flute and piano dialogues) calls to mind the notorious snowy wastes of their homeland. This is no abstract beauty, though; listen closely and you will hear the wolves howl, the beating of a fearful heart. The players' poise is just a thin line across dark chasms of feeling, a small illumination that merely emphasizes the vastness of the night. Still, a revelation'* (Graham Lock, New Musical Express*).

But what is known about the musicians themselves? In 1976 Chorus *carried an interview with Sergey Belichenko, Vladimir Tolkachev and Sergey Panasenko, who in conjunction with Yuri Yukechev were to record as* Homo Liber *six years later, in 1982.*

QUESTION: Your trio plays free jazz. How did you come to play new music and what do you like about it?

BELICHENKO: Personally I came to new jazz via the early music of Miles Davis, which I still very much value. But I first started playing avant-garde when I went to Sverdlovsk in 1971, where I heard the saxophone player Vadim Vyadro, and got to know the music of Shepp and Ayler (on record, of course). I was struck not only by their drummers, but by their music as a whole. When I returned to Novosibirsk I organized the first avant-garde group

Jazzmin – Jazz Miniatures. What attracts me most of all in new jazz is the freedom of self-expression, and also the pleasure I get from working on a tone, sound colouring and the texture of the music. And we work a great deal on this aspect of the music.

TOLKACHEV: For me this is a complicated question. I know that avant-garde definitely interests me more than all other forms of music. The deciding factor is creativity, which is not to be found in pop music. Free music gives me a chance for serious composition and original improvisation. I came to jazz as a direct result of the music of Vladimir Chekasin. It was the creativity of Chekasin which played a decisive role and gave my music impetus. When Chekasin left Sverdlovsk for Vilnius he gave me all his collection of records and it was perhaps the influence of Chekasin's personality that led me to accept new jazz.

BELICHENKO: I should like to add that at the moment all of us, musicians and audiences, have not yet understood the significance of avant-garde as a cultural phenomenon. I think that this music is one of the most significant artistic phenomena of the century. I do not accept that it should be called 'black music' – the music is above all such ethnic criteria; colour is not the most important thing. Many outstanding performers of new music are white, there are musicians of the JCOA, for example. There are, of course, black racists in new music, but if one looks at the great black musicians – Coltrane, Sun Ra, Cherry, Alice Coltrane – they are all trying to create universal music, universal art for the whole world.

TOLKACHEV: Of course demagogic attempts to alienate the white musicians from avant-garde only hinder creativity – music is music. . .

QUESTION: For some reason Panasenko is very quiet. . .

PANASENKO: I began with traditional jazz. Then I played with Vittikh and Belichenko and only then did I begin to play jazz seriously. I even played in the army. Now I listen to Shepp and Marion Brown. Free jazz gives one room for fantasies and self-expression. What attracts me? Freedom. I have been playing with Belichenko all the time since 1971.

QUESTION:I would like you to tell us about Siberian jazz, which you represent, and which is practically unknown to a wide audience in the European part of the Soviet Union.

BELICHENKO: Of course, the jazz centre of Siberia is Novosi-birsk. They started playing jazz in our city fairly recently, at the end of the fifties. Our city had great ups and down, but on the whole our jazz life is very isolated and localized. There were even jazz clubs, it's true not for long. The main place in our jazz life is Akademgorodok. Obviously the spirit of science influenced the art of Siberia too. 1968 and '69 saw a slump. We lost many musicians who went to other towns. When we started forming free-jazz groups there were a few musicians in the town, but they played mainstream and had a very narrow outlook. In 1972 a nucleus of jazz fans was formed and by 1974 we started giving lectures about avant-garde music in the House of Science: about Coleman, Art Ensemble of Chicago, and so on. To our great surprise the audiences, although not really prepared, were passionately in-terested and today on the whole life in Novosibirsk is very busy. We have at our disposal all the best venues, radio and television. Over the last year we have had thirteen gigs. We now have three big bands and recently a town jazz club was formed.

TOLKACHEV: I should like to add that in comparison with Sverdlovsk this is simply a science fiction.

QUESTION: And what about our Siberian towns and villages?

BELICHENKO: In Kemerovo there is a marvellous duo: the trumpeter Gayvoronsky and the drummer Podlipyan. They play avant-garde. All Siberian musicians try to get to Novosibirsk, but one or two swallows don't make a summer. In Tashkent, for example, there is a marvellous trumpeter, Yuri Parfenov: if he were to play with a good rhythm section he would become a star. But in Tashkent he is simply stagnating, he has no one to play with.

QUESTION: What is specially interesting in Siberian jazz?

BELICHENKO: I live in Siberia where European and Asian musical cultures, which are very different, have intermingled. For instance, I listen to the music of Touvinians – marvellous improvised music. The Touvinians are Buddhists and their music is full of echoes of China and India. I listen to Central Asian music, particularly Uzbek. It seems to me that Siberia has in concentrated form some essence of a pre-European past, thousands of years old, untouched by professionalism. A sort of musical matrix. All these musical influences could be very fruitful for the future of our jazz.

And who knows, maybe our new jazz will start spreading from Siberia.

PANASENKO: It is typical that we have no dixieland, and never did have. Nobody was interested in the music.

TOLKACHEV: As a matter of fact Siberian jazz skipped that jazz form, obviously the influence of Asia.

QUESTION: And how do you rate Siberian jazz compared to our European jazz?

BELICHENKO: Soviet and non-Soviet Europeans think that there is no jazz beyond the Urals. And if there is, then it is certainly on a lower level. However, jazz in our country has always been nourished from the distant regions of the Soviet Union. Chekasin is from Sverdlovsk, Tarasov is from Arkhangelsk, Vyadro is from Riga. They are our leading jazzmen, who have now, unfortunately, left these towns. The audience is prejudiced against our music. With the exception of Leningrad, audiences everywhere regard our music with distrust. In any case, there is still a barrier between European musicians and us. Although we have contacts with *Jazz Forum* and JCOA and other organizations in different countries. It's true that recently we have been engulfed by administration routine and jazz matters, but there is still very little good music.

QUESTION: How does it seem to you: are you playing genuine Siberian avant-garde or imitative music?

BELICHENKO: I don't accept the term Siberian, Chinese, American. It does not make sense, and only confuses the issue.

QUESTION: What? Do you completely reject national jazz schools and a whole national element in music?

BELICHENKO: But what do you call national music – a Russian theme with American improvisation? Alice Coltrane plays Indian music, and Ravi Shankar sometimes plays jazz, but each of them is aiming first and foremost for integrated creativity, and not for music which is stylistically planned along national lines. This is why they create music which goes beyond provincial limitations.

TOLKACHEV: I don't agree. There is such a thing as national colouring. Surely, Sergey, you will not deny that our music bears the stamp of our environment and our national culture? But, of course, the social and national elements must be inherent in the music.

QUESTION: And now a few words about your jazz favourites.

This will throw some light on your music and its origins.

BELICHENKO: I am interested not only in drummers (the closest to me are Graves, Cyrille, Ali, Altschul and recently Alphonse Mouzon), but Sanders, Shepp and Brown. I love Roswell Rudd, I am mad about Carla Bley's music.

TOLKACHEV: I am afraid to choose an idol. I have not been influenced by anybody except Chekasin and the music of Messiaen.

PANASENKO: Jimmy Garrison is the bass player closest to me. Coleman and Shepp influenced my general musical thinking; of course I could not have managed without the late Coltrane – 'Om', 'Meditation', etc.

QUESTION: I return to the question which I put at the beginning of our interview. Can you tell me what it is about free jazz that attracts you spiritually?

BELICHENKO: I feel very close to the ideas of Alice Coltrane, Sun Ra, Sanders, about music as an emanation of the universal spirit, as an expression of man's belonging to the cosmic world.

TOLKACHEV: For me music itself is a religion, which I value above all, as an opportunity to go beyond the limits of everyday experience, to exist in another world.

PANASENKO: For me new jazz is above all the opportunity to realize the spiritual side of my life and my experience.

The fourth member of the group Yuri Yukechev was himself the subject of an interview published by Jazz Forum, *issue 3, 1984.*

QUESTION: When did you first get into music?

YUKECHEV: At the age of six. Our neighbour was a pianist and she noticed me. We then lived in a small Ukrainian town named Lutsk. It was at the Music College where I started getting interested in composition. I was about fifteen then. Afterwards, I entered the composition department at the Leningrad Conservatory. I felt an inclination for improvisation even in early childhood. I have always been trying to reduce that gap between musical intention and its realization and I wasted a lot of paper. Since moving to Novosibirsk, I have started thinking over the future of music in general. Composers now seem to have tried all the modern systems of composition which are not based on the

physical properties of sound – the tonal systems based on the
physics of sound as an octave and so on. It was 'overheard' and
absorbed from nature. Otherwise, Schoenberg's system, mic-
rochromatics are more 'artificial'. I have a rather good view of
what they are doing in composition nowadays, at least in Europe
and the Soviet Union, and it seems dangerous to me that modern
music is losing that vibration of novelty and sincerity. If there isn't
fresh 'artistic' information in a creation of art it won't work at all.
Besides, music cannot survive without listeners, music needs their
reaction. If there is a fresh message, the reaction will come and the
act of art has happened. In modern 'classics', unfortunately, we
only see the growth of, so to speak, craftsmanship which has
become a senseless cult, the goal of which is to make more and
more elaborate musical constructions. They just have made a lot
of 'Eiffel Towers' with nothing human in them, no personality, no
communication to fascinate you! This might be the death of art.

I have thought it over and over. What should you do if you want
to be sincere in art? I came upon some remarks by Leonard
Bernstein. His idea was that music was dying and the only musical
form which still had fresh blood was jazz. It attracted me. . . I had
played jazz a bit in my youth but musically it wasn't interesting to
me because my compositional ideas had little to do with traditonal
jazz. But that mastership, that incredible skill of soundmaking,
really stunned me. Then I started thinking that written music
reproduces only about thirty per cent of the musical idea and
something different was required.

Fortunately I met Vladimir Tolkachev in 1981, and told him I
was thinking about spontaneous, free compositions where the
composer determines only the general structure and the players fill
it in freely during the performance. So we tried that and have
played together since then.

QUESTION: What kind of principles are your compositions based
on?

YUKECHEV: Sometimes we play absolutely spontaneously. As a
rule, this is the most difficult kind of creativity but most precious
and dear for us. Once you are distracted, everything immediately
fails. Sometimes we discuss in advance the general structure,
sometimes we have already worked out the 'fill-in' material during
the rehearsals. It might be an intonation, some phrases, riffs, etc.

But our supreme goal has always been to create and play absolutely spontaneously.

QUESTION: Do you consider your music to be jazz?

YUKECHEV: I don't split my music into jazz and non-jazz. To me, our music is just an 'oral' form of creativity distinct from that much more fixed 'opus-like' form of music. I am happy that I've found a sideman as good as Tolkachev, though we came into our music from quite different orientations – Tolkachev came from jazz and I came from so-called 'classical' music.

QUESTION: By the way, who are your main influences among classical composers?

YUKECHEV: You know, I remember that first record exactly, that very record after which my compositional efforts took off. It was a record with Honegger's Second and Third Symphonies conducted by Sergey Bodoux. I was about thirteen then . . . there was this real tension. I said to myself, 'Why on earth can't I do it that way!?'

Who else? Bartok, Stravinsky. . . To me Stravinsky has always been the epitome of Russian art – fresh, new, resembling nobody else's but still very profound and earthy. Also Bach, Chopin. . . By the way, Chopin's pianism had a noticeable impact on jazz pianists.

QUESTION: And turning to jazz, which musicians do you like most?

YUKECHEV: Ellington, first of all. The integrity of his musical personality and real taste – his shrewd, impeccable, faultless musical taste. In this sense I can't find a musician equal to him in the history of music in general.

I was fascinated by Cecil Taylor, mainly his later solo works. And saxophonist Oliver Lake and the Ganelin Trio. If I were to compare American and Soviet free jazz, I would prefer the Ganelin Trio for the pithiness of what they are doing. They play music of the ascendant spirit. They have luckily found one another. As for Chekasin, I think he is a phenomenon unique in twentieth-century music – his aptitude for self-expression, mastership, originality. I was particularly stunned by the concert in East Germany; the public's reaction was fantastic there.

I like Indian music very much. . . Ravi Shankar, the flautist Hariprasad Chaurasia. They are fantastic!

As for 'pure' jazz, I'm more interested in how it's played than what is played.

QUESTION: But what touches you emotionally in what you call 'pure' jazz?

YUKECHEV: You know, sometimes a musician gets into that special mood and he becomes practically a 'priest' of art. There are rare moments when he enters into some unusual religion. Those are the moments of enlightenment, refinement, catharsis. There are such moments with Ellington, the Ganelin Trio, Peterson, Basie; but it happens very seldom.

QUESTION: What kind of problems have you experienced during your musical career?

YUKECHEV: First, the lack of information. I get painfully little into my ears. Second, the problem of sidemen. Actually, Tolkachev and I are an isolated twosome now. We need allies, congenial musicians able to take part equally in the composition. Whomever we ask, they refuse to play that music. They cannot overcome their conservatism and adherence to standards. Many of them have command of their instruments, but they don't command their minds. You shouldn't play only on saxophones, you should play on 'yourself'. It seems to me very important because the precious thing is the human being, the personality, the sensations. All the rest has always been 'interpretism', producing small Coltranes.

Saxophone Diplomacy or
ROVA in the USSR

Saxophone Diplomacy *is a film that was shown in California in 1984. It is a 'people' film that dwells more on the Russians than it does on the music. 'Moscow in June of 1983 was warm, crowded and quiet. It has taken almost two years but at last we are here – the ROVA Saxophone Quartet, a few friends and family,' observes the narrator.*

In 1981 ROVA Saxophone Quartet from Berkeley, California, was voted the top combo in the unofficial Soviet critics' poll conducted by Chorus *magazine. The Contemporary Music Club of Leningrad decided to invite ROVA to come to the Soviet Union and play several gigs. The Contemporary Music Club had no resources to pay for the trip or accommodate the group; the only thing they promised was a huge audience, in spite of the unofficial nature of the visit. ROVA Saxophone Quartet decided to take up the offer. Two years later, in June of 1983, Jon Raskin, Larry Ochs, Andrew Voigt and Bruce Ackley, as well as eighteen young American poets, musicians, composers, video crew, artists, etc. were on the way to Romania and the Soviet Union. During their eleven-day stay in the Soviet Union the ROVA Saxophone Quartet played in Leningrad, Moscow and Riga for well over 2,000 people and more than 6,000 people in Romania, where they stayed for ten days. In Moscow, Leningrad and Riga ROVA musicians played together with Soviet musicians – with Sergey Kuryokhin in Moscow and Leningrad, and with Vladimir Tarasov and Ivars Galenieks in Riga. In spring 1985 the Swiss label Hat Art released recordings of these events. After the visit Larry Ochs wrote to me about their marvellous experience and the very special time they had in the Soviet Union: '. . .the response*

*was so overwhelmingly warm that, at times, I had to walk away
from it because I couldn't handle the intensity. . .'*

*But what are the impressions of an American musician who came
to play unofficial concerts in the Soviet Union? After the trip Larry
Ochs was interviewed by the broadcaster Bill Besecker on WBFO–
FM88 Radio in Buffalo, New York. Later on, the edited version of
this interview was published in* Coda *magazine, issue 196.*

QUESTION: How did this trip come about? You were invited by a
group called the Contemporary Music Club of Leningrad. Who
are they? Critics? Fans?

ANSWER: Really they are a combination of both of those things.
Before we left we didn't have a very clear picture of what was
going on over there either, so I could give you what we imagined,
but I might as well just tell you what we found out. . . In the Soviet
Union, there is a relatively small group of people known
collectively as the 'intellectuals'. Now that's not what they call
themselves and that's not what the government has branded them,
but that's the way *we* would look at it. They are very much known
to each other and they exist in small groups of artists and critics in
each city. They're writers, musicians, critics. In Moscow there are
film-makers involved, but there are no underground films in
Russia, only overground films. All these people hang out together.
In Leningrad the Contemporary Music Club consists of musicians
and critics and fans. The club may have fifty hard-core members.
Until April of 1983 they were putting on events, mostly music but
also performance art, at a place called the Dostoevsky Museum
which actually houses the official Writers' Union in Leningrad.
Then in April of '83 the president of this club put on an event that
was *too* popular. It did *too* well. There were five hundred to six
hundred people and really this museum could hold only about two
hundred when really packed. So people were flowing out into the
street. It became a sort of public happening, which is exactly what
the authorities do not want. They don't care if these clubs exist, as
long as they know about it, but if they become too popular, then
they're disbanded. So in April of '83, the Contemporary Music Club
was informed that they couldn't put on any events for a while. Now,
apparently, they'll start to operate again later this year.

■ Boris Grebenshchikov with (left)
Igor Butman

■ Boris Grebenshchikov

Aquarium (left to right) Alexander
Kondrashkin, Sergey Kuryokhin and
Boris Grebenshchikov

■ Sergey Kuryokhin and Eleonora
Shlykova performing for a recording

■ (Left to right) Sergey Kuryokhin, Eleonora Shlykova and
Vladimir Chekasin at the Yaroslavl Jazz Festival, 1981

■ Nikolai Levinosky (trumpet) leads a jam session at the
Composers' Union *(HANS KUMPF)*

■ Last rehearsal for the Yaroslavl Jazz Festival, 1981 (left to
right) E. Shlykova, S. Kuryokhin (keyboards), V. Labutis,
P. Vishyauskas, I. Butman, A. Alexandrov and S. Belichenko

■ Alexander Alexandrov (bassoon) with Anatoly Vapirov

■ Anatoly Vapirov *(HANS KUMPF)*

■ Vapirov with Jan Garbarek — Contemporary Music Club,
October 1979 *(A. PETROCHENKOV)*

■ Igor Butman *(HANS KUMPF)*

■ Alexander Alexandrov

■ Vladimir Volkov *(V. PESHKOV)*

■ Sergey Lyetov *(HANS KUMPF)*

Yuri Yukechev (top left), Vladimir Tolkachev (right) and Sergey Belichenko of Homo Liber

■ Vyacheslav Gaivoronsky *(V. PESHKOV)*

■ Alexander Kondrashkin (drums) with Vladislav Makarov on cello

■ 'Improvising Trio' of Novosibirsk (left to right) Sergey Panasenko, Sergey Belichenko and Vladimir Tolkachev

■ Archangelsk with their leader
Vladimir Rezitsky on the right
(BERT NOGLIK)

■ Vladimir Rezitsky

◀ 'Zero musicians' Ivan Sotnikov (left)
and Timur Novikov with their
'ironophones' *(HANS KUMPF)*

■ Lembit Saarsalu (left) with Hans
Kumpf — Niguliste Kirik, Tallinn, 1984
(KERSTI UIBO)

EXERCISES   VLADIMIR CHEKASIN

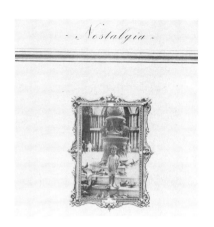

Nostalgia

INVOCATIONS ANATOLY VAPIROV

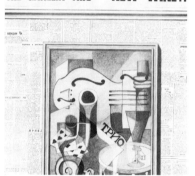

THE GANELIN TRIO   NEW WINE..

GANELIN. TARASOV. CHEKASIN.   VIDE

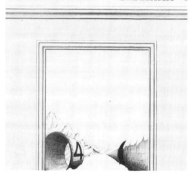

HOMO LIBER   SIBERIAN 4

■ Some Leo Records covers

QUESTION: What kind of event was this April '83 happening?

ANSWER: There's a musician and performer there in Leningrad named Sergey Kuryokhin, who happens to have several records out on Leo Records. Sergey plays piano and is beginning to play saxophone. I'm sending him mouthpieces and reeds.

In fact, in Leningrad – when we finally got to play, which is a long story – his group opened for us. Bruce Ackley, ROVA's soprano saxist, played with them as part of this performance. Sergey put on a performance piece in April '83 with ten musicians, along with actors and dancers. It was a big event and everybody came. There was just too many people.

Anyway, in 1981 I started getting letters from the president of the club. They were just hand-written letters; they don't have typewriters there. They're very hard to get hold of. They don't have Xerox machines. It's a whole different world. It's an incredible place for any American to go to, because it's . . . it's the 'enemy', right? The other big power. And, what's really been incredible since we came back is to realize that not only did we not really have a very good picture of what was going on over there, but so few Americans, relatively speaking, go there. It's not Western Europe. Moscow and Leningrad are very heavily influenced by Eastern culture, especially Moscow. It's a very 'foreign' place. And of course the way the government has the country running itself makes it very different from any democratic country. At the same time, just to talk about Russia for a second, the cities are beautiful. They're enormous, on the kind of grand scale that it's hard to imagine. It's real different from New York City, which is a big city, with enormous buildings. Leningrad would be comparable to New York if you could imagine the Empire State Building, Grand Central Station and the World Trade Center as the only enormous structures, with all the other buildings wiped out and replaced by a giant broad avenue seven times larger than a truck, with canals down either side of it. You could just stand back and take in just how big these buildings are. That's the difference. I guess it's because Russia is so big, they build these cities on this incredible scale, at least in their centres. Once you got outside the centre of the city – and we would not have had we not met people and gone to talk with them at their houses, to see where people lived – it's like the Bronx, rows of faceless apartment buildings. Inside, they're comfortable, but it's a very drab kind of modern architecture.

QUESTION: How did the Contemporary Music Club find out about the ROVA Saxophone Quartet while so few Americans know of you? How did they know about your group?

ANSWER: Their president read about us in a magazine and read about our concerts at Moers. He thought our music sounded interesting. We were at the Pori Jazz Festival in Finland in 1980, which is very close to Leningrad, just an hour-and-a-half boatride from Helsinki, really. He wrote me at that time saying he'd like to get some records from us, which is very common. I get letters from Eastern Europe all the time, especially since I run Metalanguage [Records]. So I sent him the records. In his next letter he said he was the head of this club . . . well, there's clubs all over in Eastern Europe. Every town has a club. He knew we'd been to Pori and invited one of us to come to Leningrad to give a lecture the next time we were in Finland, which doesn't happen every day. So I wrote back and said, 'Well, how about everybody in the group? What can we do?' He thought that would be great, but there's absolutely no way for us to get any funds to pay you . . . so you'd have to come on your own.

Ever since I was a kid, I've always been fascinated by Russian history as well as politics. I went to college as a political science major. So Russia's always been my dream to go to. So I wrote, 'We'd love to come but we'll have to raise the money. So send us an official-looking letter that we can use to get grants!' At that point they wrote us that letter. They probably invented some stationery. The letter said we were 'Number 1' in the jazz critics' poll of the Soviet Union! Really, the jazz 'critics' consist of about twenty-five people. They 'were sure' that if we could come to the Soviet Union, that our concerts would be attended by thousands of our fans and we would have as much of an impact as the Duke Ellington concerts of the late sixties. So this letter was very impressive-looking and we attempted to raise some money using it. Well, actually, and somewhat to our surprise, we had a very difficult time, and in fact, no foundations came through until the last minute. Then we just got a little bit of money from a couple of foundations on the west coast. And no corporation – in spite of all the press coverage and talk about the importance of cultural exchange between these two countries. We'd seen quotes over the last year and a half from Armand Hammer, from Occidental Petroleum and all kinds of pretty important people, but when it came down to it, our fund-raising effort just didn't fit any of these foundations' criteria. And nobody was willing to bend the rules a little bit. We ended up raising the money mostly from private individuals who were enthusiastic about our music and the idea of touring Russia. I borrowed a little bit at the end to make the trip. I was really committed to the idea, and when we got close there was just no way that I wasn't going to borrow the last couple of thousand dollars to do it. It was worth it, completely. We've done seven tours of Europe, and this thing was the kind of great experience that you read about in people's travel books where they say, 'This is the greatest experience of my life.' It's going to be a long time before I can top this thing. The amazing thing is that we were only in the Soviet Union for eleven days, but it was so intense, it was so personal and everyone there was so warm and open. Really, this is like the first jazz concert by a group. Gary Burton had been there as an individual and performed at the American Embassy for forty privileged musicians and forty critics. But these were the first 'public' concerts by a real jazz group in the Soviet Union since 1978, when the Thad Jones/Mel Lewis band was there. You can imagine what that's like. Imagine having one jazz concert every six years. Also, this was the first concert by a contemporary music group since, well . . . I don't know when the last one was. I don't even know if there was one! Most of these people, as you said, stay 'on top' – they have access to records, they have friends sending them magazines. There's a guy there who is a rock critic. He lives in Moscow. At the end of our trip he gave us twenty letters addressed to Arto Lindsay, Lydia Lynch and others in the New York rock scene. My sister (who's a photographer and film-maker, on the trip to help document it) brought them back and gave them to Arto Lindsay to give out. He read his and he read a few of the others, and every letter was completely personal and the questions were really interesting – for twenty different musicians! Which means that this guy, in spite of having very little access to their art, was able to ask questions that these people would actually be interested in answering, as opposed to: 'I'm a fan, tell me how you do your music', which is the way most

letters like that are. It made the trip very intense because every
time we had a conversation with people, time was so short and it
was so precious to them, it was like, instantly, you know, let's
connect! Let's get to the central question right away about what
you do. At the same time, almost every conversation we had was
about art in the West, or music. We did not talk about politics. We
didn't have time and they weren't interested. We did ask them a
few questions about how they related to the way their government
worked. For them, this was the way things were, and it wasn't a
problem . . . it was just the way things were. They were fairly
comfortable, nobody was starving. The food situation over there,
for an American, was not particularly terrific, but no one's
starving. There's not nearly the variety we enjoy. They just don't
think about that kind of stuff. Well, this is the way things are and
it's not going to change. The one question somebody asked us at
one point while we were walking through a market was, 'Tell me
something. Do you really have access to all kinds of vegetables all
year round?' When we said 'Yes', he stood . . . like, that was
amazing, now *that* was amazing! But other than that, we never
really got involved in those kinds of conversations. It was about
art.

QUESTION: How much did that conversation on art, and the
Soviet awareness of Western art and music carry down from the
'intellectuals' to the general audiences that attended your concerts? Were your concerts for general audiences or for 'select'
audiences?

ANSWER: In Moscow we did two concerts. We played for 1,300
people between two concerts. In Riga, which is the capital of
Latvia – and a different story actually, it's a little more
Westernized there – we played two concerts. The first was for over
eight hundred people. The second concert was a relatively
unpleasant experience in the jazz club there. It was an exclusive
jazz club. If you didn't belong, you could not get in. We played for
about a hundred people. There were people who had come from
Arkhangelsk and Odessa, and they wouldn't let them in. It was
ridiculous, but this was one of the scenes our video crew filmed
which was not particularly pleasant information for the Russians to
let out. The guys who ran the club really couldn't let them in.

In Leningrad we played for about two hundred people.

Leningrad was another story because the official concert that we were supposed to do was cancelled because, we were told, the government there is very conservative. Probably they didn't like the fact that we were coming there at the request of this (defunct) Contemporary Music Club. The CMC was not sponsoring the concerts. As things worked out, we ended up working with an organization from the United States, called Friendship Ambassadors, who organized these concerts.

The official concert was cancelled so we played an 'unofficial' concert. That's significant, 'official' and 'unofficial', over there. We played at the Writers' Union in the Dostoevsky Museum, and the place was packed! It was not a big place, it would hold only two hundred people. And that was a sort of exclusive audience of writers and artists because it was really word of mouth. It happened at the last minute, but still there were two hundred people. The concerts in Moscow and the big concert in Riga were general audiences. Most of the people there don't speak English, so it would be hard to say how much they knew Western culture. But in these larger concerts, I would say, certainly, the majority of people who were there were there because we were Americans and they had no idea of what we were going to do. This made things very interesting because our music wasn't jazz. It's billed as jazz, but when an average person thinks of jazz, they don't think of ROVA Saxophone Quartet. I would be the first to say that I think that what we do is 'derived' from jazz and is more jazz than anything else, but if you are just some guy thinking 'jazz', then you don't think of what *we* do. So we were real interested to see what would happen. Then we went to Romania and did seven concerts for up to 4,000 people. Those were really general audiences. We were playing on the bill with three or four Romanian groups. One of them was avant-garde but the rest of them were backwater, man. There were like barbershop quartets with a rhythm section and stuff. We were playing in giant gymnasiums for thousands of people and out walks ROVA with just four saxophones playing all this high-energy kind of music. We did play our so-called 'intellectual' pieces, but we held that to a real minimum. Most of the time we played the real energy stuff, with melody and things like that. But still, not your average accessible jazz, and the response was really incredible. People really dug it. It was

incredible to see this happen, it was great. It made us feel like if
the powers that be could give this kind of music more of a chance,
it would definitely get across to a more general audience, which we
always felt was true anyway. But this was a real test for it, because
this was like coming in cold to an audience that really had no idea
what they were getting. They were just coming because we were
Americans, and it's very rare to see Americans at all.

So most of the conversations we had (in Romania, too) were
with musicians, critics . . . not your average person, because your
average person just doesn't speak English, there, and right there
that's going to be a barrier. We can always work with translators,
but that's the way it worked.

QUESTION: Gunther Schuller, who toured the Soviet Union with
the New England Conservatory Ragtime Ensemble, mentioned
that Soviet audiences will walk out of a concert if the music is not
what they expect. When the performers are Americans, they
naturally expect 'rock' or 'jazz' music. When they discovered the
Schuller tour was presenting 'ragtime', a certain percentage got up
and walked out. Did you find anything like that happening during
your tour?

ANSWER: Oh sure! But we find that happening at every concert
we do! [laughter] So, for us, that's nothing. When we play a
concert anywhere, if there's eight hundred people there, after the
first fifteen minutes, seventy-five of them are gone. So, that's
nothing for us. What we were worried about was eighty per cent of
them walking out, but it was never like that, the response we got
from the ninety per cent who stuck around was overwhelmingly
positive. People were really excited about it. Hell, I know we had a
really significant impact on the direction that a lot of musicians are
going to take, especially in Russia. We had every musician and
composer, including classical and rock musicians, along with
everybody who knew about these concerts. Remember, they
weren't publicly known about. Although once the community of
artists knew that we were coming, I'm sure that the word spread,
but there's no billboard or radio publicity or newspaper announce-
ments, nothing like that. These concerts are held in a large
auditorium, and if you don't get wind of it, you don't know about
it. That's the way things work there. Because we were in
communication with the Contemporary Music Club and because

Friendship Ambassadors were helping us get these concerts together, there was a lot more underground publicity information about these concerts than might normally be the case.

On our second day in Moscow, we did an afternoon concert. At 1 p.m., for a 4 p.m. concert, they moved it to the other side of town. They just moved it to a different hall. Well, the hall was still packed, and there were still people who couldn't get in, outside. We had to make a big deal to get certain people we had met, in. Even though they moved the concert, and for what reason we don't know, maybe in an effort to keep the audience down, instantaneously the word went around.

QUESTION: Did you get to visit any record stores there?

ANSWER: Very little. What you get in State-operated stores. There's not very much. In Russia there's almost nothing. There's an official Russian label. They don't have Western music in the stores. There might be a huge pile of 'disco'. 'Disco' is very big, for whatever reason, they like this disco stuff. Probably for the same reasons that they like it over here. It's good for the masses, keeps them from doing too much thinking, having this sort of groove. The official label will have some good classical music and actually the Ganelin Trio, which is an officially recognized free-music trio that's very good. They have one record that's available sometimes in the stores, but it's very hard to get things.

In Romania, you've got all the Eastern European countries' labels, they all have one official label, and the stores were pretty good. I bought a lot of records there. They were a dollar apiece. You can't go wrong for a buck! We sort of went crazy in Romania and bought a lot of Romanian folk music. Some great stuff!

QUESTION: I was under the impression the Soviets had released a number of LPs by Oscar Peterson, Duke Ellington and others. . .

ANSWER: When they do release something like that, they just release it, and it's gone. It's not like you've got a Tower Records, full of records and when the stock runs out, it's refilled. It's hard to get things. When something comes out, you've gotta know about it and snatch it up pretty fast.

QUESTION: I'm wondering, even though you were in the Soviet Union only eleven days, did you get a chance to formulate your own viewpoint as far as why the Soviets are so fascinated by American jazz and American performers?

ANSWER: I really want to recommend a relatively new book that came out last spring, called *Red & Hot* by an older musician who plays New Orleans music. I think he's actually President of Oberlin College. His name is Frederick Starr. It's about the history of jazz in the Soviet Union. But actually it's a much bigger book than that. It deals with jazz history and how it got from the United States to Western Europe and then to Eastern Europe and finally to Russia. Then it goes from there and talks about how jazz survived, or did not survive, through various political histories over the past sixty years. It's a very warm, personal book, and the guy who wrote it is really committed to the idea that for people in Eastern Europe, jazz, because it's real pluralistic, kind of democratic, free – at least with the implication of a free kind of music – has a spirit in it that they don't get to experience. I did an interview one night, very late, with the 'father' of Soviet critics. Over there if you're a generation older, the younger generation will say this is my father, even though there is no relationship. We did this interview. We were talking about a particular type of music that's very popular in the United States, right now. Even though it's an art music, it's doing very well. I won't mention any names. He was very down on this music and he said, 'You know, Larry, these people are making a very big mistake with the kind of music they're making. I understand why they're making a mistake, because for us, American music is the only way that we can experience the other world.' What he meant was the 'free world'. For them, by listening to jazz and improvised music, that's how they experience the free world, and that's why it means so much to them. And it really knocked me out at the time especially since he was interviewing me in his car, in an empty square . . . in the middle of the night, because we weren't in his home town and he didn't want to interview me in a hotal because he thought someone might be listening. And it's very bad, often, for Russians to be heard talking 'English' to Americans. It sometimes can go the wrong way for them. It was a very enlightening moment.

QUESTION: I've read through most *Red & Hot* and I'm left with the impression that the government over there doesn't really know how to deal with jazz. Did you get that impression first-hand over there?

ANSWER: We didn't have any first-hand experience with the

government because as it worked out our official status was 'tourist' and we were officially 'amateur' musicians. We'd raised the money. No one was paying us, and this is how we were allowed to do these concerts at all, because there is no official cultural exchange between these two countries. So I can't really say. We certainly felt a 'presence' the whole time we were there. I felt like I was back in eighth grade, being a rebellious kid, and for some reason, I had to throw a rock through a window and make a scene. I couldn't put my finger on it, but I could feel that all the time. But as far as anything direct, no! . . . except for the fact that our concert was cancelled in Leningrad. But again, we never talked to anybody. Of course, that never could have possibly happened. So it's hard for me to talk about that.

QUESTION: One of the original intentions for going over there with your group, as quoted in *Jazz Forum* magazine, which is published in Warsaw, was to 'demystify the peoples of the US and the Soviet Union'. I think by coming back and doing these kind of interviews, that's exactly what you are doing.

ANSWER: I'd really like to be able to do more. On our trip we took a video crew and we got the video back out. We shot a lot of very questionable stuff. There were just some incredible experiences that we had which were not particularly positive. If we were being watched closely, some of the things that got shot were really of dubious value to the Russian government.

I hope this video show will eventually get done. They're hoping for national television, so I hope that happens because the people we met were great. Sure, their government has intentions that may not be in our best interests, but you know I'm sure, looking at it from the other side, that they feel the same way about our government. What really has to happen in both countries is that the people have to take over. Our two governments are playing a very dangerous game that's not doing any of us any good. The only way that things are really going to change, especially between these two countries, is for them to come here and for us to go there, and for there to be more exchange so some kind of understanding can happen. Then there can be pressure put on our government. There'll be more people here who'll be able to say, 'Hey! There's humans over there, just like us, and we don't need to blow them up.' Basically, that's what it comes down to.

Leo Records – Reviews in the Soviet Union
Efim Barban

One of the most important factors in the development of new music in the USSR was the sole Soviet jazz magazine Chorus *(Kvadrat) which was first published in 1966. The publication of the magazine was approved by the Leningrad Committee of Komsomol, which at that time was supervising the activity of a Leningrad jazz club with the same name 'Chorus'. Several years later the publication was officially closed, but it continued to exist in the underground, and has been published in typewritten form ever since. Every issue of the magazine was typed and retyped and by the time the magazine reached Siberia or the Central Asian Republics its circulation reached a great number of copies. The magazine was unique not only because of its form, but because of its content as well. It covered an extremely wide range of topics and ran articles from many contributors. Though it existed in the underground it was not a political magazine. From time to time there appeared translations from* Down Beat *and other Western publications. 'Will Jazz survive till 2000?', 'Panic on Titanic', 'Polythematics at Different Textures', 'Aesthetic Borders of Jazz', 'Anatomy of Jazz Reality' – these are just a few titles taken at random from the 1981 issue of* Chorus, *which consists of more than 150 typewritten pages without photographs or illustrations. With the emergence of new music in the Soviet Union* Chorus *became an integral part of the music scene.*

It is impossible to think of an equivalent publication in the West. Unlike all Western publications it did not depend on the market, subscribers, advertisers, etc. It catered for a small but extremely educated audience with considerable knowledge of literature, philosophy, psychology, linguistics, and so on. As a result, the magazine developed several unique genres of writing about jazz, one of which is the record review. Reviewers were given unlimited space, and consequently each review became a separate philosophical/musical essay. The four reviews which follow were written by Efim Barban and are taken from various issues of Chorus. *They will help the reader to understand the phenomenon of new music in the Soviet Union. They may also give some idea of the erudition both of the reviewers and the audience to whom they address themselves.*

Vladimir Chekasin: *Exercises* **(Leo Records, LR 115)**
   Vladimir Chekasin – alto, tenor saxophone, double saxophones, clarinet, voice, guitar, percussion; Sergey Kuryokhin – piano, voice, flute, percussion, drums; Boris Grebenshchikov – guitar, voice, percussion

The work of the trio in which Vladimir Chekasin (born 1947) has played with Ganelin and Tarasov has been well documented; over the last five years ten of the trio's records have been released in the Soviet Union and abroad. In recent years Chekasin has frequently appeared in public as a member of other jazz groups. His music has been performed both by the Vilnius Conservatory big band, which he directs, and by ensembles of other musicians. The lack of a permanent core of musicians has often compelled Chekasin to make use of the fortuitous opportunities provided by festivals and concerts by assembling mixed groups for single performances (the Yaroslavl Festival, the 'New Jazz Spring Concerts' in Leningrad, and others). His last endeavour of this kind was an ensemble he tried to bring together in April 1983 during the FMP Meeting in West Berlin, and which he led, including P. Brötzmann, T. Kondo, A. Tomlinson, D. Galas and other stars of the avant-garde. The temporary nature of such ensembles, the impossibility of proper rehearsals and language difficulties do not facilitate the realization of the composer's intention at its best. Nevertheless, this side of Chekasin's musical activity, which has become an inalienable part of his creative career, deserves to be put on record, since the Vilnius saxophonist has for a long time been one of the accepted leaders of Soviet, and indeed of European jazz.

The recordings in the album *Exercises* date from the end of 1982. The first side of the record is taken up by one of the many versions of Chekasin's composition 'Exercise', called here 'Exercise I', and performed by a trio – Chekasin himself with S. Kuryokhin and B. Grebenshchikov. The second side consists of two pieces, a duet with Kuryokhin, 'Exercise II', and the solo saxophone 'Exercise III'.

The music in 'Exercise I' is deeply ironical in relation to its own content, openly parodies available means of expression and, occasionally, is bluntly nihilistic about the notion of musical art itself. The human voice has a frequent and varied function in the composition. Chekasin's voluptuous muttering after the 'acoustic outburst' in the introduction gives way to Kuryokhin's recitation – a mannered imitation of English poetic intonation (a meaningless selection of sounds). After the pointillistic clarinet/prepared piano duet, which is also sprinkled with vocal effects, Chekasin's voice produces something resembling a parody of a melodrama, using meaningless double-Dutch to express passionate invective and declarations of high-flown pathos, in turn interrupted by a ballad – Chekasin has forgotten about his parody and is playing solo tenor sax. The effect is of a fantastic episode, fantastic because of its emotional content and dramatic inventiveness. But the listener, who has already received one set of signals to interpret, and has no time to adapt his perceptions, interprets Chekasin's ecstasy as a parody and does not pick up the serious feeling in his music. Out of its context, this episode would certainly have been understood in a different way. Subsequent musical events only reinforce the total irony of 'Exercise I'.

A prepared piano solo follows the guitar duet (Chekasin-Grebenshchikov), based on an ostinato repeat of a rhythmical dance figure, overlaid by a tenor solo, soon replaced by the sound of two saxophones in unison, playing variations on the rhythmical piano formula. There is a metrical disruption, then a pause before a vocal passage for three voices, which can be perceived as a fit of sickening pathological yawning. Suddenly the piano begins a staccato light-hearted Viennese waltz and the tenor sax joins in. The contrasting juxtaposition of various aspects of the subculture (avant-garde–pop music) is comic because it produces a rhetorical effect by their incongruity – at this point, there is usually an

Homeric roar of laughter from the hall. Kuryokhin sings along in falsetto. The coda: the musicians continue mistreating the unhappy Strauss, usually accompanied at concerts by the delighted whoops of the audience.

'Exercise II' is an improvisation on the theme of the well-known standard 'Bye-bye Blackbird', recorded at a Moscow concert in 1983. It opens with a tenor solo, playing a variation, without the traditional statement of the theme. A story 'explanation' between tenor and piano follows, passing into a mood of tranquil dialogue. Here Chekasin introduces his characteristic stamping, repeating this exotic 'instrumental' device several times in different rhythmic and pitch variants. At the same time he plays the hi-hat with his foot, throws out quotations from jazz standards and classical music (Mussorgsky?), puffs, like an engine letting off steam, seized by a paroxysm, which is orgiastic in the true sense of the word.

The structure of the piece recalls 'Exercise I', but here, instead of a waltz, the mainstream tune 'That's a Wrong Time' in a virtuoso performance by Kuryokhin is dovetailed into the music's avant-garde style of execution, with the same calculated rhetorical effect of semantic incongruity. The audience, naturally, are gasping with delight. The humour turns into the most biting sarcasm when Chekasin begins to superimpose the harshest grating tone his tenor sax can produce on this classic jazz tune, playing the title theme.

'Exercise III' could be called an improvisation on the theme of the Garner standard 'Misty'; at least a considerable part of it is harmonically and melodically derived from that source. The first part is an harmonic and rhythmic figuration of the theme. Chekasin alters rhythms, tempi and register in a masterly way, constantly using a collage technique and quoting jazz and non-jazz 'literature' lavishly. Once more, the 'foot' accompaniment figures. Among the themes incorporated into the work is a folk tune which recurs in the compositions of the Ganelin Trio, from 'Con Anima' to 'Catalogue'. After a talented imitation of turkey gobbling (which provokes wild uproar in the audience), Chekasin creates a free-for-all of musical banalities, a catch-as-catch-can including 'Mein Lieber Augustin' and the 'Dance of the Little Swans' from Tchaikovsky's ballet. Before us is the clown, who, while demonstrating his clumsiness in the circus, proceeds to pull off stunning

acrobatic feats. If its content is discounted, Chekasin's music in
'Exercises III' is skilled acrobatics.

When one tries to place Chekasin's music in the Russian artistic
tradition one is involuntarily reminded of the Oberiuti (The
Society of Real Art – Kharms, Vvedensky and others) aesthetic,
which derived from the art of Russian futurists. The absurd
grotesquerie of their perception of the world, their eccentric,
critical attitude to academic art, the black humour, the counter-
culture antics, irony as a cure for self-satisfaction – they have all
these in common. The basis of the Oberiuti's art, as laid down in
their manifesto, was 'the concrete object, with its literary and
habitual skin peeled away'. It seems we have here the first instance
of a native musical Oberiuti 'happening'.

Listening to Chekasin, one is distinctly aware of the rebellious
nature of his music. An unsubdued consciousness shines through
the grimaces of a clown playing the fool and the screen of parodied
exercises, and wages a constant struggle against musical idolatry,
lying illusions and the banal code of corporate musical ethics. If
one is to believe Malraux's assertion about 'the death of classical
man', one can discern in Chekasin's antics a new stature, which
includes the debased and the sensual.

Another characteristic of Chekasin's music is its profound erotic
quality. We recognize this as an attribute of jazz; the intensity of
swing in jazz has always been seen as an index of the music's
eroticism. But in new jazz, intelligible musical components have
effectively crowded out this immemorial element of jazz. For this
reason Chekasin's eroticism, in the terms of new jazz, is seen as
classical, if not reactionary. As it happens, the Russian philosophical tradition invests artistic genius of whatever kind with high
erotic potential. 'Every product of true genius is erotic,' asserts
Berdyaev in *The Sense of Creation*. He adds: 'Genius is permeated
with the erotic.'

However, the central focus of Chekasin's aesthetic is its
comprehensive ironic quality. Irony in his music is a mode of
thought, a frame of mind, a relation to musical and other reality, a
means of existence. The sublime gnostic negativity and the
deconstructed artistic quality of his music are evoked by its
profound irony. Essentially irony is a specific kind of negation,
which proposes the non-acceptance of reality. The ironic mode of

negation, as distinct from serious non-acceptance, which sets another reality against the negated reality (position or system), opposing one principle with another, does not admit positive substitution, and dissipates any positivity. External reality loses all meaning for ironists, since truth for them is a purely subjective concept. However, this is true only of romantic irony; Socratic irony, among whose practitioners Chekasin must be counted, denies even the subjectivity of truth, since it quite simply does not affirm anything; it is absolutely negative. It is this position of absolute negation which drives ironists beyond the bounds of the reality in which they live, beyond the bounds of their time and epoch. They have no link with reality, they are entirely locked up in themselves.

Ironists take nothing on trust, are not capable of a real act or positive behaviour, since this necessitates choice, a halt to their 'endless reflections'. Essentially, theirs is a tragic predicament: they will not admit the historical reality in which they live, nor can they see any way out of it. As Kierkegaard wrote, '[The ironist's] relation to their epoch can be expressed in the Biblical saying "those who are to carry you away have already entered".' Incidentally, Kierkegaard also distinguishes self-satisfying (romantic) irony from tragic (Socratic) irony.

The laughter and guffaws from the hall, which accompany Chekasin's performance, and are audible in this recording, can at times be interpreted as laughter in time of plague – as the reaction of an amused public to the sufferings of a clown, who is actually dying in the ring, and whose mask turns him into a figure of fun. More than once the music of 'Exercises' lifts this mask a little. Chekasin's 'transcendental buffoonery' (Schlegel) constantly towers over his audience's wretched sense of humour, sacrificing his own art and genius to his negation.

It is against this background that Chekasin reduces the common sense of jazz to inspired lunacy.

But it seems that the chief cause of Chekasin's ironic attitude to his own music is the understanding (or the sensation) of the unavoidable disparity between his creative intention and its realization, the end result of music-making. Irony is invoked to underline this disparity, demonstrating the superiority of Chekasin's subjectivity over musical objectivity. In this there is at once a

tragic fate and the only freedom possible for the artist in relation
to his own music. An 'ironic superiority' is the only possible way of
expressing one's dissatisfaction, not only with everything made,
but also with every final outcome. But, being his own creation, his
musical 'finality' unavoidably turns even his own self-mockery
against its creator, making him parody himself.

One of the aspects of Chekasin's use of irony, where the serious
and the comic are organically and inextricably mingled, is directed
against musical philistinism, against a reactionary 'philharmonic'
tradition which cannot tolerate a free approach to musical ritual.
This kind of musical philistine cannot endure Chekasin's music. 'It
must be a good sign that harmonic vulgarians do not know how to
react to this constant self-parody, where the listener must first
trust what he or she hears, then distrust it, until the head begins to
swim. . .' (Schlegel).

The habit of irony, since it destroys any positive sense, also
destroys ironists' personalities. Unfettered by any positive ethical
or aesthetic order, they have no greater end in view than pure
play, delighting only in their own talent for free (nihilistic) play.

Gradually irony replaces reality with playing at reality.

Ironic players are not concerned with the content of music;
there is nothing higher or more significant than the ironist. Neither
truth, nor tradition, nor morality have any meaning for them; they
are their own canon and demiurge. For this reason ironists are
inevitably immoral; they have no moral stance, since morality is a
belief in an actively vindicated principle, while irony is above all
the refusal to take anything seriously, and the consequent
negation.

But in renouncing aesthetic ideals and artistic truths ironists
exceed the limit of human creative capabilities – another facet of
their tragic natures – not understanding that human genius by itself
is capable only of destruction. The creative act achieved by purely
subjective efforts, without the assistance of the truths and ideals of
one's time, is impossible. In their self-satisfaction ironists forget
that man is not the master, but only the shepherd of his time
(Heidegger); it is not given to him to trespass against his own fate
(his time). In order to go beyond the limits of their own nihilistic
Nothingness, ironists must have a positive link with their time,
with the age, and with the lived experience of the age.

Chekasin is by no means the only musician to make irony the central principle of his aesthetic. Tracing the meaning of musical irony is the current problem for new jazz. In the European neo-avant-garde irony has become, perhaps, the main element in the semantic structure of music. It has emerged as a distinctive feature of the music of outstanding new-jazz masters like Bennink, Mengelberg, and Breuker in Holland, Christman, Brötzmann and Carl in Germany, S.A. Johansson in Sweden, Beresford and other members of the London Musicians Collective in England and Portal in France. America has not escaped infection: among others, Carla Bley, the Bowie brothers and members of the Charles 'Bobo' Shaw group.

If the semantics and philosophy of Chekasin's music are more or less clear, its structure is less susceptible to analysis by traditional musicological criteria. It is not merely a matter of the lack of structure, or the mixture of standard jazz and other musical structures in *Exercises*, but of the number of meanings encoded in the text.

To paraphrase the Oberiuti thesis, one could say that Chekasin is clearly trying to peel the 'musical skin' away from his work and put the concrete object at its centre. For this reason, listening to and looking at Chekasin's performances (his music's visual dimension is often as semantically important as the acoustic dimension) we see distinctly that some elements belong to artistic reality, while others belong to concrete reality. Frequently, his pieces are structured as a game with the listeners' perceptions of a different kind of reality; then the musicians in his ensemble leave the stage and enter the hall, the realm of the commonplace.

The displacement, or switch from one system to another, is an important generator of meaning in this music, accentuating the play factor in the text, revealing its character as a game, its ironic, parodic and theatrical aspects. When this happens, the significance of the boundaries of a musical text, which separate it from the non-text, is at the same time impaired and strengthened (more often than not Chekasin's music lacks canonical form). This juxtaposition of the real and the conventional is a perfectly ordinary example of a 'text within a text' (a play within a play, a picture within a picture, the literary device of a story within a story). The double encoding of certain sections of Chekasin's music means that one part is perceived as reality (the context), while the other is perceived as convention (quotations). His text often deliberately 'pretends' to be reality, which invests it with a life independent of its author, breaks the spell of its fictitious character, making it into a concrete object of the real world. This is where Chekasin's 'collage games' come from, creating a tense structural fact/fiction opposition. In his music a quotation is the sign of an object, not of the composer's making, which refers the listener to another epoch, or another kind of music. At the same time it gives the fictitious element an almost documental authenticity. But reality sometimes appears in Chekasin's music as a distorted, caricature reflection of the fictitious, as a sham, so that what it excludes as fictitious, becomes the true, authentic reality. Chekasin's rooted aversion to official rhetoric is, naturally, the source of this. For this reason, lifelike (lived) behaviour incorporated into his music – naturalistic effects like stamping, retching, the imitation of speech and so on – turns into 'operatic' art behaviour, and the conventional (quotations) turns into lived reality, into acoustic pictures and statues, hung or placed in musical space. As a result, there occurs what Yu. M. Lotman describes as 'the ascent from the distorting semblance of the ostensibly real world to the authentic essence of the world mystery'.

This semantic refinement is an undoubted consequence of Chekasin's ironic sensibility; his favourite musical occupation is plucking the peacock feathers of fiction from the crow of reality.

In general many of Chekasin's works are conceived not as performances of well thought-out, invariable music (which is his theoretical bent), but as various kinds of games with the listener. His style clearly has an affinity with that of Pototsky and Bulgakov, who wrote novels within novels. Their logical and prosodic techniques are analogous to the structure of Chekasin's pieces.

When I had finished listening to *Exercises*, a strange, apparently irrelevant idea occurred to me: if Chekhov had died young, he would have gone down in the history of Russian culture as a literary clown. . .

Sartre asserted that every human life is the history of a defeat, and interesting for that reason alone. Art disguises and compensates for (or reveals) this unavoidable defeat. 'Poetry,' according to Sartre, 'happens when the person who is losing, wins. The true poet chooses to go on losing until death, in order to win . . .' In this sense the music of *Exercises* is a defeat.

Homo Liber *Siberian 4* **(Leo Records, LR 114)**
  Vladimir Tolkachev – alto saxophone, flute; Yuri Yukechev – piano, vibes, flute, percussion; Sergey Panasenko – bass; Sergey Belichenko – drums

Thoughtful musicians have always been few and far between in jazz of all periods. This makes the appearance of an album from the Novosibirsk ensemble Homo Liber an even greater surprise. A first-class ensemble has emerged from the jazz desert of Siberia, playing serious and mature music. Perhaps there might be some truth in Chaadaev's statement in one of his letters: '. . .everything great comes from the desert'? The music in question, furthermore, does not derive from any of the relics of jazz style; it is free jazz, whose intellectual level and content is comparable with the work of the pillars of the European avant-garde.

The ensemble's first album, called *Siberian 4*, was released by the English company Leo Records in the summer of 1983. Homo Liber appears as a group in two guises, as the Tolkachev–Yukechev duet and, with the addition of Sergey Panasenko on bass and the drummer Sergey Belichenko, as a quartet. The album's make-up reflects this binary existence: on the first side is the composition 'Bona Fide', played by the duet, the second has a three-part composition for the quartet, called 'Trivium' (a meeting of three paths).

The basic structural method of 'Bona Fide' is free collective improvisation. The improvisation process takes the form of an evenly balanced dialogue between two disputing voices – a violent interaction, packed with musical events. An instinctive tendency towards polyphony as the proper structural embodiment for dialogic content has made the musicians include a 'third party' in the duet, by occasionally playing two instruments simultaneously.

The composition opens with the buzzing sound of the vargan, an instrument better known in Siberia by its Yakut name *khomus*, accompanied by a faint folk tune on a wooden flute, coming from far away. Small percussion instruments – little bells, blows on the piano strings, the tom-tom or tambourine – give a pointillist texture. A slowly developing crescendo: the music becomes more vigorous, the piano enters, the faint bumble-bee drone of alto grows louder. The central passage of the piece opens, irradiating the most diverse spectrum of expressive states, and combining the swinging emotional quality of jazz with the rhythmical (logical) refinement of post-Webern chamber music. This refinement is introduced by the pianist's departure from the standard metrical paradigms of old jazz. The timbre and phrasing of the alto are close to traditional jazz to start with, although the rhythmical basis of the alto's thought moves away from the insinuating sound of Johnny Hodges's grandiloquence, and recalls, from time to time, Oliver Lake's lapidary rhythm forms. The turbulent passion of the saxophone attack achieves the frenzy of paroxysm – only the 'classic' avant-garde of the 1960s brought themselves to such a pitch of ecstasy. This passage contrasts with the moving wooden flute dialogue which follows, calming the music's volcanic eruption for a time. A splash of violent tectonic activity displaces this quasi-fairytale mirage. This time Tolkachev has renounced his archaic sound for good; the pure layers of phonetic colour of free jazz are audible. The piece's finale divides into two. The turbulent flood of sound, dying away, carries the music out into the meditative peace of a piano prelude. This sound-painting is clouded somewhat by the muddy undertone of the alto, but the piano solo's impressionism lulls and soothes. After a short monodic alto retort, a return anew to an expressive dialogue – the tom-tom accompanies the saxophone's 'shadow fighting'. The coda recalls the beginning of the piece, although the vargan is replaced by the tom-tom, which accompanies the fading flute melody – the conventional silent-film ending: the two embrace and walk off into the distance.

'Trivium', in keeping with its title, falls into three contrasting parts. In this suite form the composition solves its own kind of fairytale 'knight at the crossroads problem': three paths are explored, possible routes for the development of a new jazz quartet's improvisation. Unusually dramatically developed, the first part, although it is overflowing with potential expressive tensities, is somewhat fragmentary, disintegrating in the second half into a series of short duets: percussion/bass, piano/percussion, alto/bass, alto/piano. Here, unfortunately, the dialogic content, so vividly expressed in 'Bona Fide', does not develop. The second part of the composition is extraordinary in its emotional penetration; it is undoubtedly the best section of the album. The central role in it is taken by the saxophone. If the work's musical development is built, for the most part, on the juxtaposition of tension and resolution, here a distinct melodic theme is employed, with constant variations by the alto. A profoundly Russian note of lament (moaning, suffering) is at the heart of the melodic complex. Beginning as a lyrical ballad, the tempo increases and the music passes into the stormy lament of the saxophone scherzo. The rhythm section provides active swinging polymetric support for the alto. Here the infectious sincerity of unforced feeling is combined with a surprising compositional integrity and a masterly realization of the idea of comprehensive development. We join in the musician's most intimate inner experiences. Coltrane's deepest poetic intuition, Ayler's mystical fire and the elegance of Dolphy's formal creativity are fused together in the music of the alto. The saxophone's ardent rhetoric leads one to the firm conviction that Tolkachev (born in 1951) has become over the last five or six years an exceptional musician.

The third part of 'Trivium' contrasts with the second part and its structural conception, and with the emotional tone of the whole composition. Remote recollections of the style of Lake's work occur in the alto's approach to the elaboration of the musical material: unexpected rhythmical pauses, dynamic tempo overfalls, the aphoristic quality of the musical rejoinders. The musicians' solo statements, which follow the collective passage, do not contribute to formal consolidation, and look like a concession to the traditional 'break', justifiable only in music based on rhythmical regularity.

While semi-jazz or pseudo-jazz might be a possible description of the first side of the album, for all its artistic significance (in point of fact it is an excellent example of 'third-stream music'), one cannot doubt the jazz pedigree of 'Trivium'. And although the ensemble's music does not come within the framework of standard jazz form, it contains almost no 'noise' (untempered sounds) or 'sonorous storms'. The musicians seek to set a primitive creative intuition against the formal rationalism of the European musical tradition, and succeed in controlling the high spontaneity (charisma, myth-making) of their creative method with the help of an intensified sense of form. The most absolute aesthetic pitch enjoyed by Y. Yukechev (born in 1947) plays a considerable part here, as does his superlatively developed sense of proportion (measure). Despite the lack of jazz experience, a real authenticity distinguishes his improvisation – the absence of middle-brow musical clichés, borrowed phrases and ideas. S. Panasenko (born in 1949), the quartet's bass player, is, unfortunately, squeezed out on to the periphery of musical events; it may be that a certain musical inertia, and emotional detachment from what is going on account for this. The style of the veteran Soviet avant-garde drummer S. Belichenko (born in 1947) is akin to that of Sunny Murray; he creates a close-textured polyrhythmic foundation for the ensemble's improvisation, although the architectonics of his solo are not always sufficiently varied.

In terms of ensemble playing, the duet is head and shoulders above the quartet. Any of the ensembles of our jazz rearguard – Melodiya, Diapason, Jazz-Comfort and others – will appear, next to the Homo Liber duet, as a mechanical collection of individuals, a social, rather than a musical association. The duet demonstrates that particular type of organic musical unity in which the individual not only finds him- or herself, but realizes his or her emotional and spiritual potential, a unity which is a goal in itself, and not the means of 'interpretation' or 'realization' of other people's music.

Naturally, enormous courage is required on the part of the musicians, to bear the burden of their absolute creative freedom. They have rejected all guarantors of this freedom (functional harmony, variation, regularity, etc.) so that they risk losing it or being destroyed by it. Each time they improvise they choose themselves anew, freely, and reject systems of musical organization imposed from outside. Their music springs from the depths of their self-awareness. There is certainly one flaw (or virtue) in this artistic method: it immeasurably heightens the responsibility of the artists for what they create, demanding of them, as the old jazz did not, great individual maturity. It seems that the members of the ensemble are well aware of this, since the ensemble's name embraces both its aims and an allusion to a simple and immutable truth: 'a man's ability to be the bearer of culture, that is, to understand it and to act in its name, depends on the degree to which he is at once a thinking, and a free being' (A. Schweitzer).

The solution to the riddle of the appearance of a first-class free-jazz ensemble 'in the depths of the Siberian mines' lies in the presence of these individual qualities in the musicians of Homo Liber.

Translated from Russian by Sylvia Trott

The Ganelin Trio: *New Wine. . .* (Leo Records, LR 112)
Vyacheslav Ganelin – piano, basset, el. guitar, percussion; Vladimir Tarasov – drums; Vladimir Chekasin – alto, tenor saxophone, basset horn.

'It may be that history is the history of a handful of metaphors' – the first sentence of J.L. Borges's miniature three-page essay entitled 'The Fearful Sphere of Pascal'. In the same way, and with much greater truth, it might be said that the history of traditional jazz is the history of a handful of musical themes. With the appearance of the new jazz the old store of standards on which performers drew for the inspiration and material for their improvisation is losing its significance – each performer now tries to play his or her own music and nothing else. In this way the new jazz has discovered an escape from variation-form. It seems as though the first-class thematic material accumulated by jazz is becoming nothing more than the property of jazz history. Of recent years there has of course arisen among the neo-avant-garde a noticeable interest in the thematic heritage of classical jazz. Air's album based on Joplin ragtimes, Georgi Gaslini's record based on themes by Thelonious Monk and Oliver Lake's record making use of themes by Eric Dolphy – these are only some of the symptoms of this nostalgic tendency. The new album of the Ganelin Trio, *New Wine. . .*, released by Leo Records, provides still further evidence of this new interest in 'standard' classics among new jazz players and also a magnificent example of the skilled use of traditional jazz themes in new aesthetic conditions.

The record includes Part Two of Ganelin's two-part 'Non

Troppo' which the trio performed during 1982–83. J. Bock's well-known standard 'Too Close for Comfort' was the thematic foundation of this piece, but at the same time *New Wine*. . . does not follow the traditional jazz pattern, with an obligatory exposition of the theme. Ganelin does not in fact introduce the theme openly until the final section, which becomes a kind of recapitulation without an exposition. The method of development used by the players may be said to be one of the variants rather than variations: thematic reminiscences and harmonic allusions are fundamental aspects of their development of the musical material.

The work begins with an extensive percussion solo in which rhythmic paradigms of the theme appear from time to time. There is a basset solo, the piano joins in, while the percussion provides no more than a soft 'brushing' accompaniment. The basset imitates the 'walking bass', and there is an allusion to the tonal music of the classical jazz piano trio playing an ordinary harmonic theme figuration. And suddenly the music is cut short by what seems to be the ironical, wheezing aside subtone of the saxophone gloomily humming a variation of the theme in the low register. Stop time: and the tenor sax perpetually accelerates the tempo, stepping up the atmosphere of emotional tension already charged with intensive swing. The climax of the first half of the piece comes in Chekasin's solo, which is close in style to that of classical bebop. A polyphonic group improvisation of the greatest incandescence is followed by an unexpected rarefying of the texture and a fall in the emotional temperature, an episode in which only the small percussion (plus tom-tom and cymbal) are used, bringing the first side of the record to a comparatively quiet end.

The second half of the work opens with a duet between 'bassetized' piano and percussion. Virtuoso variation of the theme alternates with the solo preludizing of the piano – one of the best of Ganelin's recent solos, with the two hands executing simultaneous variations on different phrases from the theme. An absolutely brilliant constructive idea! The piano starts 'skidding' and a stuttering version of the theme appears with witty caesurae. The piano executes innumerable different versions of the thematic material, most of them either reductive (melodic 'commentary' or harmonic resumé) or complementary (individual 'postscripts' or rhythmic 'footnotes' to different phrases of the theme). As the duet goes on in its carefree way, it is almost noiselessly, surreptitiously joined by the alto sax, whose insinuating blueslike solo forms an extensive episode, in which piano, clarinet, guitar (rhythmical sliding crab-movements up and down) and small percussion provide the accompaniment. The purity of tone and classical harmony of this solo recalls the 'Desmond sound', its phrasing the rhythmic precision of Sonny Rollins. Almost reluctantly Chekasin embarks on the variation of a single phrase of the theme, extending it into a solo full of ecstatic revelations with the quarter-note chords of the theme broken up into sixteenth-notes. In the finale first the piano and then the tenor sax play the theme straight, without melodic deconstruction of any kind. The work ends with an energetic, swinging unison of the trio.

A feature very unusual in contemporary jazz is the ensemble's use of an initial musical text. Ganelin's approach to the theme might be described as a 'polemical interpretation' – parodying, censoring and making critical allusions. And although as a composer he seems to question the musical material of the theme – rhythm, tempo, tonality, proportions, form – in actual fact *New Wine. . .* resembles in genre a suite, the sections of which are constructed as a 'free translation' from the language of mainstream to that of new jazz. The players successfully avoid literalism and the superficial stylization of mere epigones, and they catch the spirit and general content of the original, revealing a nice and exact grasp of its significance in the context of the recent history of jazz. This is particularly important for the comprehending of any musical tradition, because 'every understanding is the correlation of a given text with other texts, and the rethinking of that text in a new context. . .' (M. Bakhtin).

As a rule, musical metaphor arises at the junction of two languages, and it is precisely for this reason that the music of *New Wine. . .* is rhetorically so highly saturated, something matched only by the high degree of its inner polemical nature – cultural, historical and stylistic. And in spite of a few zones of alienated (anonymous) text on the first side of the record (e.g. the percussion cpisode in the finale) the trio's album is unquestionably one of its best, together with *Live in East Germany* and *Poi Segue*.

It is significant that the players' brilliant instrumental technique is profoundly functional – their performance is free of all meaningless ornamentation and mere virtuosity. Unlike the majority of contemporary 'guardians of the jazz tombs' these Vilnius players, while pouring their new wine into old skins, are before all else concerned with the general structural plan of their music rather than with demonstrating their performing skills in a succession of solos.

The attitude of today's avant-garde to the classical jazz heritage cannot really be called nostalgia for the old stylistic unity and simplicity of outlook. Its cause is rather to be sought in a kind of jazzman's 'inferiority complex' that has gradually developed among a number of new-jazz players. An ill-realized search for justification and for arguments in the long, unspoken struggle against tradition, the attempt to assert the claim of one's music to be authentic jazz – all these were clearly the cause of new-jazz players turning to the only legitimate principle for art jurisdiction of the old jazz – precedent.

Thus the avant-garde's initial verdict on standard jazz was not only final but it was unjust. On the other hand the reinterpretation of the classics is a perfectly legitimate feature in the development of any art. The panthematicism of the old jazz presents limitless possibilities of this kind. The theme in jazz is a kind of 'open sense'. Only improvisation (development) confers individually significant content on the jazz theme, converting the prototext of the theme into the metatext of the musical composition. But the most amazing thing about the music in this new album of the Ganelin Trio is the creation of such a wide and many-faceted world of ideas by means of no more than a few musical intonations. The end of Borges's essay is an almost literal repetition of its opening (a jazz structural scheme in fact) – 'It may be that universal history is the history of the different intonations given a handful of metaphors.' It looks as though the Ganelin Trio decided to demonstrate this by their music.

Sergey Kuryokhin: *The Ways of Freedom* (Leo Records, LR 107)
  Sergey Kuryokhin – solo piano

Sergey Kuryokhin (born 1954) was introduced to new jazz by

Anatoly Vapirov, who included him in his quartet as long ago as 1977. *The Ways of Freedom* is his first solo record and was released in 1981. The seven pieces on this record give a very fair idea of both his artistic personality and his 'keyboard philosophy'.

One of the central aesthetic antinomies of his music is clearly shown in the first piece, 'Theory and Practice': the organic combination of a romantic meditativeness and a constructivist revealing a device, e.g. developing musical material of intricate intelligible labyrinths and rhetorical 'puzzles' by means of 'hitting' (purely rhythmic) technique. Kuryokhin does not employ the standard homophonic piano style of old jazz, and there is often no sign of the conventional division of the player's task between left hand (accompaniment) and right (melody); nor does he use the traditional jazz form of variation.

Pieces 'The Wall' and 'Rules of the Game', which are close to each other in terms of artistic climate, are well provided with all the features of Kuryokhin's style – the quick succession of different musical landscapes (of the dynamic of development), fantastic 'machine-gun' glissandi and pianistic devices of all kinds, including the use of a 'prepared' instrument and considerable use of the technique of collage. In the last piece the tempo is even artificially accelerated, and this often exaggerates the piano style to the point of caricature. Artificial acceleration of this kind, which is also employed in 'Another Way', is plainly due either to the producer's negligence or to some strange whim of the sound engineer. In either case this inexplicable acoustic trick came as a surprise to the musician himself.

'Archipelago' opens with a series of grinding, metallic-sounding chords in the dark lower register of the piano where the plucked strings produce a 'wiry' glissando. Heavy pedalling creates the effect of a curtain of sequences hanging in the air, and a skilful use of rests corrects the admirable rhythmic balance of the music. Having reached the height of uncontrolled fury the music often verges on hysteria. The range with which the resistance of the material is overcome finds expression in tempestuous and ecstatic 'bursts' of energy.

The beginning of 'No Exit' recalls conducting by means of nails and wooden block in Stockhausen's 'Intensität' from the *Seven Days*. After a series of romantic reminiscences the music takes the form of a smoothly flowing stream of sound whose monotonous dynamic is disturbed by occasional moments of turbulence. 'Inner Fear' is the most traditional piece on the record, and is in fact constructed like a sonata allegro, with variations of the first and second subjects clearly distinguishable in the development section. Classical in form and tonal in idiom, this piece is chiefly interesting for its melodic development which is marked by emotional immediacy, clear musical definition and a dreamlike meditativeness.

The last piece on the record is an extensive one, 'Another Way'; and here the music is again artificially accelerated. The work sums up the structural ideas of the foregoing pieces. The musical events follow each other in logical succession like a series of episodes in styles of different value. There is no 'beat', the rhythmic brand-mark of old jazz that guaranteed its belonging to pop culture. If this music shows clear indications of having a sexual character – moments at which the material is tempestuously mastered, of wild violence and intoxicated aggression resembling a sadistic 'rape' of the instrument (reminding one of the subtitle of Luc Ferrari's 'Société II', 'And if the Piano were a Female Body'), its chief contents are associated with escape and conquering fear. Escape from reality, from existence, from fate or destiny, from music itself in the last resort, flight as withdrawal and refusal. And herein lies the profound social significance of Kuryokhin's music. 'Another Way' thus turns into a drama of the man who can see no aesthetic escape from musical nonconformity. There are hysterical episodes in the piece, obviously arising from inability to find an escape, 'another way'. Into the coda there floats, unexpectedly, a blissful bucolic landscape, a serene pastoral – a kind of musical variety of a 'false beard'. And no sooner does one begin to think, 'Well, here is just another one of those people who find consolation in the hypocritical celebration of some "golden age" of music of nature' – when the whole of this confectioner's idyll is turned upside down – once again we encounter the wild, indomitable range of the piano's body – the play on its wooden parts and strings, the tempo screwed up to a presto – struggle and flight breaking out with renewed violence. The negative dialectic of Kuryokhin's thought allows of no self-deception.

The works on this record show a strange inclination to unite into a single text. It is possible to regard them as parts of an 'open' musical narrative; their autonomy is conditional (formal). It is possible to explain this in detail by the fact that the new pieces are not so much new works as montages of fragments from earlier works; what is chiefly new in them is the arrangement of the 'musical micro-modules' within the framework of the piece. Here, in fact, we have the most important feature of Kuryokhin's musical poetics. A structural principle of this sort is more creatively fruitful than the forms of traditional jazz variations, which have become clichés, and it offers an improviser greater formal potentialities. By rejecting the standard variation form, and indeed all the 'framing formulae' of the old jazz the player obtains great possibilities for limitless stringing together of musical episodes and the building of a musical structure like an 'open text'. It is precisely here that we are aware of the improviser's inventiveness and sense of form, for the absence of any 'development from a seed' obliges him to replace such development by a living and coherent linking of musical events (conflicts). The player's thinking becomes more pluralistic, his mental perspective freer and less prejudiced because he is not driven by the logic of musical development into the dead end of variation-spinning and does not surrender to the power of a one-dimensional musical subject. It is true that the absence of standard form, aleatory procedures and 'unpremeditated' structures in general do sometimes lead in Kuryokhin's sense to cyclic or 'recurrent' forms. But inert structures of this kind were deliberately cultivated in the old jazz as an artistic method (naturally in other rhythmic conditions).

Every jazz performer creates his own forerunners. Kuryokhin reminds one of Taylor, Schlippenbach and Conlon Noncarrow. His music does not by any means spring from a genetically pure jazz tradition. The significant absence of jazz from some of his works appears as a kind of rhetorical figure in his aesthetic system. In this way his music can enter into playful relationships with the jazz-orientated audience, can bring together ideas that could never have met in the old jazz world and discover analogies and equivalents in quite disparate musical worlds (which is the essence of the aesthetics of the avant garde). Kuryokhin is not alone in his struggle for musical pluralism and variety. Among other European pianists with the same aim are the Dutchman Fred van Hove and the Englishman Keith Tippett.

The Ways of Freedom was much reviewed abroad – in the whole jazz press (*Down Beat, Coda, Cadence, Jazz Forum*, etc.) and a number of papers of world importance, such as *The Times* and *New York Times*. The majority of these critics attempted to consider Kuryokhin's music from existing aesthetic standpoints, stretching it on the Procrustes bed of the stereotyped cultural associations of Russian jazz and frequently giving its content a quite unwarranted political interpretation. This is particularly ludicrous because what Kuryokhin's record most recalls is – to paraphrase Borges – an entertaining 'collection of musical coins'.

The character of Kuryokhin's quotations and his fondness for collage – which is clearly due to the influence of Chekasin – deserves special notice. His frequent use of quotation, both open and concealed, reveals his listening habits. It is typical that, apart from the Joplin ragtime in 'The Rules of the Game', he never quotes jazz; so that he must either have a poor knowledge of the old jazz repertory or else wish deliberately to emphasize his abandoning of the 'black tradition', a symptom of jazz self-alienation. And yet his jazz is by no means bound by formal rules but is created by his particular life feeling: his 'blackness of being' and 'Harlemism of life' (Ellison).

There are of course occasions when Kuryokhin's music is excessively mechanical or excessively speculative and lacks emotional vibrations aiming at a cultural rather than a natural completeness. Lévi-Strauss maintains that 'music dares to go further than nature, and further than culture', but a hen is not a bird and Kuryokhin is not Lévi-Strauss. Even so it is always possible to discover in his music, side by side with a variety of different cultural reminiscences, powerful cells of expressive 'physiological' tension, though these are not linked to any hedonistic kind of sensibility.

Why use sophistry? 'Talent is like money – you either have it or you don't' (Sholom Aleichem). But had that great Jewish humorist been able to hear the new jazz, he would have realized that his formula was not so accurate. Talent is sometimes more like the conditions of human freedom, the ways of which are inscrutable indeed. The value of talent (and freedom too) does not lie in itself, but in the possibility to use it in order to realize artistic truth. And without that realization the talent itself is something like a lever without a fulcrum.

Translated from Russian by Martin Cooper

A 1984 Panorama of Soviet Jazz
Virgil Mihaiu

It was not until the 1960s that the world of arts witnessed some timid signs reflecting the already rich tradition of jazz in the USSR (birthdate: 2 November 1922, Theatre Institute Hall, Moscow, when the First Eccentric Jazz Band of the RSFSR performed under the leadership of Valentin Parnakh). The first appearance of Soviet jazz musicians abroad – pianist Vadim Sakun's sextet – took place at the Jazz Jamboree, Warsaw 1962. Only Igor Bierukshtis, the group's bassist, had a full musical education. The leader was a physicist working at the Academy of Science in Moscow, trumpeter Andrey Tovmasian was still studying music, Alexander Kozlov played the baritone sax but was credited as a professional architect, guitarist Nikolay Gromin worked as an economist in a big department store, and Valery Bulanov was still a student at the Moscow Polytechnic. The record produced by the Muza-Polskie Nagrania label on that occasion sounds very lively even today. Three years later, another beautiful surprise: altoist Georgi Garanian's quartet (with Gromin on guitar, Bulanov on drums, and Andrey Egorov on bass) presented a jewel of jazz lyricism, entitled *Ballad*, which was released by Supraphon after the 1965 Prague Festival. In 1967 the Estonian capital Tallinn hosted an international jazz festival which was to mark a decisive step in the development of Soviet jazz.

During the next decade East European audiences became more aware of the potential of Soviet jazz. But the scarcity of records able to document an almost immeasurable wealth of talents still hindered a proper assessment. Then, in the beginning of our decade, Leo Records started releasing music from the Soviet

154

Union, which transcends any local, 'exotic' significance, providing that one must no longer expect progress in art to be generated from certain established, privileged areas.

The Soviet critics' jazz poll published in Riga by the newspaper *Sovietskaya Molodyozh* (Soviet Youth) in 1984 gives as winners the names of musicians from Leningrad, Moscow, Riga, Tallinn, Vilnius, Smolensk, Alma-Ata, Tbilisi, Novosibirsk, and other towns. The geographical spread of these towns emphasizes the development of jazz in different parts of a country covering one sixth of the globe. Maybe in other places such developments wouldn't matter that much, but here we are witnessing a process of cultural groundbreaking into areas of rich musical traditions, where modern improvising techniques were previously unknown. Therefore, regardless of their intrinsic value, or of our possibility of ever listening to them, it is indeed very touching to read international magazine reports about the existence of the Semyon Mordukhayev Quartet in Uzbekistan, the Quarta group in Moldavia, the Kestutis Lushas group in Latvia, Kursk pianist Leonid Vintskevich, Armenian jazz pianists Mihail Zakhazian and Vagan Karapetian, and so many other interesting jazz groups extending from Byelorussia and Ukraine to Siberia, or from Azerbaidjan to the Baltic Republics. The record coverage of such rich music is utterly inadequate. Even worse is the distribution. Consequently, one has enormous difficulties in keeping in touch with all the developments inside Soviet jazz. For that reason, this essay is to be considered as a Romanian critic's point of view of a recent musical phenomenon still improperly documented.

As in any other country, we may find some sort of stylistic stratification among Soviet jazz musicians (a multiple one, if we are to take certain national or local schools separately – think of the Baltic Republics, of Moscow and Leningrad, of Siberia, etc.) There are traditionalists, mainstreamers, boppers, soft-core or hard-core avant-gardists, and so on and so forth. But one is forced to recognize from the very beginning the high professionalism of those who play jazz in Stravinsky's homeland. This is due mainly to a traditional respect for culture, which is kept alive in that country, and an extended system of excellent musical education. Even if many jazz musicians produce what is generally known as 'derivative music', it is unlikely that as far as their mastery of the instruments is concerned one could find any technical faults. Of course, I do not wish to lay myself open to the accusation that I am advocating dull correctness instead of sparkling creativity, which after all is the whole point of jazz! What I want to stress is the fact that, if we are to accept a certain amount of accessible jazz as a basis for attracting new audiences, of accustoming young listeners to a *new sound system* (and such 'propaganda jazz' is present everywhere), then at least that jazz should sound 'accurate' from a professional musician's standpoint.

The problem of emulating Western (i.e. American) models was still a major issue two decades ago. But if we compare the understanding of the big-band concept as illustrated by two Melodiya records – Iosif Veinstein's Leningrad orchestra, and Oleg Lundstrem's Moscow big band playing homage music to Ellington and Miller – we may notice that there is not only a difference of some years between the two recording sessions – the difference is qualitative. While the first orchestra gives a rendition of something that had already achieved its authentic climax under different socio-ethnic-historical conditions, the Oleg Lundstrem variants (especially two extended creative arrangements of 'It Don't Mean a Thing' and 'Caravan') showcase an inner transformation; the real essence of orchestral jazz is delivered in refined formulae, avoiding extravagances, but with a keen contemporary scrutiny. Energetic collective passages render Ellington's immortal themes, while the solos of trombonist Victor Budarin, saxophonist Stanislav Grigoriev, pianist Vagif Sadychov and drummer Ivan Yurchenko add profoundly personal insights to the swinging ensemble work.

In truth, there is a tradition of 'respecting the established patterns', which could by no means be restricted to the country we are talking about. And there have been continuous quarrels between the traditionalists and the modernists going on in every field of art (sometimes as fiercely as civil wars), not only since Victor Hugo's *Hernani* . . . So, OK we have Veinstein, Leningradski Dixieland, Allegro, or Igor Brill's ensemble, which could be confused with so many similar groups from Australia, Japan or Denmark. Is such a fact always that scandalous? Willis Conover's VOA broadcast – for years on end a major source of information for Eastern jazz fans – is actually saturated with mainstream products. So what? Beginners may get accustomed to the sound of music, and old addicts can have their daily dose of chord changes. On the other hand, who would a musician like Kuryokhin rebel against, if these (what he perceives as) negative stimuli did not exist? 'More lunacy, absurdity and shocks – this is what is needed to stir things up, not dinner jackets, black ties and dixieland,' he said in an interview with *Jazz Forum*.

A typical blend of virtues and mistakes is the *Labyrinth* album produced by the Melodiya ensemble under the leadership of G. Garanian in the mid-seventies. Anyone accustomed to the State-owned label's maniacal dread that a record wouldn't sell unless it contains a certain percentage of compromise, cliché-haunted, 'fashionable' music will, however, admire the Garanian & Co. achievement on this LP. The record's concessions aside, we may listen to a fine Garanian composition entitled 'Lenkoran', a musical evocation of the exotic Azerbaidjani town on the Caspian Sea shore. The orientally modulated theme is set forth by a powerful wind section. Then follows a tenor sax launching into an inflammatory solo in which every note is attacked con brio, thus emphasizing the typical virility and warmth of that instrument. The irresistably swinging section leads to an explosion, where all the sounds are scattered, divided, lessened, as if each were led by an inner logic towards unforeseeable territories. After a brief respite, the chaotic sound-bits, resulting also from overdubbing and echo effects, resume their search for each other, and the theme is stated again, in its full eloquence, at the end.

A record where some ebullient new wine is poured into almost classical forms was dedicated to George Gershwin by Leonid Chizhik – piano, Alexey Kuznetsov – guitar, and Alexey Isplatovsky – drums. The music's apparent simplicity concentrates wealths of feeling and highly rewarding interplay of three impeccable technicians, who know how to deliver Gershwin's message to today's listeners. The outcome is at once bracing, soothing and very dense in its musical substance. The fact is that Chizhik avoids here becoming pleonastic (is that due only to the tempering influence of his companions?) As ill luck would have it, things change when he finds himself in a completely unrestricted format. The *Reminiscences* solo piano double album was recorded live in Moscow and Leningrad in 1980. Programmatically, this solo effect is meant to pertain to the same confessive vein as Keith Jarrett's (or, in my country, Johnny Raducanu's) individual confrontation with the concert grand. The parameters of Chizhik's musical world reflect an ego rejoicing at its own technical perfection. Long passages of narcissistic ostinati are the trademark of his *Reminiscences*. The particular angle from which the Moscow-based pianist views jazz is classical inspiration, evident for instance in his elaborate three-part suite, made up of Prologue, Monologue and Epilogue. His brilliant craftsmanship makes Chizhik some sort of Soviet Oscar Peterson. There are superb moments of skilful interweaving of three or more melodic lines, hammering riffs, and tender tinklings of single notes, all of them smartly chosen and mixed. The weak point of this double LP is that, once at ease with the space he has been granted, the pianist becomes rather self-indulgent, lacking the concentration and precision which turned his previous disc into a landmark in the reinterpretation of Gershwin's tunes. Therefore, it is not surprising that the most impressive track on *Reminiscences* is Chizhik's version of 'The Creole Love Call' by Ellington. In only six minutes, the pianist sums up an entire treatise of blues simplicity and sophistry, demonstrating his aptitude for preaching the neo-classicist lesson to the new generation of listeners.

Alexey Kuznetsov's excellent guitar playing meets that of Nikolay Gromin's on a duo performance devotedly entitled *Django*. The pure, controlled, uneffusive sound of the two guitars is subordinated to an all-embracing melancholy, suggesting two solitary forms lost in the infinity of the steppe. Another fine record by Kuznetsov is *The Blue Coral* with some tensional electric guitar solo pieces, among which 'Summertime' is really memorable. This musician, though not an innovator, is a skilled, intelligent improviser, with a polished, easily recognizable timbre, giving his listeners as much joy as he himself seems to have while playing.

One might speak of a real tradition among many Soviet jazz musicians of venerating the celebrated masters of this music. One more example: David Goloshchekin, who in 1983 celebrated fifteen years of leading the Leningrad Jazz Ensemble by releasing the record entitled *Fifteen Years Later*; it contained 'evergreens' by Gershwin, Ellington, J. van Heusen, etc. Vladimir Feyertag's liner notes spare us any other comments: 'Musicians came and went, one style replaced another, but Goloshchekin did not change: he is still true to hard bop – a traditional trend of modern jazz. His virtuoso mastery of several instruments, improvisational skill and good taste make each concert of this ensemble an unforgettable musical performance which is unfortunately difficult to convey on a gramophone recording. However, it is always interesting to follow his improvisational ideas. His musical speech is rich in original turns of phrase, sparkling with witty quotations. Besides, he is an excellent director who can adroitly use even the subtlest nuances in his partners' styles, who inspires them with his dedication and at the same time dictates to them the form of the compositions, the order of their improvisations and the overall tonal scheme.

'During the fifteen years he has taught a lot of musicians, some of them now playing together with him. The eldest of them is pianist Piotr Kornev, a subtle accompanist; the youngest is the guitar player Andrey Ryabov who joined the ensemble shortly after his graduation from a musical college. The double bass player Dmitry Kolesnik, drummer Evgeni Huberman, and percussionist Viktor Shcherbin provide the precise, driving rhythm of the ensemble.' In the end, Feyertag mentions Goloshchekin's conviction 'that classical jazz has not exhausted its artistic and aesthetic values, that music must be expressive, comprehensible, kind and beautiful'. The fact is that most of the records discussed up to now just . . . keep on swinging, regardless of their age. And for those who are sceptical as to whether such a thing matters a great deal today, I should mention that I taped Goloshchekin's album during my visit to Sweden in the autumn of 1984. How come? Well, there was a young Swedish researcher who had just discovered the hidden splendours of Soviet jazz by purchasing that record in a Petrozavodsk shop. And, as I was eager to listen to any recording from that field, he offered to help me on the spot. On the other hand I could also relate quite a few authentic stories about fans of Leo Records' Soviet musical documentation, whom I met in the most unexpected places and situations. It is clear that – regardless of styles – Soviet jazz is rising to a powerful position on the world scene.

Another source of vitality is the multinational character of Soviet culture. It is a pity that I have neither the space, nor the proper means to discuss this issue in its broad implications. That is why I have chosen to concentrate on the really impressive achievements of jazz musicans from two of the Soviet Republics (Azerbaidjan and Estonia) with which I have become familiar through records obtained with considerable difficulty.

Vagif Mustafa-zade (born 16 March 1940; died 15 December 1979), one of the world's most original pianists of the post-bop era, embodies the very notion of jazz in Azerbaidjan, situated on the western shore of the Caspian Sea. The above-mentioned Swedish jazz fan showed me an item in *Pravda*: it told of the organizing of a festival *in memoriam* Mustafa-zade, held in his home town Baku, five years after his untimely death. Azerbaidjan, 'the hearth of the fire', has been renowned since Zarathustra's times for its columns of burning oil welling forth from the depth of the earth, while its capital Baku ('town of the winds' in Persian) gradually developed into a very cosmopolitan centre for oil companies, run by the likes of Rothschild, Deterding, Gulbenkian, Assadulaev, etc., at the turn of our century. Nowadays, this twelve-century-old city has the charm of a southern metropolis, containing about two million inhabitants, the fifth largest city in the USSR. Baku's contrasts – oriental scenery, historic monuments and the boisterous rhythms of modern civilization – fascinated Mayakovsky, who saw in this 'town of flames' a dynamic metaphor of a society aspiring to its emancipation through industrialization. Being born in a territory with deep Islamic cultural/artistic roots (the Azer language is most closely related to Turkish), Vagif Mustafa-zade succeeded in giving a vivid and beautiful expression of his people's sensibility through the universal language of jazz. He started playing the piano when only five years old, and at the age of twenty he had already earned a reputation as a jazz pianist in the artistic milieu of Azerbaidjan. *Jazz Forum* provided some more facts about Mustafa-zade's career in the obituary published in 1980: 'In the early sixties he led his own jazz trio, Kavkaz, in Tbilisi, eventually winning national acclaim through appearances at the 1966 and 1967 Tallinn jazz festivals. In those years it was difficult for musicians to make a living playing jazz full-time, so Mustafa-zade opted to work with different show bands as well as the Azerbaidjani Radio and TV Band. Yet he also recorded some nine albums for the local branch of the Melodiya label, more than any other

Soviet jazz musician.' It is to be regretted that these records are almost unknown to the large jazz audience. Just before his tragic death this phenomenal pianist-composer did start to become known abroad: after the ten-day festival of Tbilisi, in 1978, *Jazz Forum*'s editor Pawel Brodowski wrote a laudatory account of Mustafa-zade's too-long-neglected qualities: 'Appearing with his tight, disciplined quartet, Mugam, Mustafa-zade showed himself to be an unassuming Bill Evans-type of musician – lyrical, introspective, and full of exceptional feeling for rhythm and harmony. His piano reminiscences are permeated with the oriental colours of Azerbaidjani folk music. This is a modal and improvised music, particularly well suited for a fusion with jazz. Mugam is the word used to describe the essence of this music, the rhythmic and melodic models which can be repeated any number of times, very much like an Indian raga. Mustafa-zade has fused these folk elements, notably the scales and melisma, with his original rhythmic conception, and the audience responded very warmly to the results.' This success prompted Mustafa-zade to give up his job at Baku Radio-TV, and to devote all his energy to jazz. After getting the first prize at the 1979 International Competition for Jazz Themes in Monaco, he was also awarded the title of Honoured Artist of Azerbaidjan, the first time a Soviet jazzman was ever so honoured. Shortly before his death, Vagif Mustafa-zade released a double album on Melodiya, which reveals a personality of enormous resourcefulness, wonderfully supported by Georgian bassist Tamaz Kurashvili. The Mustafa-zade–Kurashvili collaboration, as evidenced by the Melodiya double LP, is one of the notable feats of piano/bass jazz since 1965. Sumptuously adorned formulae, a sophisticated sound architecture made up of vigorous touches and contrasting variations, dexterously blended into colourful fabrics – as if suggesting Islamic decorative art – all this keyboard labour finds its adequate, stimulating complement in the springiness and consistency of the bass lines. Amazing in Mustafa-zade's playing is his capacity for rendering on the keys those contortions specific to Central Asiatic and Middle Eastern music, usually generated by the human voice or by instruments capable of producing gliding sounds (con arco or winds). The irresistible succession of notes is like a sonorous overflowing, a hot magma taking into possession ever new emotional horizons. Mustafa-zade's creation was vim, it is full of surprises, then again it knows when, how and to what extent to let itself be permeated by the ineffable Oriental melancholy. Jazz is alloyed here with the vast *mugam* tradition (*makam, mukam, makom* are some alternative spellings, denoting these modes characteristic of Central Asiatic folk music). Seldom have I heard a more significant transposal of a people's spiritual/musical resources into jazz.

Just one month after Mustafa-zade passed away, another 'jazz godfather' – this time from Estonia – also left the scene for ever: Uno Naissoo. He was only fifty-two, but he had managed to do a lot for Estonian and Soviet jazz music. Suffice it to mention the fact that he was the main organizer of the much-hailed Tallinn Festival of 1967. His diversified activities, from playing to composing, teaching and writing, made him known as a kind of symbol of Estonian jazz, although the latter celebrated its first successes three years before Naissoo was born.

Today, in spite of its size (smallest of the seventeen Soviet Republics), Estonia boasts a rich jazz scene. Tonu Naissoo (born in 1951, the son of Uno) appears, together with bassist Taivo Sillar and drummer Peep Ojavere, on a Melodiya record made in 1981 and entitled *Turning Point.* Although structurally the tracks do not seem to contain anything out of the ordinary, they demonstrate that the trio is full of musical ideas. It is a soulful jazz, music whose intricacy in its melodic and rhythmic patterns reveals a captivating introspection. Of course, one may see certain similarities between this record and the sound created by Paul Bley, together with Peacock or Swallow on bass, and Altschul on drums, some time in the sixties. There are also Jarrettian accents, and the acoustic/electric piano alternations are much in the manner of Bill Evans or, again, Paul Bley. Nevertheless, an unprejudiced listener cannot but remark the freshness of the sound visions created by Naissoo, Sillar and Ojavere.

Other significant Estonian jazz records include *Tiit Paulus and Friends*, setting off the fruitful collaboration of guitarist Paulus and saxophonist/clarinettist Arvo Pilliroog, and *2x Rustic Waltz* by the Lembit Saarsalu Quartet. The first LP reaches its highpoint in a stirring 'Pastorale', composed by Uno Naissoo, which beautifully evokes the dreaminess of the misty North. Paulus, Pilliroog and their friends, bassist Unt, pianist Tonu Naissoo and drummer Ojavere, may sound very familiar to ears that are accustomed to the ECM sound, but the veracity of the players' Estonian heritage poses the following question: was it the Northern musicians who adapted to Manfred Eicher's requirements, or were the latter actually inspired by the typical atmosphere of Scandinavian music? I am inclined to favour the second supposition.

As far as Saarsalu is concerned, he is an energetic, dynamic saxophone player, as well as a composer and arranger, carrying out successful investigations into the aesthetic heritage of Estonian folklore. Throughout their troubled history, the Estonian people, as well as their Baltic neighbours – the Latvians and Lithuanians – have learned that, in order to assert and preserve their national identity, they must above all pay due respect to culture. As a result, though numbering two million, the Estonians are always thought of as progressive-minded promoters of culture, people famous for their huge choral feasts – which have been taking place every five years, for more than a century now – a singing nation.

The most important Soviet contribution to the advancement of jazz resides in its many-sided avant-garde movement. As standard-bearers and founders of this *new music* from the Soviet continent, wonderfully (though only partially) documented by Leo Records, three names should be hailed: Vyacheslav Ganelin, Vladimir Tarasov and Vladimir Chekasin. They deserve a separate analysis, which I have already attempted in this book. There have been plenty of Western reviewers who, despite their sincere efforts to understand this phenomenon, have missed the point. They endeavoured to explain things with no previous knowledge of Russian and Soviet cultural developments. Therefore, it was good to read Norman Weinstein's comment in *Jazz Forum*, on Vladimir Chekasin's collaboration with pianist/avant-gardist Sergey Kuryokhin: 'If Mayakovsky and Khlebnikov were alive today, and jazz musicians as well as poets, this is what I would imagine they would sound like together.' Indeed, the Ganelin Trio revived the spirit of artistic eclecticism which prevailed in the Russian (and later Soviet) avant-garde for about a quarter of our century, after 1905. It is the spirit resulting from the desire to unfetter man's creative potential in the field of the arts. It is a totally sincere creation, grounded in the naïve Utopian belief in the perfectibility of the audience. The latter should be freed of their inhibitions and of taste-corrupting didacticism and commercialism. The term Utopian is not employed pejoratively here. On the contrary: without such vision the wide scope of today's arts would have been inconceivable. The terrible hiatus imposed in the 1930s, casting its shadows over the next two decades, was not able to suppress the fantastic artistic resources of Europe's biggest country. In the beginning of Tarkovsky's film *Nostalgia*, the main character, a Russian writer travelling through Italy, disappointedly asks his Italian mistress: 'What do you, Italians, understand of Russia?' The particular situation of Russia: the most Eastern defender of European values, was underlined by quoting from a Pushkin letter, in Andrey Tarkovsky's masterpiece *The Mirror*. The Russian intelligentsia has always had this sense of being involved in a mission to promote the individual ideal, a luminous Renaissance inheritance worthy of being preserved, against far-Eastern despotic/gregarious 'models'. Hence, a high value is put on spontaneity and naturalness in artistic endeavour. And isn't jazz our century's freshest and most spontaneous musical expression?

Ganelin–Tarasov–Chekasin have overcome prejudices and conquered new realms for jazz. Their works are pervaded by the unique force of Russian masterpieces. The specific problem of relating art to a vast environment is brilliantly solved. The Ganelin Trio have created new relationships between music and the space it was nourished from. Consequently, their new forms are hard to grasp for a cold, rational mind, limited to its occidental *parti pris*.

The Americans have developed a very advanced system of information, and yet their jazz (perhaps their most genuine contribution to the history of arts) is going through a period of decline. Representatives of jazz from Eastern Europe have their own faults, with the difference (and excuse) that they possess fewer means of being properly informed. If we are to speak of mistakes, then the Ganelin Trio made one during their tour of England and Wales (the first ever visit to Britain of a Soviet jazz group), by choosing to perform the 'Non Troppo' suite. Not that the piece is in any way inferior to their previous masterpieces, but its connotations and motivation were hard to convey in a concert to a foreign, unknown audience. Let's dare say that Vyacheslav

Ganelin, a great jazz musician, thinker and diplomat, thought the choice of this piece might disarm the often-heard criticism concerning the trio's inability to play 'in the tradition'. As a relative newcomer, he neglected the fact that critics in the Bloomsbury Theatre were ready to put down their impressions as some ultimate judgement on the Ganelin Trio, without any knowledge of the trio's other works! Trying to placate in advance all possible hostile reactions, the musician from Vilnius put forward his most (stylistically) conciliatory work – the title is eloquent enough in this respect. The consequence was that the tradition-bound critics were glad to identify 'breathy romantic saxophone, bursts of ragtime piano and a drum solo straight out of the Buddy Rich book', while an otherwise rigorous expert in new jazz, Eddie Prévost, jumped to a conclusion that would sound ridiculous, were it not dramatically unjust: 'Given that all industrial societies of the world seem to be producing their own contemporary improvised musics – with regional/national emphases, then it seems strange that the Ganelin Trio should appear so musically reactionary – so dependent upon outmoded American stereotypes.' A musician may be excused if he cannot, by force of circumstances, inform himself about what critics from another part of the world might be pleased to listen to. None the less, there is no excuse for a critic spoiling the image of one of the last fifteen years' decisively innovatory jazz forces, by apparently taking one concert (whose meaning he misunderstands) as representative of the immense variety of artworks by the Ganelin Trio.

After its British tour, the Ganelin Trio reportedly decided to play again only on very special occasions. It is true that so many years of togetherness can become pretty tiresome. Chekasin seems to have felt it most strongly. Accordingly, he got involved in many other projects. Two of them have been recorded: his frantic *Exercises* with Sergey Kuryokhin (piano, voice, percussion, poetry, flute) and Boris Grebenshchikov (guitar, voice, percussion), are a delightful mixture of jazz innuendo, parody, and the pure pleasure of theatrical extroversion. The other record features the Vladimir Chekasin Quartet, and is called *Nostalgia*. This time we regretfully discover certain limits of Chekasin's departure from the Ganelin Trio: his new partners seem absolutely unable to match the value of their leader. And, being no longer challenged, the latter appears unexpectedly repetitive and self-indulgent. The very fine introduction spoken by Chekasin in Russian ('We have all loved something or other/ in the past, at one time or another./ The years have passed. . ./ We try to feel the same love now/ but we can't – although we really want to/ . . . for we are different'), the beautiful cover design, the long, masterfully constructed saxophone progressions, all promised a musical counterpart to Andrey Tarkovsky's Italian film of the same name. Yet, alas, these promises were ruined by an inhibited, at times even awkward, rhythm section. Perhaps we still could come to terms with pianist Oleg Molokoedov and drummer Gediminas Laurinyavichus, but the thundering drone of a bass guitar stuck into pop-rock ostinato formulae is an insurmountable handicap even for a genius like Chekasin. Which does not mean that we are not to expect other marvellous achievements from this 'prodigal son' of the new Soviet jazz. And, as Gustave Cerutti puts it, in his view of *Nostalgia* (*Jazz 360°*, No.75), the unprejudiced listener may find '*du plaisir sans problème*' in this record, something not entirely undesirable, after all.

My conviction that the Ganelin–Tarasov–Chekasin unit is the expression of collective genius remains as strong as ever. And it has only been confirmed by the *Catalogue* reissue, previously known as *Live in East Germany*, and the excellent *Strictly for Our Friends*, containing recordings made in March 1978. These two 1984 releases by Leo Records are confirmation of their producer's opinion that the Ganelin Trio's greatest innovation lies in 'the merging of the suite form with polystylistics, which seems to be the only way out of the stalemate of American mainstream and the deadlock of European avant-garde'. And how incredibly fresh Chekasin sounds here! His great playing on the reeds, brass and other instruments, brilliantly emphasized by the unique interaction of Ganelin/Tarasov/Chekasin, only makes his own quartet appear all the more amateurish.

In response to Chekasin's 'treason', the other two members of the trio produced a duo record, entitled *Opus a 2*. It is an intelligently constructed suite: in the absence of the reedman's emotional outbursts, Vyacheslav Ganelin concentrated upon the minimalist dimensions of experimental jazz. He switches by turns from the piano to double bass, guitar, percussion, organ, swings here and there on the basset and meanwhile – through a tense interplay with Tarasov's 'intellectualized' percussion – rich moods are imperceptibly born from tiny details. The water gently purling at the beginning and at the end of the forty-one minute piece reminds us that Ganelin's universe is very close to Tarkovsky's damp worlds of nostalgic Russian metaphors. The culmination is reached in some kind of implosion, during the half pathetic, half distanced expiry of the accordion. Ganelin thus demonstrates one of his major qualities: his ability to approach all musical instruments with equal sureness of touch, endowing them with ever new resources, which he is able to arouse even if he has no conventional knowledge of playing those instruments. After listening to *Opus a 2*, I am afraid Ganelin could even convince me of the 'friendliness' of those fantasy-killers called synthesizers. This record, though less impressive than the bulk of the Ganelin–Tarasov–Chekasin *oeuvre*, once again shows how much at his ease a conceptual jazzman like Ganelin feels in the studio (this subtle sound alchemy very much resembles the trio's fascinating suites 'Concerto Grosso' and 'Poi Segue').

As was hinted before, Soviet avant-garde jazz is comprehensive, but only too few of its representatives have had a chance to appear on record. Sergey Kuryokhin has been luckier than many of his contemporaries. At the age of thirty he is already well-known, both from Leo issues and through his eminently sensible opinions, expressed in various interviews. Actually, the Leningrad pianist and *enfant terrible* belongs to the category of musician-thinkers, whose role is primarily to facilitate the flow of the progressive currents of a certain culture. He once confessed in an interview: 'There has to be a sense of spirituality. Without it the musicianship has no meaning at all, it's quite naked.'

As far as Kuryokhin on records is concerned, Graham Lock has noted perceptively: 'Reputedly the leading avant-garde pianist in the USSR, he's been compared to Cecil Taylor, though he doesn't really have the mainman's torrential passion. A little too chill and flashy for me, he's yet to find the substance to match his style.' Really, Kuryokhin's solo album *The Ways of Freedom* is not totally convincing; not only because of the debatable speeding-up-of-the-tapes question. While Ganelin–Tarasov *Opus a 2* gains from each new hearing, these *Ways* remain flat, in spite of the outstanding quality of the musician. Fingers are running up and down the keyboard but, after all, the effect is surprisingly static. To my mind, the most meaningful comparison would be with Anthony Davis's solo record *Past Lives*; but the disappointment I feel in both young pianists is perhaps due to my having nourished too-great expectations.

The situation changes when Kuryokhin joins other jazzmen with related idea(l)s. Now he suddenly heartens up, reacts and sends forth impulses himself. Sergey Kuryokhin's true personality is filled with the joy of affective communication, a specific Slavic feature. His contribution to Chekasin's *Exercises* is spellbinding. The same could be said of *Sentenced to Silence*, an exciting record featuring the profound and intense tenor sax/bass clarinet explorations of Anatoly Vapirov, supported by two other remarkable musicians: bassist Vladimir Volkov and bassoonist Alexander Alexandrov. In fact, Kuryokhin claims to be a frustrated saxophonist: 'This is . . . why I work only with saxophonists – Anatoly Vapirov, Vladimir Chekasin, and with two others, younger, but marvellous musicians, who have appeared relatively recently: Igor Butman and Pyatras Vishnyauskas. I base everything on the saxophone as the main instrument – I mean I think in a linear way, not harmonically but melodically.' The major principle in Kuryokhin's conception of jazz is that of the freedom of improvisation. He tries to create paradoxical 'happenings', where the actions are secondary to the development of the music. A real artist, belives Kuryokhin, is always a nonconformist. That's how his view of the piano as 'an anachronism' should be understood.

Kuryokhin's avowed influences belong to another sphere than that operating on the previous generation of jazzmen. It is interesting to notice that, after varying degrees of admiration of Dolphy, Muhal Richard Abrams, Taylor, Braxton, Bailey, etc., Kuryokhin, like other avant-garde pianists, got very interested in Thelonious Monk. In this way the new-jazz representatives develop along similar paths, the *Zeitgeist* imposes its 'vibes' regardless of boundaries.

Some years ago, who would have thought of a Siberian variant of avant-garde jazz? And yet, there it is! The *Siberian 4* LP recorded by Homo Liber gives only a taste. The players are young intellectuals who explain the radical orientation of jazz in Siberia by the fact that the dixieland jazz form has been skipped in that part of the world. A heavy burden, as it were, was thus lifted from their hearts. They had as a result a more direct access to the truly contemporary spirit of jazz.

The spirit of Stravinsky, as much as the spirit of Diaghilev, Mayakovsky, Khlebnikov, Meyerhold, Malevich, Kandinsky, Chagall, and their peers, forms the core of today's Siberian experiments. What should be stressed is the fact that, no matter how 'crazy' such progressive trends might appear to their detractors, a closer analysis will always show that Soviet jazz avant-gardists have a strong sense of content in everything they create. This should be remembered when the majority of the Soviet new-jazz experiments are considered. They avoid any elements of vain, shallow, boring irrelevancies. These musicians reject what painter and jazz musician John Fischer exposed as the following syndrome: 'free musicians who have to blow to feel good, and there is no structure and no communication. After two times of identifying with those people's freedom, or their right to be free, you suddenly wish they would say more. You wonder why it always stays the same. It's because they cannot accept organization as a necessity to creation. . . The therapeutic get rid of the pressure type of freedom – that's not freedom. Freedom is the thinking and doing and the ability to do all the things you have to do to get to that goal. That's freedom. It means mastering what you're doing.' (*Jazz Forum* 89/1984).

Living in an area of intermingling musical cultures, the Siberian jazz avant-gardists are closer to the ancient sources of artistic improvisation than many of their predecessors (even Shepp's pan-African sessions sounded a little artificial, in their attempt to prove by all means that jazz was going back to its roots. It sometimes looked much more like a trip than a serious investigation.) The musicians on *Siberian 4* deliberately use their peculiar position in order to absorb as many influences as possible. For example, Belichenko studied Central Asian music, particularly Uzbek, and Touvinian Buddhist folklore, full of echoes from China and India. He confessed: 'It seems to me that Siberia has in concentrated form some essence of a pre-European past, thousands of years old, untouched by professionalism. A sort of

musical matrix. All these musical influences could be very fruitful
for the future of our jazz.'

Distance from big cultural centres is no reason to be insensible
to the newest developments. Yukechev declared in his *Jazz Forum*
interview: 'I was fascinated by Cecil Taylor, mainly his later solo
works. And saxophonist Oliver Lake and the Ganelin Trio. If I
were to compare American and Soviet free jazz, I would prefer the
Ganelin Trio for the pithiness of what they are doing. They play
music of the ascending spirit.'

A new jazz of *pith and moment*, this is what we have been
receiving from the Soviet Union, during these last years. The *Jazz
Forum* 'Festival Fever' issue (*JF* 90/1984) informs us about the
very busy ninth Moscow Jazz Festival. Alexey Batashev, one of its
producers, speaks of having deliberately avoided the booking of
leading Soviet jazz groups, in order to leave more space for some
of the newer faces, especially from the eastern part of the USSR.
Among the highlights of the festival, Batashev mentions Herman
Lukyanov's Kadans group; the Gayvoronsky/Volkov duo 'playing
a gently tinted, avant-garde jazz raga', the trios led by tenorists
Vapirov, Raubishko, Alexander Pishchikov, and by pianist
Mikhail Okun; the newly founded Moscow Saxophone Quartet
sporting Alexander Oseychuk's arrangements. 'The Valentin
Rusakov Trio from Tomsk was a delightful surprise. These
newcomers play "art-jazz", basing their original compositions on a
Victor Hugo drama or the local folklore of Siberia.' Such pleasant
news reminds me, for instance, of Rolf Reichelt's report from the
1980 Leningrad Autumn Rhythms festival, where, after playing
due respect to the Ganelin Trio, the competent German critic
wrote about altoist Vladimir Rezitsky's Arkhangelsk as showcas-
ing 'a unique group concept. The band . . .`offered convincing
collective music with irregular metres, exciting sounds, interesting,
melodically complex structures, interwoven ostinato patterns and
free interplay.'

Exciting reports like these are to be heard quite often, and they
should stimulate extended debates and closer examination of the
facts. The contribution of Soviet musicians to the extension of the
horizons of the jazz world cannot be summed up in a few pages.
Our major purpose was to direct the attention of people who
believe in art's fundamental values towards a most rewarding

phenomenon: the emergence and consolidation of an impressive new 'school' in jazz.

Notes of a Record Producer
Leo Feigin

There is only one reason why these notes of a record producer form the last chapter in a book on Soviet jazz. Leo Records has become inextricably linked with the fate of jazz in the USSR, and strange though it may seem, the attitude of the Soviet authorities to jazz in their country is in many ways similar to the Western establishment's attitude to Leo Records, with a few honourable exceptions.

I would be willing to bet that there's never been, and probably never will be, a record label like Leo Records Ltd, which broke the story of the new music from the Soviet Union to the whole world. However, the full story of Leo Records will never be told, especially its cloak-and-dagger activity. We shall have to take to the grave certain secrets and names, for fear that some people, who are still living in the Soviet Union, might be punished or persecuted for their courageous actions in preserving and smuggling out to the West works of art which would otherwise have been, inevitably, lost.

I happen to be the producer of this label. For better or worse, I was placed in this position by circumstances, or by God, if you like. I had to take all the decisions related to the release of the records and I am prepared to take responsibility for all the mistakes, successes and failures.

Decisions

The most important decisions, however, had nothing at all to do with music. From the very first moment I got hold of the first Ganelin Trio tape I was confronted by legal, moral, ethical and aesthetic issues. I am continually obliged to question myself. If I release this tape what will be the consequences for the musicians? Will I endanger their lives, or ruin their musical careers? Will they be thrown in prison, or kicked out of the Soviet Union? Will they be allowed to perform again? Will they be allowed to travel abroad?

Do I have the moral right to release their tape?

On the other hand, it was obvious to me that the first release of tapes from the USSR in the West would be a tremendous morale booster for the musicians in the Soviet Union. Since the Soviet State-owned Melodiya label could not care less about the new music, such a release could change the whole atmosphere of free music inside the Soviet Union. It could help the musicians to overcome feelings of total isolation and doom. It could revitalize the jazz scene and give Soviet musicians new hope and incentive to live, play and create.

From my very first hearing of the Ganelin Trio recording *Live in East Germany* I realized I was holding a masterpiece which would make jazz history. Did I have the right *not* to release it?

Unprecedented

It's never happened to music before. In the past there were many manuscripts that had to be smuggled out of the USSR and published in the West. *Doctor Zhivago* by Pasternak, *The First Circle* by Solzhenitsyn . . . examples were abundant. Some of the writers who were living in the Soviet Union were thrown into prisons, some were expelled from the Writers' Union, some were kicked out of the country. What a mad world!

PRS, MCPS

There were legal problems as well, which up till now, five years later, have still not been sorted out. From the very beginning I was made aware of the organizations which control royalties. The PRS

(Performing Rights Society) is supposed to pay royalties to a 'publisher' (so-called 'needle time') for broadcasting and public performances. Theoretically, as 'publisher', Leo Records could expect to get these royalties.

Another organization, MCPS (Mechanical Copyright Protection Society), is supposed to collect royalties (so-called 'mechanical rights') from record companies on behalf of the musicians, providing the musicians are members of MCPS. Since there was very little chance for a Soviet musician to become a member of MCPS (that would be criminal from the point of view of Soviet laws), Leo Records could hardly be expected to pay 'mechanical rights' to MCPS. However, the reality was less simple. Not only was Leo Records denied royalties by PRS for broadcasting its records, but, from the very first release onwards, MCPS was after Leo Records demanding payment of 'mechanical rights'. A mad world, indeed!

VAAP

In 1973 the Soviet Union decided to join the Universal Copyright Convention and created the All-Union Copyright Agency (VAAP). It was declared that VAAP was a *public organization*; at the same time it was declared that in the Soviet Union there existed a *State monopoly* on foreign trade. The act of selling to a foreign company the rights to use works of Soviet citizens was a foreign trade operation, which a private individual in the USSR was not allowed to carry out. It could be affected only through VAAP. On top of this there was no evidence whatsoever suggesting that the musicians in the Soviet Union belonged to this organization. There was no legal procedure, no membership, no regulations.

It was obvious that the creation of VAAP constituted the formation of a criminal organization. On the one hand, it was a *public*, and not a *State* organization. On the other, the monopoly on foreign trade belonged to the *State* and only to the *State*.

The leading human-rights supporters and dissident writers in the Soviet Union were very much alarmed. They wrote an open letter to UNESCO, saying that VAAP '. . . is striving to become – if it is not stopped – a tool of our censorship in the whole of the outside world, a censorship which aims to suppress freedom of information and the exchange of spiritual values between peoples'.

Paradox

Thus, VAAP enjoys complete monopoly on the export and import of spiritual values. This means that the Soviet Union cannot be an equal partner with the other adherents of the Universal Copyrights Convention. And yet, both PRS and MCPS accepted VAAP as their collective member. That is why, according to PRS, all royalties from broadcasting Leo's records were due to VAAP, and that is why Leo Records was supposed to pay 'mechanical rights' to MCPS. And here we come to the most incredible paradox: the only reason Leo Records started releasing new music from the 'Soviet underground' was that the State-owned Melodiya would not do so. In real terms it meant that Leo Records was supposed to subsidize VAAP, and as such the Soviet authorities, through PRS and MCPS, for suppressing new music. In 1981 saxophonist Anatoly Vapirov was sentenced to two years in prison. Leo Records released his album and, according to the MCPS law, was supposed to pay royalties to the Soviet authorities for putting him in prison. In short, Leo Records was supposed to pay for suppressing human rights. That was totally absurd. Could I be a party to this? Of course, I refused to pay. MCPS bureaucrats keep on sending me letters, saying that I have very little choice. I shall either have to pay, or they will take me to court and put me in prison.

First Releases and Response

The release of the first records from the 'Soviet underground' attracted an entirely different response in the East from that in the West. The response from the East was overwhelming. I was thrilled to read dozens of congratulatory letters from Poland, Czechoslovakia, Hungary, Romania and the USSR. All these letters underlined the extraordinary significance of the label, which represented unofficial culture in the Soviet Union. At last musicians in the USSR had a chance to release records that were not censored by the authorities. At last they had hope – the realization that their music could be heard in the West, that everything was not so gloomy. At last they could make a tremendous jump over the gulf separating East and West. They had a real chance to overcome the feeling of cultural isolation and get rid of their inferiority complex.

Response from the West

The response from the West was totally disappointing. The political, social and cultural significance of these releases was completely overlooked. As far as the music of the Russian players was concerned, it was not understood. As one of my friends noted: 'The feeble West failed to cope.'

There is a saying: 'Each nation deserves its government.' If it is fair to paraphrase this saying, then 'jazz music deserves its critics'. It sounds like a curse, but I am convinced that no other field of art has such ignorant, mediocre, and irresponsible critics.

Betrayal

It is not difficult to recall the immediate response of the jazz media to the music of Charlie Parker, Ornette Coleman, John Coltrane or Albert Ayler. As a matter of fact, it has become a tradition on the part of jazz media that anything new or innovative should be put down and proclaimed anathema. New music from the Soviet Union was not only innovative in the sense that it was developing an entirely new identity, new Slavonic feel and new approach to structures; it provided an additional, unprecedented edge – free music was played in one of the most totalitarian countries in the world. It was a miracle. As Norman Weinstein put it in one of his reviews: 'That such awesome music emerges from the midst of such political and artistic repression is miraculous.' However, his was a lonely voice in the wilderness. Western jazz critics did not have the necessary experience and knowledge to understand that there was a great deal of difference between playing free music in a free society and playing free jazz in a dictatorial regime. The significance of this event totally escaped them. As a result they failed to provide even minimal support both to the label that was documenting this music and to the music itself. Their reviews bear witness to the fact that new music in the Soviet Union was betrayed. Western jazz media do not understand that by betraying freedom somewhere else they are betraying freedom in their own country. The majority of people in the West take freedom for granted. And jazz critics happen to be no exception. They are like the fish in an aquarium, which does not understand that the water is the sole medium for its freedom. As soon as the water is removed from the aquarium the fish dies.

No Sponsorship

Is it not surprising, therefore, that Leo Records could not find anybody, either an individual or an organization, which would be willing to provide the label with any financial support or sponsorship. Tremendous efforts and precious time to find a sponsor were totally wasted. How ironic, then, and how pathetic that the documentation of the Russian new music, and indirectly the fate of new music in the Soviet Union, depended entirely on the efforts and finances of *one Russian emigré*, who had to work full-time elsewhere and save every penny to run the label.

All this was happening at a time when the recording industry seemed dedicated even more single-mindedly than usual to the pursuit of profit, when Michael Jackson was selling dozens of millions of his record *Thriller*; the pop star Boy George was collecting awards for 'outselling' his competitors (not 'outplaying', notice); when the tabloids in the UK were regularly giving away one million pounds to attract more readers to their newspapers and make many more millions. I never got any replies from such prospective sponsors.

Litmus-paper

New music from the Soviet Union, documented by Leo Records, proved to be a litmus-paper. When it was dipped into the Western jazz media it registered a chain of wrong reactions. The essence of the music was misunderstood, its innovations were unnoticed. What this litmus-paper really did was to expose many weaknesses of the jazz media and the whole of the jazz industry.

Unavoidably, any accusations of this kind must be supported by some evidence – otherwise these accusations are not valid. The trouble is I have so many examples, I could write a separate book.

Crossed Wires: One

After the release of the first album from the 'Soviet underground', *Live in East Germany*, this is what Max Harrison wrote in *Records and Recording*: 'The three men named played tenor saxophone doubling clarinet, piano and drums, and there are *two unidentified participants* on bass and guitar.' What surprised me most in this phrase was not the fact that the critic forgot to mention alto saxophone, double alto, basset horn, wooden flutes and ocarina. I was surprised that a jazz critic was not really interested to know how these three musicians played up to seven instruments simultaneously. Had Mr Harrison got in touch with me (the address of the company was on the record sleeve, and both of us lived in London, after all) I would have been happy to explain to him how Ganelin plays simultaneously piano, basset, and electric guitar. Instead he chose to reproach the producer for not mentioning two other imaginary musicians on the record sleeve. I wrote to Mr Harrison and sent him another album of the Ganelin Trio, *Con Fuoco*, suggesting that he could correct his mistake in the review of *Con Fuoco*. This is what Mr Harrison wrote in *Music and Musicians*: 'When commenting on their previous LP, *Live in East Germany* (LR 102), I did V. Ganelin, V. Tarasov and V. Chekasin an injustice, assuming, because of the variety of instrumental sounds, that other, unnamed, participants were present. In fact they play everything themselves. Not that this is a good record. . .'

In 1983 Cecil Taylor with his Unit gave one of the most outstanding, illuminating performances of his career in London's Roundhouse. The next day *The Times* carried a review by Max Harrison in which he put down Cecil Taylor and his music. It is obvious that the aesthetic of new music remains a deep mystery for Mr Harrison. One of his favourite clichés, while writing on new music, is 'it doesn't jell'. The obvious answer to this is that it is not supposed to!

Crossed Wires: Two

Another example of great journalism was provided by the heavyweight of jazz criticism Mike Hennessey of Billboard Publications, who writes for a big American monthly, *Jazz Times*. When it became clear that the Ganelin Trio would be touring England I went to see Mr Hennessey personally for a friendly chat. I brought my catalogue and promotional material, I explained the activity of the label, and I was very proud that by that time there were ten releases from the 'Soviet underground' in my catalogue. This is what appeared in the February 1984 issue of *Jazz Times*:

From Russia with Jazz
Next month sees the first British tour by jazz musicians from the Soviet Union when the Ganelin Trio, a free jazz unit from Leningrad arrives to join the Contemporary Music Network, a touring program arranged by the Arts Council.

The Ganelin Trio – Vyacheslav Ganelin (keyboards), Vladimir Tarasov (drums, percussion) and Vladimir Chekasin (saxophones, flute, clarinet, basset horn, trombone) – has appeared at a number of European festivals with considerable success. Chekasin's saxophone work has been described as reminiscent of Albert Ayler and German critic Joachim Berendt has described the trio's music as 'the wildest and yet the best organized and most professional free jazz I've heard in years'.

The Ganelin Trio has two albums available on the highly dynamic and enterprising Finnish label, Leo, which is owned by drummer Edward Vesala. They are *Live in East Germany* (LR 102) recorded in 1979, *New Wine . . .* (LR 112) and *Con*

Fuoco (LR 106) recorded in Moscow and West Berlin, and *Vide*. The Ganelin Trio is also featured on a (LR 117) interesting forthcoming release from Leo, *New Music From Russia*, a five-album package which presents a large number of contemporary Soviet musicians, together with a book of reviews, interviews and photographs.

Though little more than three years old, Leo is an extremely active label whose catalogue also includes recordings by the Ethnic Heritage Ensemble, Tomasz Stanko (a brilliant Hungarian trumpet player), the excellent Finnish flautist, Juhani Aaltonen, and Frank Foster's Living Color (an ensemble which includes Mickey Tucker, Charles Persip, Virgil Jones and Earl May).

For more information on the Ganelin Trio and Leo Records you can write to P.O. Box 193, 00101 Helsinki 10, Finland.

I shall spare the reader the details of my correspondence with Mr Hennessey – the notes of both parties might be of great interest to a student psychiatrist. But what about putting the record straight? In the next issue of *Jazz Times*, tucked in the bottom corner, there appeared several lines which were supposed to be an apology:

> In my piece last month about the Ganelin Trio from the Soviet Union I falsely attributed Hungarian nationality to Tomasz Stanko, whereas he is from Rseszow in Poland. I also confused the Leo label, on which the trio records, with the Finnish label of the same name. The Leo Records I should have referred to is based at 130, Twyford Road, West Harrow, Middlesex, England. My apologies to readers. As Ronnie Scott has been known to say, 'I've gotta stop smoking that stuff'.

Needless to say, the Finnish label Leo Records received several letters of inquiry about the Ganelin Trio, and I received several letters from some American radio stations with apologies for misinformation. I even received a cassette-copy of a broadcast announcing the Ganelin Trio to be the product of the Finnish label. What a mess!

A Real Let-down

Jazz Times is supposed to be especially important because this publication is one of the main sources of information for American disc-jockeys. For years I have been writing letters to the publisher Ira Sabin begging him to commission an article on new music from the Soviet Union. However, Mr Hennessey's piece was the only article on Leo Records during the five years' existence of the label. The attitude of the publisher can be best illustrated by the following event: I was sending to *Jazz Times* two copies of all my new releases hoping they would be reviewed. It was a tremendous financial burden on me, because postage was not cheap, and to send records to reviewers I always had to save money by refusing myself other necessary things. One day there was a letter from the publisher: 'Lend me your records. I'd like to hear them.' That was a real let-down. I was paralysed by a feeling of total uselessness. I wrote back to Ira Sabin saying: 'What have you been doing with my records? Using them as frisbies?'

From that moment on I realized it was useless to write, to send records, information, etc. This publication was, as far as I could see, deeply into bebop. Its publisher didn't seem to care about new music from the Soviet Union or about new music at all.

Down Beat

There was another big publication which was competing with *Jazz Times* in hiding information about Russian jazz from the world jazz community: *Down Beat*, of course. To be fair I have to admit that *Down Beat* lost this battle to *Jazz Times*. It did not misinform. But as far as hiding information was concerned *Down Beat* was doing a great job. It took this magazine almost four years to publish an article on Leo Records and the Soviet jazz scene, but the credit for this should go to Francis Davis, who is one of the most conscientious jazz critics in the USA.

In spite of my three visits to *Down Beat*'s office in Chicago its editor was determined to keep silence. Finally *Down Beat* reviewed two Soviet albums. Both reviews were so inadequate they were totally misleading. Reviewing the Ganelin Trio's album

Ancora da Capo Peter Kostakis failed to discern a very rigid
structure in this two-part suite. He wrote: '. . .the trio plays a
desultory series of episodes, all seemingly improvised'. Another
Down Beat reviewer, Jon Balleras, tried to give Sergey
Kuryokhin's album *The Ways of Freedom* a political interpretation: 'At best, this is a culturally and politically significant
recording, one which illustrates the proposition that mixing
politics and music can, at times, result simply in uninteresting
music.' What a ridiculous statement!

Stereotyped Mentality

There was one serious obstacle preventing Western jazz critics
from fully understanding and appreciating new music from the
Soviet Union: the stereotyped American (Western) mentality.
Even such a conscientious, sympathetic, and serious reviewer as
Bill Shoemaker could not get over this obstacle. He wrote in *Coda*
magazine: 'no strains of the proverbial Volga boatmen are to be
heard in Vladimir Chekasin's outrageous *Exercises*. . . On the
contrary, Chekasin and Ganelin frequently quote jazz standards.'
   There is no question that in order to write about Chekasin's and
Ganelin's music one has to have some basic knowledge of Russian
culture, history, traditions, etc. *Exercises* is, in the opinion of
knowledgeable reviewers, the most 'Russian' record in the entire
Leo Records catalogue. The 'Russianness' of this recording is not
in 'strains of the proverbial Volga boatmen'. It is expressed
through links with Russian avant-garde culture of the first quarter
of this century. However, if one has no knowledge of this, one has
to follow stereotyped routes: in blues you hear the cries of field
workers of the South. In the Russian jazz one must hear the cries
of Volga barge-haulers.
   What escaped the attention of almost all American reviewers
were the most characteristic features of Russian improvisers: the
suite form of their works, thought-out structures, the polystylistic
and polythematic nature of their music. Only after the Ganelin
Trio's concert in London did British jazz critics start writing about
the special way, neither American nor European, in which the trio
puts together its music.

Why Doesn't Melodiya Release Their Records?

In November 1983 I went to New York trying to promote my records. After many efforts I got an invitation to show my ten Soviet releases to Gary Giddins, whose reviews of the Art Ensemble of Chicago's and Willem Breuker's Collective's concerts in the *Village Voice* were fascinating. This was my great chance to attract the attention of a good writer to new music in the USSR. I put *Live in East Germany* on his turntable and three minutes later I felt I had him really hooked. His questions about music and musicians were very sharp. It did not escape his attention that the pianist was playing basset and electric guitar simultaneously, and he wanted to know how the musician was doing it. The power and wit of the Ganelin Trio's music really grabbed him, and I was secretly rejoicing. All of a sudden he noticed the inscription on the record sleeve: 'The musicians do not bear any responsibility for publishing these tapes.' He was looking at the inscription, and then there came the question: 'If they are such good musicians, why doesn't Melodiya release their records?'

Very seldom in my life had I felt so tired and disappointed. I was sitting on a comfortable sofa in his beautiful apartment full of records and books in the heart of Manhattan. But the burden of this comfort was too heavy to bear.

I left his appartment hardly noticing that I was walking in the pouring rain. My confidence was badly shattered. I was not sorry about the ten albums I left in his apartment. I was horrified at the thought of what he might write about Russian music. Fortunately, Gary Giddins never did.

Questions

Not everyone was as generous to the music from the 'Soviet underground' as Gary Giddins. The worst ever remarks on this music appeared in the American magazine *Cadence*. The review of the Ganelin Trio's *Vide* was written by Alan Bargebuhr. It opens with the words: 'I don't really see the point of the new Ganelin Trio concert recording.' The review of Mr Bargebuhr is structured in the form of questions. He does not comment, he does not analyse the music, he asks questions: 'But is there structure? And is there a clearly focused artistic vision? At such length, doesn't it stand to reason that there will be some moments of brilliance amidst the dull and ordinary? On this LP, these liberated Russian players might be said to be musically compensating for the repression they feel politically and artistically. But how do we know how they feel, and isn't that our myopic fantasy? How repressed can they be artistically? The tape of this concert did not have to be smuggled out of Russia, did it? There was an audience at the concert, so it's clear that they are not exactly performing in a vacuum. Was the audience arrested and transported, after the concert?' Mr Bargebuhr ends his review with the words: 'I hope I never have to hear it again.'

On the face of it, these are amusing remarks. But do they demonstrate any real attempt to understand the music, or merely the reviewer's satisfaction with his own facetiousness?

Unfair Play

But what was hurting me most was the fact that the records from the 'Soviet underground' were not reviewed in the biggest publications. As soon as I released an album by an American musician it was immediately reviewed in *Down Beat*, *Jazz Times* and all others. There were excellent reviews of Amina Claudine Myers's records, John Lindberg's, Keshavan Maslak's, Marilyn Crispell's. The Russian albums from my catalogue were surrounded by a thick cloud of silence. This seemed very unfair, and I could not understand it. It used to drive me to despair because distributors did not want to take my records for distribution, and those distributors who did take them could not sell them to the shops. This point was expounded by Francis Davis in his article published by *Down Beat*: 'What makes my colleagues' failure to comment meaningfully on the Russian musicians an aesthetic as well as a moral oversight is the overall quality and originality of the music.'

Controversy

In the same article which appeared in April 1984, Francis Davis wrote that on the basis of *Vide* and *New Wine*, 'It is fair to say that the Ganelin Trio is one of the premier jazz ensembles not only in Europe, but in the entire world. The most remarkable thing about the music made by these men is that it sounds not at all derivative, even if American ears like mine can count off any number of obvious precedents (Taylor, Shepp, Kirk, the Art Ensemble, even Desmond and Brubeck).'

One month earlier *Vide* was reviewed in another American publication, *OP* magazine. The reviewer, John Baxter, wrote: 'This record features two extended AACM-influenced free improvisations. There are Lester Bowie-style trumpet solos, George Lewis-style trombone solos, Muhal Richard Abrams piano solos, etc. AACM fans may find the Ganelin Trio's music too derivative to be interesting.'

So, there we are. Two reviews published at the same time proclaim completely opposite ideas. This kind of controversy surrounded the music from the 'Soviet underground' all the time. However, now, looking back at these controversial reviews I come to only one conclusion: controversy is a sign of great art. Mediocre or bad music never arouses controversy.

Thank You

Of course there *were* serious, conscientious jazz critics who were writing about new music from the Soviet Union. Norman Weinstein in the USA, Charles Fox, John Fordham, Graham Lock, Ron Atkins, Barry McRae in England, Misha Lobko in France, Gustave Cerutti in Switzerland and Mark Miller in Canada. However, their voices were drowning in the deep sea of silence. Their efforts were not enough to help me to attract the attention of distributors and bring my records to shops.

I have nothing but thanks to Pawel Brodowski of *Jazz Forum* for supporting this music, to Bill Smith of *Coda* magazine, to Gustav Cerutti of *Jazz 360°*, to Graham Reid of *Passages* (New Zealand), and Anthony Wood of *The Wire*. I wish their publications had as many subscribers as *Down Beat* or *Jazz Times*.

New Aesthetics

The emergence of the new music was a great musical revolution, which led to a crisis of perception. The new music created an entirely new aesthetic, and the features that had kept jazz music in the field of entertainment were lost. After about three quarters of a century jazz music had become a serious art form. This music embraced all the features of jazz and all the features of modern classical music. It became, in my opinion, the richest music in the world. However, the jazz media failed to cope with this development. The music of Ornette Coleman and other free improvisers created an uproar among jazz critics. Leonard Feather and the like rejected this music (I am using the name of Leonard Feather as an example in a collective sense, because as a recognized authority he epitomized the point of view of the Establishment). Even now, a quarter of a century later, some critics do not understand this new aesthetic. They were forced to accept it, they had to learn to live with it, but they never really understood it. Yet they continue to write about it. That's why Leonard Feather feels more comfortable declaring Miles Davis's music of the eighties to be an artistic achievement (which to my mind it isn't) than commenting meaningfully on the music of the Art Ensemble of Chicago.

The new music needed new writers. The new musical language needed new ways and means of describing its aesthetic, because the language of the old jazz was no longer adequate. However, this has not happened, and this is one of the tragedies of new jazz.

In the case of new music from Russia the situation was even worse, because very few writers knew anything about life in the Soviet Union, the history of Russian art and culture. That's why the majority of critics failed to discern the 'Russian spirit' in the music of the Soviet improvisers.

Alliance with the Left

To my mind, another great misfortune of the new jazz was that its exponents from the very beginning tried to identify themselves with the political left. This was especially true of European musicians. The FMP catalogue proclaimed: 'In the midst of

capitalism, on the field of capitalism, playing against capitalism. . .' I remember what a shock I got in the mid-seventies when I
arrived in England after living in the USSR for thirty-five years.
The Roundhouse, the most important venue of the time, staged a
series of concerts of new jazz with all the receipts going to the
Communist Party of Great Britain. I could understand that the
musicians, who were dissatisfied with the attitude of the Establishment and public at large to their music, were forced to join the
leftist movement, but here there was a great paradox. On the one
hand, the musicians considered themselves to be in the forefront
of the counter-culture and anti-Establishment. They were in
opposition and it was exactly for this reason they had leftist
tendencies. On the other hand, they did not realize that where the
communists, whom they were supporting, had come to power, the
playing of free jazz was discouraged.

Disaster for the Music

In Britain and other European countries this alliance of new music
with the leftist movement resulted in a total disaster for the music
and musicians themselves. The leftist movement, being by nature
impecunious and unsubsidized, could not give the new music
either financial or moral support. And though the musicians had
taken this anti-Establishment stance they could not survive
without the help of the Establishment. They had to apply for
grants and bursaries, but the grants were small and hard to come
by and the exponents of new music had to play in dirty little pubs
and badly lighted, unheated places like the London Musicians'
Collective. Derek Bailey, Evan Parker, Trevor Watts, John
Stevens, Barry Guy and many other fantastic musicians deserve to
play on big stages in front of huge audiences. After all, their music
is not inferior by any standards to the music of modern classical
musicians, who have entirely different relations both with the
Establishment and their audiences. They do not have to sacrifice
their artistic freedom, and they enjoy great financial support.

What was different about new music in the Soviet Union was
that its exponents managed to raise themselves above any political
or dissident movements. True art, to me, is always above politics.

Interviewing the Ganelin Trio during their tour in England Graham Lock asked Vyacheslav Ganelin what he thought of Joachim Berendt's quote that their music was 'a cry for freedom'. (The naïveté of Graham Lock is surprising. I wonder what kind of answer he expected from a person who knew that with one unguarded answer he could forfeit all his chances of future performances abroad.) And yet, Ganelin replied with great sincerity: 'If Joachim Berendt wants to see it that way, that is his opinion. For us, music can't express anything but itself. There is no question of anything political, it's just music.'

And this is exactly what sets Soviet musicians completely apart from their European and American counterparts: the ability to elevate themselves above any politics, the surest sign of serious art.

Communication

In August 1984 Bill Smith, the editor of *Coda* magazine and a musician, visited London. He was very excited to go and see Evan Parker perform with a trio in a West End pub. Bill Smith brought his family and a couple of friends for the gig, but apart from our small company there were four people in the audience. It was most embarrassing.

This lack of audience is destroying one of the most important functions of jazz – the function of communication. British musicians have developed the habit of playing without an audience. They play by themselves for themselves, and it is always painful to see them suffering on the stage. The lack of the habit of communicating with an audience is one of the reasons which has brought their music to an impasse. Probably that's why some British musicians were really embarrassed to witness the act of communication between the audience and the Ganelin Trio on the stage of London's Bloomsbury Theatre, which, for a change, was not only filled to capacity, but could not accommodate all those who wanted to see the trio. It must have been the most ridiculous congregation that new music in London has ever witnessed. Soviet Embassy representatives, the Arts Council of Great Britain, members of the GB–USSR Society, the Russian service of the

BBC, Russian emigrés in London, students of the Russian language, Russophiles, Russophobes, jazz critics and radio broadcasters, even the cream of the KGB. Naturally, very few seats were left for jazz fans. The majority of the audience was attracted to this performance for reasons other than the desire to hear the music. It was only natural that the members of the trio felt as if they were being exhibited in a zoo.

They started playing their tragic suite 'Non Troppo', but the vibes from the audience were totally wrong. The audience was surprised, amazed, astonished, stunned, but remained absolutely alien. It did not understand, it was not moved. Probably that's why in the second set Chekasin was determined to get a response from the audience by hook or by crook. For a short time, while 'New Wine' was developing on the stage, he became a buffoon, a mountebank – the only person who in medieval Russia was allowed to take the mickey out of the Tsar and get away with it. There was parody, self-parody, irony and humour. The banality of 'Too Close for Comfort' interspersed with avant-garde screams was splashed all over the stage. The audience was delighted. There were encores and even flowers. Some British musicians, however, were disgusted. They refused the invitation to have a drink with the Russian musicians after the performance. Evan Parker told me he wanted to get on the stage and give Chekasin 'a hell of a beating'. The drummer Eddie Prévost wrote in *The Wire* magazine: 'Above all, I feel that the relationship of the Ganelin Trio with its audience is not a healthy one.'

Local Heroes

In the meantime there was another development that proved to be crucial both for new and old jazz: the breaking up of the big musical scene into small localized movements. The first half of the eighties was the time for 'local' heroes. On the one hand it was a truly democratic process, the decentralization of the new music, which gave birth to many small groups, units and individuals playing highly original music in an incredible variety of styles. On the other hand this process was damaging to the music because the smaller the units, the less exposure they were getting.

From this point of view the new music from the Soviet Union was in the most unfavourable position. Soviet musicians, with the rare exception of the Ganelin Trio, could not get any exposure in the West because they could not travel and perform at will, in spite of many invitations from festival organizers there.

Soviet Bureaucracy

Soviet bureaucracy was a bad partner in this game. It was fascinating to watch how awkward, how ridiculous their efforts were. On the face of it, they had a great chance to use this outburst of new music in the Soviet Union for propaganda purposes. Every time the Ganelin Trio performed in the West the Soviets were killing two birds with one stone: first, a performance of the trio implied that free jazz existed and flourished in the Soviet Union. Moreover, indirectly the Soviets were saying: 'Look, free jazz not only exists, but our musicians are actually as good at it as yours, if not better.' Second, the Soviets were making quite a bit of money out of it. Sometimes they asked incredibly high prices for the trio and paid derisory sums to the musicians. However, being the most bureaucratic of all bureaucracies, they were constantly spoiling their own chances.

It seems that they impose some kind of quota for letting musicians out of the country. The invitations for the Ganelin Trio to perform abroad were pouring in from festival organizers in each European country. And yet the Soviet bureaucrats would not allow the trio to perform more than three times a year. For several years festival organizers battled with the Soviets to get Sergey Kuryokhin and his orchestra to perform in the West, but these efforts failed.

Substitution

What the Soviets were doing instead was sending other bands to perform instead of the Ganelin Trio, Kuryokhin's orchestra or Rezitsky's Arkhangelsk. It is very difficult to understand how Soviet bureaucracy works, and it seems there are two possible explanations. First, Soviet bureaucrats dealing with culture are so unqualified and outdated in their views and tastes that they can't see any difference between a highly original group like Arkhangelsk and a second-rate entertainment band which is registered with the state agency Gosconcert. Another explanation could be corruption in the Soviet Ministry of Culture, with civil servants pushing the group of their preference.

As a result, instead of the Ganelin Trio and Sergey Kuryokhin's Crazy Music Orchestra the Soviets were sending to the new music festivals abroad their mainstream groups, such as Allegro or Kadans. Unavoidably, it led to confusion. Allegro, which had very strong musicians in its line-up but played rock–jazz fusion music, looked utterly ridiculous on the stage of Le Mans jazz festival, which caters exclusively for highly original, adventurous new music. Paul Acket, the organizer of the biggest festival in Europe, the North Sea Festival, had been trying to book the Ganelin Trio for many years without getting any official response from the Soviets. Then one year, in 1983, out of the blue, instead of the Ganelin Trio they sent the group called Kadans. Fortunately this was a strong group, which played its own rendition of 'Round Midnight' and wasn't ashamed of it. However, it was a mainstream group which wouldn't get any points for novelty and originality.

Bad Organization

On top of everything else, it takes ages for the Soviets to process an invitation. Usually negotiations go on for months and months. As a rule many people are involved in these negotiations: cultural attachés in both countries, societies of friendship, the Ministry of Culture, the Gosconcert agency and many other people.

And yet, too often, the tours of the Ganelin Trio are very badly organized. The worst examples were two tours of Italy, arranged by the Society of Friendship of Italy and the USSR. They were conducted without any publicity, and as a result the trio had to play to empty houses.

Publicity

They say that bad publicity is better than no publicity at all. I have always doubted the validity of this. Again, the Ganelin Trio is an example. Their tour of England generated a lot of publicity, and one film company decided to jump on the bandwagon and make a film about them for the 'South Bank Show' while the trio was in London. Later on the film was sold to other countries.

However, I am convinced that the film did more harm than good. It was shot the day before the departure of the trio after an exhausting tour. The musicians were dead tired and during the shooting there were many things that went wrong. But the most unfortunate thing was that the producers of the film had no idea about the music of the trio. As a result what we saw on the screen was three exhausted, strange-looking men, sitting close together on a bench trying to answer the questions of the interpreter. This interview was from time to time interrupted by bits of music, which were taken out of context and were, for that reason, incomprehensible. The suites of the trio were totally unsuitable for studio recording, and the tricks of the cameraman, who probably thought that he was making a disco film, didn't help us to understand the music of the trio. Any film about the Ganelin Trio should be made during a live performance, because the audience plays a very important part in their work. All in all the music of the trio was grossly misrepresented.

Timing

The timing of the emergence of Russian jazz was very unfortunate because the best years of the new music were over. It seemed that this music peaked at the end of the seventies, which happened to be a time of considerable economic stability both in Europe and America. That's why there is every reason to believe that socio-economic factors are mainly responsible for the relative flourishing of new jazz in the seventies. When people have jobs and some money to spare, when they have security, they can afford to go on a more adventurous musical journey. They are not afraid to look into themselves, and they are not afraid to make discoveries. The avant-garde of the seventies provided jazz fans with this opportunity, for the music of this era was all about the personality of a performer, the individuality of an improviser. The personality of the performer in the new jazz is an inseparable part of the content of the music. And this explains the incredible amount of solo avant-garde records that were released in the seventies.

However, the end of the seventies brought a big economic crisis, unemployment, insecurity and financial hardships for many people, whose position had seemed safe in the seventies. It is in the nature of a human being that in times of economic insecurity he or she does not want to look inside, does not want to make any discoveries. What he or she wants is to forget the unpleasant reality. Instead of serious, challenging music, a nice background noise. Pleasant entertainment is wanted – instead of jazz a 'soap opera' of jazz.

Soap Opera of Jazz

There are several labels that deal with the 'soap opera' of jazz, and the best examples are, for me, ECM Records and Windham Hill. ECM has many important and beautiful albums in its catalogue, but a large proportion of its product, with its immaculate sound, has already been called 'music without substance' by some jazz fans. ECM sound, 'the most beautiful sound next to silence', came just in time – the world was subsiding into a recession. Insecure people wanted a beautiful background noise which would help them to forget, even for a short while, ugly reality. The most striking example in support of this suggestion is the fact that the most ECM records per capita have been sold in Israel – the country with the greatest insecurity factor in the world. Israel is a poor country with the rate of inflation running at times at 400%. The country is in a permanent state of war with its Arab neighbours. Music fans in Israel were buying ECM records faster than in any other country in the world.

Another amazing example is the extraordinary financial success of Windham Hill records, which are even more 'soapy' than ECM. The demographic market research made by this label revealed that the label's major consumers were female, in a very wide age bracket (a market hitherto untapped by any record company).

Music from the 'Soviet underground' provides a complete alternative to the 'soap opera' of jazz. It is music full of guts, wit and structures. Instead of the 'most beautiful sound next to silence' it provides a roar of live recordings. However, the time for this music is gone, and there is only a hope left that one day the time will come again, as happened in the past. Everything moves in cycles in this world.

Editorial Policy

I have often been asked: 'What is your editorial policy?' This is a simple question, and yet I always had difficulties in answering it. Sometimes it seems to me that the answer is pretty obvious: whether a producer wants it or not his or her label is a precise reflection of his or her personality. One look at the catalogues of ECM Records, Hat Hut Records, or Black Saint is enough to see the personality of the producer behind it, or the editorial policy of each of them. Of course, this applies only to independent producers.

Needless to say, every producer has certain principles on which he or she builds his or her work. I had principles too. I have never released a record to make money, or solely to please the critics or the public. I have always thought of producing a work of art rather than making a record, and I am very happy that there are only a few records in my catalogue which circumstances obliged me to release. From this point of view Leo Records' catalogue is a reflection of my taste, principles and outlook.

Most of the time I produced records for art's sake. I knew from the very beginning that I was producing records for a very small dedicated audience, real connoisseurs. The public at large seems, if past musical innovations are a reliable indicator, to need at least ten years to catch up. And ultimately there is only one criterion to judge the validity of the record – whether it stands the test of time.

Principles

Of course there were other principles too. Very important was the principle of discovery. I never worked with an established artist, or a big name. Almost every record in my catalogue is a discovery of a new musician, a new exciting talent. I took special pleasure in giving a boost to young, unknown artists, in spite of the fact that this way is the hardest and most unrewarding. I am happy that I was able to record Amina Claudine Myers, Keshavan Maslak, John Lindberg, Sakis Papadimitriou, Marilyn Crispell, Borbeto-magus, Phil Minton/Roger Turner, for the first time as leaders, and some others, apart from the musicians from the Soviet Union and East European countries. All of them had recorded before, but Leo Records gave these artists a push as leaders and individual performers. By the mid-eighties Leo Records had already formed an identity as an innovative label breaking new names into the new-music scene.

Independence

What was especially important to me was the principle of independence. By that I do not mean that nobody could tell me whom to record or which records to release. First and foremost I saw Leo Records as an alternative to big business, which was brainwashing the public. What fascinates me even now is the fact that one person, with very limited financial resources, single-handedly, can produce records as good, both in terms of the quality of the production and the quality of the music, as those of multi-million corporations. It is a miracle that several helpless individuals, separated by thousands of miles and the Iron Curtain, can beat a huge State machine in the East and big business in the West, both of which are trying to smother individuals and turn them into brainless robots. In this sense I shall always see Leo Records as the ultimate triumph of the individual over the State machine. This label was born out of a need to record the under-privileged and the oppressed. And I shall always see it as the 'conscientious objector' of the record industry.

Basic Rules

Every year jazz critics from many countries vote in the international critics' poll of *Down Beat.* Among other things they choose the
best record producers of the year. For years we have been seeing
the same names: Manfred Eicher, Giovanni Bonandrini, Michael
Cuscuna, Norman Granz. All of them are great professionals who
know their business inside out. I guess they know pretty well
where to put the microphones, and they have their own ideas
about the way their records should sound. All of them are strong
personalities, and this is the trouble, because most of their records
sound the same.

I think my ideas about producing records are different from
theirs. To be honest, I would be ashamed if somebody told me that
my recordings of Amina Claudine Myers, Sakis Papadimitriou and
Marilyn Crispell sound the same. I would be equally ashamed if
someone told me that all Ganelin Trio albums sound the same.

As far as producing records is concerned, I follow three basic
rules. A record producer is first and foremost a mediator. He is a
middle link between the musician and the listener. That's why the
main task is to present the listener with a product which sounds
exactly like the original. Not to change the sound, not to make it
better or worse, but to preserve it the way it is. Another task of a
producer is to create the atmosphere which helps musicians to
show their best qualities and to reveal their talents. The producer
should help the musicians to rise. That's why I never work with
musicians with whom I don't feel a certain affinity or rapport. But
where the producer can be really helpful is in the overall strategy
of the recording. The sequence of recording can be of crucial
importance, and so is the sequence of the compositions on the
record. It can either make or break the record.

Tapes

Delivery of the tapes from the Soviet Union is the most mysterious
and secret element in the operation of Leo Records. Every tape
that has (or hasn't) become a record has its own story. There were
tapes that took several years to reach me, and there were tapes
that used to turn up out of the blue, without any dates of

recordings, names of the musicians, titles of the compositions and so on. Since the tapes were arriving in the most unpredictable fashion it was impossible to introduce any reasonable planning of new releases. It is obvious that the impact of Leo Records could have been much stronger had it been possible to introduce a rational element into the running of the label. Moreover, I could not possibly avoid making some mistakes concerning titles, dates of recordings and instruments played.

Some discrepancies didn't escape the attention of the critics. Reviewing the Ganelin Trio album *Con Fuoco*, Kevin Whitehead wrote in *Cadence* magazine: 'A wonderful record. (By the way, nowhere does Ganelin play electric guitar, as listed on the liner. Note – the other Leo record by the trio claims to have been recorded in East Berlin on the same day as this Moscow concert. They must work their musicians like slaves over there.)'

Kevin Whitehead was absolutely right, but why and how this mistake happened is a fascinating story in itself.

Total Mess

I received two letters from the USSR saying that a tape was on the way. Both letters mentioned that the tape was recorded live, but gave different dates of the recording, different instruments, etc. Some time passed and the tape never arrived. I was beginning to forget about it.

Then, one morning, I discovered a huge box on the doorstep of my house. The box was covered with labels saying that it had been opened by the Customs to check its contents. There were other labels too saying that the Royal Mail had been trying to locate the addressee for several months because the sender of the parcel missed out one part of the address. Picking up the box from the doorstep I noticed that it was unusually light for its size. Having opened the box I discovered another, smaller box inside. The smaller parcel was sent from West Germany and contained a reel of tape in the original Soviet-made box. The address read as follows: 130 Twyford Rd, Middlesex. The part of the address West Harrow was missing. For curiosity's sake I looked up the street index of London and discovered that there were a dozen Twyford

Roads in Middlesex.

The tape was the Ganelin Trio's masterpiece, beautifully recorded. But now I was in a real mess. I had two different letters referring to one tape. On top of everything both letters were written in coded language to beat Soviet censorship. I decided to go on with the release, but to minimize the possibility of mistakes I decided to put as little information on the record sleeve as possible. The album was entitled *Live in East Germany*, but the date of the performance was wrong. The music of the trio was so powerful, and the number of the instruments they played simultaneously was so large many critics did not believe it was a trio. To correct the mistake, and to put the record straight this album was rereleased in 1984 as *Catalogue*.

More Charades

In the beginning of 1982 an English student of Russian brought two tapes from the Soviet Union. Both tapes were fifteen minutes long and were absolutely identical. They were recorded by the Anatoly Vapirov quartet. I realized that if I were to release Vapirov's album there should have been more tapes, because fifteen minutes of music is not enough even for one side of a record.

Then came the news that Anatoly Vapirov had been sentenced to two years in prison for so-called 'private enterprise'. The release of his album became a necessity. But what could I do? I decided to add Sergey Kuryokhin's solo music to the album to make it a reasonable release. The trouble was that I had left-overs of Kuryokhin's music from three different tapes of different recording quality. It took me several weeks of hard work to put these tapes together and to edit them in such a way that Kuryokhin's solo piano on Side Two of *Sentenced to Silence* was perceived as one continuous composition. The album was released in March 1983. A year and a half later, in autumn 1984, the other tapes of Anatoly Vapirov turned up. They were sent from West Germany without a return address, and they were the missing parts of his 1981 recording that were meant for his first release. Later on these tapes were included in the next Vapirov album *Invocations*.

Pure Luck

More often than not the fates were generous to the people who tried to help deliver the tapes. In 1983 one English musician went to the USSR as a tourist. While he was there he took part in a spontaneous jam session with Soviet musicians. Probably for that reason he attracted the attention of the KGB. Before he left he was asked to smuggle out a reel of tape. At the airport, as soon as he approached the Customs, he was separated from the group, taken into an empty room and thoroughly searched. By sheer luck the tape was in the handbag of his companion, who was allowed through the Customs without being stopped. The tape happened to be the recording of a live performance and was released the next year.

As far as I know during all these years only one tape has been lost. All other tapes reached me safely sooner or later. I was very fortunate to deal with very decent people who were doing it of their own volition without asking for any rewards. There was only one exception. A Russian woman who lives in the UK tried to extract money from me for bringing the tapes to London. Six months later, having listened to them, she returned them. She didn't like the music.

The Quality of the Tapes

Most of the tapes that arrived from the Soviet Union had to be remastered. They were recorded on quarter-track machines that were very old. Very often the characteristics of the tapes and the recording-machines did not match. The combination of high-quality Western tape and outdated Soviet equipment gave the worst results. After the release of Sergey Kuryokhin's album *The Ways of Freedom* some critics wrote that the tapes were 'electronically speeded up'. Unfortunately, neither the engineer, who was recording Kuryokhin, nor myself, possess electronic equipment to speed up the tapes. All Kuryokhin's solo piano music was recorded at one go on the same equipment, but during the session they used tapes of three different makes. The worst sound was achieved on Ampex tape, which is considered to be the best. Normal, average sound was produced by BASF. However, the third type, Racal, gave over-bright effect to the sound, which some people confused with the speeding up of the tapes.

Probably the most painful decision for me was the release of *Ancora da Capo*, which, I believe, is one of the greatest works of the Ganelin Trio. The quality of the original quarter-track recording was very bad and could not be greatly improved. Ultimately, after long hesitation, I decided to release it. Some time after the release I received another copy of *Ancora da Capo*, Part Two, which was beautifully recorded. What made me feel guilty was the fact that musically it was a superior performance to the concert in Leningrad, which I had released.

Monstrosity

The same thing happened later on, when ENJA released *Non Troppo*, which was recorded in the studio in the Soviet Union. It was an uninspired recording without an audience. Some time later I had in my possession a superbly recorded performance of *Non Troppo*, which easily overshadows anything that the trio had recorded before. The same happened with *New Wine*.

At that time I used to wake up sweating in the middle of the night. The monstrosity of the whole thing was beginning to become clear to me – the best concerts of the Ganelin Trio, both in terms of artistic achievement and the quality of recording, were still unreleased. What was I doing? Was I doing the musicians a disservice?

But what could I do? It was totally impossible to plan any releases in advance. The whole thing was in the hands of fate. The only consolation left for me was that I was doing everything possible to bring to the world the new music from the 'Soviet underground'. Another consolation is that one day, when the Ganelin Trio and other Soviet musicians have been established as a new force in music, all these recordings will be released. The best is yet to come.

Identifiable Design

Soon after I had started the label I met Kim McCroddan, who worked as a studio manager. Gradually he got involved with the label, and he was doing wonders with remastering the tapes recorded in the USSR. Later on he introduced me to his friend Chris Gray who was an architect and designer. The idea of giving Leo Records an instantly identifiable design was hanging in the air. Kim and Chris came up with a strong and simple design which cost very little. They did a lot of work on a voluntary basis and I am convinced that Leo Records is the cheapest label to run. We have been doing everything ourselves, and we survive only because of that. However, we never sacrifice the quality of the records.

Financial Difficulties

The most difficult and unrewarding job for me was publicity, promotion and distribution. I had started this glamorous enterprise as a record producer, but I was finishing as an accountant, secretary, driver, salesman, loader, shipping agent, and so on. Perhaps keeping the accounts of your own company can be a very satisfying job, providing the company makes a profit. With me it was different. I saw it as a total waste of time, and there were times when bookkeeping, delivering sleeves and pressings, sleeving the records, packing them, writing invoices, shipping parcels, chasing distributors, etc., made me really furious. There was one main reason why I could not give the label proper publicity and set up a proper distribution: I was a *beggar.*

The company operated on overdraft facilities given to me by my bank. The house was mortgaged and remortgaged to provide the guarantee for the overdraft. A part of my salary went to repay the interest on the overdraft. After three years of operation the company was twenty thousand pounds in the red.

I lost count of how many times I saw the same awful dream: a knock on the door, the bank's solicitor in the doorway with a piece of paper saying the house had become the property of the bank (this is no doubt an analogy with my nightmarish past in the USSR).

To avoid any misunderstanding I have to confess that I was not starving. But very often I had to refuse myself some necessary, basic things, because there was no money. What made it really awful was that very often I didn't have money to send my records to reviewers, which was of crucial importance. My personal situation was especially frustrating because the image of the company did not correspond with its desperate financial situation. Once I overheard a conversation of two musicians, who were talking about Leo Records and how wonderful it would be to record for this label. In their opinion Leo Records was a major label dealing with new music. It was very flattering to hear their conversation, of course, but I wish they had known what they were talking about. Another time I was introduced to an Arts Council official as a record tycoon. The introduction was done as a half-joke, but it was exactly this kind of half-joke that sticks for ever.

Distribution Problems

During the five years of the company's existence I have failed to set up a reliable distribution. I have worked with small distributors in several European countries, such as Switzerland, Finland, Norway and Austria. But I have never had distributors in Italy, France, Germany, Sweden, the Netherlands, Spain, Australia and many other countries. Leo Records is in a vicious circle.

There is a direct correlation between the number of live performances of a musician and sales of his or her record. The more often artists perform, the better known they become, the more records they are capable of selling. The trouble with the Soviet musicians was that they didn't perform in Europe. The Ganelin Trio was the only exception. That's why it was impossible to sell the records of the Soviet improvisers. Their names were difficult to pronounce, their music was impossible to promote on the radio because of the huge structures they play. Who could afford to play a whole composition on the radio which lasts at least twenty minutes? In times of inflation and economic instability there were very few people in the world who dared to buy records by unknown musicians from the USSR. For example, Homo

Liber's album *Siberian 4* got outstanding reviews all over the world. *Down Beat* and *Jazz Times* were the only publications that never reviewed this record. And yet, in spite of the outstanding reviews, it was impossible to sell more than 200 copies of their record.

The resistance from distributors and shops was amazing. They did not want to hear the words 'Russian Jazz'. When I released *Live in East Germany* Ray's Record Shop in London refused to take this album for sale from my distributors. Only after Brian Case's review in *Melody Maker* did they change their minds. The review finished with the words: 'Buy this album immediately.' And they bought. One copy.

In December 1984 I went to Dobell's Record Shop in the centre of London to persuade the owner to take my records for sale. I didn't want him to buy my records. I would be happy to leave the records on a sale or return basis. The owner looked at the catalogue and said: 'I know these records. I don't want to have this music in my shop.'

Crooks

I have been fortunate to work with some honest distributors, but unfortunately, the distribution business is full of crooks. I had my share of bad luck, especially with French distributors. In the very beginning Leo Records, among several other companies, was hit by a company in Bordeaux. It was too expensive to take this distributor to court, and apart from that I had no time. I turned for help to the British Commercial Consul in Bordeaux, but the owner of the distribution firm managed to outwit the Commercial Consul for more than two years, until we all got sick and tired of the whole affair.

They say one learns by mistakes. With the next French distributor, I signed an official agreement. I gave him twenty-five promotion copies of each of my albums, 500 albums altogether, and two months' credit to pay the invoice. Six months later, after many unsuccessful telephone calls to France, I was chasing him in my car all over France. It cost me several hundred pounds to get my money back, but I wouldn't have been able to get it without the assistance of the British Embassy. All 500 promotion copies were lost. The same story in Germany. I got my money from the company there only because I had an unforeseen chance to blackmail them. All this was happening when I desperately needed money. The overdraft was growing, the interest on the overdraft was growing, and I could not go on with new releases. But what was really driving me crazy was that by robbing me these people were robbing the underprivileged.

And yet there were many people who were looking for my records all over the world. I was receiving letters from the most improbable places – Gabon, South Africa, Japan, Australia. Many letters were very encouraging and they helped me to go on. Here is an extract from a letter from a jazz fan in Palaiseau, France.

> I finally found your records in Paris (in 'Les Mondes du Jazz' but you had certainly guessed that) and I hope they will receive the consideration they deserve.
>
> *Piano Plays* is a pure jewel; I just can't stop listening to it! I haven't yet listened to the other records (*Vide, Exercises* and *Rhythms Hung in Undrawn Sky*) I bought.
>
> Would you be kind enough to send me your new catalogue? I wait impatiently for January to buy *New Music from Russia* from you. Please keep me one!

Later on I found out that the record shop in Paris mentioned in the letter was buying my records from New Music Distribution Service in New York. This is something I shall never be able to understand about the record business, because I was shipping my records to New York, and my distributor was shipping them back to Europe. I wonder how much my records cost in that shop in Paris.

Consequences

When I started the label I was worrying about the consequences for the Soviet musicians. Especially painful was the decision to release Anatoly Vapirov's album *Sentenced to Silence*. What would be his fate? As it happened he was let out of prison ahead of time. I can't claim that the release of this record helped him to get out of prison, but it is obvious that it didn't harm him very much. To be honest I never tried to make a political issue out of my records, and it seemed that the Soviets responded 'in a silent way'. None of the musicians has been harmed so far. The Soviets seem to understand that they have overlooked something important where jazz is concerned. Traditionally Russian talents have never been appreciated in Russia. Now the Soviet bureaucracy seems to be incapable of recognizing that they have a galaxy of talented musicians there who could make a serious contribution to world culture.

Sometimes, when I think about these records from the Soviet Union, I find myself in a very curious position. Whether I want to or not I am promoting Soviet jazz. Many times I have heard the suggestion that the Soviets should pay me for doing this job. With my friends it has become a standing joke: 'You need money, why don't you send them the bill?'

Sometimes, however, I wish it had not been necessary for me to start the label in the first place. Would it not be marvellous if Soviet musicians had the opportunity to record their music and perform in the West when they feel like it? Let us hope that one day it will happen and the Soviet authorities will give these musicians the credit they fully deserve.

It is obvious that I have only 'scratched the surface'. There is a small army of new-jazz musicians in the Soviet Union. For years I planned to release an *Anthology* of new music from Russia. I saw it as a box of five or six records with a beautifully printed brochure inside. I have all the material ready, but shall I ever have the money to fulfil this project? At the moment it seems like an unattainable goal.

Heroic Ring

The work of avant-garde jazz musicians in Russia has a truly heroic ring about it – the almost total lack of musical information, of adequate musical instruments, the impossibility of recording one's music, the impossibility of living by one's art, the severe censorship of the authorities, the untutored audiences. To some extent these accompany any serious art form which is not very

popular, even in the West. But what is startling is that even in such
unnatural and hostile circumstances, from the depth of nowhere,
from the outside edges of the country, appear some really creative
musicians, who do not lose their optimism and creative energy.
Russia is truly a country of jazz miracles!

What is also miraculous is that jazz has once again proved to be
true to itself. It has resurfaced in a fresh, innovative form when
bebop has reached senility and the new music of America (with
very few exceptions) cannot offer anything new or exciting. It has
resurfaced at a time when European new music finds itself in a
deadlock. What is more, jazz has resurfaced in the most unlikely
spot of the globe, in the midst of the most cruel spiritual
oppression. Such is the nature of this most democratic music on
our planet. It can't be restrained. It was born out of slavery, and it
will reappear wherever there is a demand for freedom.

Epilogue

The West loves success stories. It loves soap operas and new
millionaires, and the music world is no different. Richard Branson
of Virgin Records, Manfred Eicher of ECM. . . They came to the
scene and achieved financial success and publicity. The West loves
and respects such people, for we live in a world of ready cash, and
we are forced to understand the language of money. For the public
at large financial success becomes the most important criterion in
the evaluation of art. It becomes a measure of artistic success.

Well, with Leo Records it did not happen. It is not a success
story. It is a story of financial hardships, disappointments,
frustrations, anguish and fury. It is a story of great sadness,
because financial difficulties, dishonest distributors, semi-illiterate
critics and indifferent media have prevented me from breaking the
news about Russian jazz the way it deserves to be presented. And
yet, it is a story of great personal satisfaction. From the very
beginning I realized that I was doing something very special,
something very important for those people in the East who, like
myself in the past, were subjected to one of the most inhuman
regimes in the world. After all, spiritual values are the only thing
that prevent this regime from turning a human being into a

brainless creature.

My life had a meaning, and I did not have to ask myself the question which one hears around all the time: 'What have I done with my life?' I knew exactly what I was doing, and I was happy to do it. Was it worth it, then? Would I do it again? The answer to this question today, five years after I started, is clearer than ever. *Yes*, of course.

Select Discography

Muza-Polskie Nagrani; Vadim Sakun's Sextet; L O396
Ballad; Georgi Garanian Quartet; Supraphon SUA 15732
Labyrinth; G. Garanian; Melodiya C60-05277
The Reminiscences; Leonid Chizhik; Melodiya C60–16157
Django; Alexey Kuznetsov; Melodiya C60-11247-48
The Blue Coral; Alexey Kuznetsov; Melodiya C60-15527-28
Fifteen Years Later; David Goloshchekin; Melodiya C60-20507 007
Vagif Mustafa-zade; Melodiya C60-12277-80
Turning Point; Tonu Naissoo; Melodiya C60-16147-8
Tiit Paulus and Friends; Melodiya C60-15457-8
2 x Rustic Waltz; The Lembit Saarsalu Quartet; Melodiya
  C60-13563
Con Anima; The Ganelin Trio; Melodiya C60-07361-2
Concerto Grosso; The Ganelin Trio; Melodiya C60-14433-4
Poi Segue; The Ganelin Trio; Melodiya C60-17485
Opus a 2; Ganelin/Tarasov; Melodiya C60-19651-008
Setkani; Vladimir Chekasin/Rudolf Dasek/Klaus Koch; Sup-
  raphon 1 15 1308
Vyacheslav Ganelin Trio; Poljazz Z-SX 0628
Jazz Jamboree '71 Vol I (Sampler); Vyacheslav Ganelin Trio;
  Poco A Poco (fragments); Muza SX 1454
Jazzbuhne Berlin 1979 (Sampler); Vyacheslav Ganelin Trio;
  Katalog (fragments); Amiga 8 55749
Catalogue; Ganelin/Tarasov/Chekasin; Leo Records LR 102
Con Fuoco; Ganelin/Tarasov/Chekasin; Leo Records LR 106
The Ways of Freedom; Sergey Kuryokhin; Leo Records LR 107
Ancora da Capo; Part 1; Ganelin Trio; Leo Records LR 108

Ancora da Capo; Part 2; Ganelin Trio; Leo Records LR 109

Sentenced to Silence; Anatoly Vapirov/Sergey Kuryokhin; Leo Records LR 110

New Wine; Ganelin Trio; Leo Records LR 112

Siberian 4; Homo Liber; Leo Records LR 114

Exercises; Vladimir Chekasin; Leo Records LR 115

Vide; Ganelin/Tarasov/Chekasin; Leo Records LR 117

Nostalgia; Vladimir Chekasin Quartet; Leo Records LR 119

Strictly for Our Friends; Ganelin Trio; Leo Records LR 120

Invocations; Anatoly Vapirov Quartet; Leo Records LR 121

On a Baltic Trip; Hans Kumpf; Leo Records LR 122

Non Troppo; Ganelin/Tarasov/Chekasin; ENJA 4036

Baltic Triangle; Ganelin Trio; Leo Records LR 125

Jam Session Leningrad; Hans Kumpf + Anatoly Vapirov Trio; AKM Records, AKM 003

Jam Session Moscow; Hans Kumpf with Fischer, Chizhik, Zubov; AKM Records, AKM 005

Index

Zelenov, Valentin, 92–3
Zen Buddhism, 103

Zubov, Alexey, 69, 78